Robert Mugabe

ROBERT MUGABE

A LIFE OF POWER
AND VIOLENCE

STEPHEN CHAN

Ann Arbor
The University of Michigan Press

All rights reserved
Published in the United States of America by
The University of Michigan Press

ISBN 0-472-11336-4

A full CIP record for this book is available from the British Library
A full CIP record for this book is available from the Library of Congress

Typeset in Ehrhardt by Dexter Haven Associates, London
Printed and bound in Great Britain by MPG Books, Bodmin

Contents

Glossary

FRELIMO	Frente de Liberacao de Mocambique (Mozambican governmental party)
MDC	Movement for Democratic Change (recent opposition party to Mugabe)
RENAMO	Resistencia Nacional Mocambicana (rebel movement in Mozambique)
ZANLA	Zimbabwe African National Liberation Army (armed wing of Mugabe's party)
ZANU	Zimbabwe African National Union (Mugabe's party)
ZANU–PF	ZANU-Patriotic Front (coalition party formed from Mugabe's and Nkomo's)
ZAPU	Zimbabwe African People's Union (Nkomo's party)
ZIPRA	Zimbabwe People's Revolutionary Party (armed wing of Nkomo's party)
ZUM	Zimbabwe Unity Movement (opposition party led by Edgar Tekere in 1990)

OTHER ACRONYMS

ANC	African National Congress (anti-apartheid party; Nelson Mandela's party)
CIO	Central Intelligence Organisation (Zimbabwean secret police)
CODESRIA	Council for the Development of Social Science Research in Africa
IMF	International Monetary Fund
MMD	Movement for Multi-party Democracy (Zambia)
NAM	Non-Aligned Movement
NCA	National Constitutional Assembly (NGO consortium from which the MDC grew)

OAU	Organisation of African Unity
PAC	Pan-Africanist Congress (anti-apartheid party, South Africa)
PF	Patriotic Front (negotiating vehicle for Mugabe and Nkomo before independence)
SADCC	Southern African Development Coordination Conference
SAPES	Southern Africa Political Economy Series
UANC	United African National Council (Muzorewa party vehicle)
ZANU-Ndonga	(minority party of Ndabaningi Sithole)

22 Years of Robert Mugabe

I was a member of the Commonwealth Secretariat from 1977 to 1983. I was not a senior member and I cannot claim to have been intimately involved in the diplomatic manoeuvres of Secretary General Sir Shridath Ramphal, either preceding or during the Lancaster House talks that were a prelude to Zimbabwe's belated independence. Nevertheless, as a tangentially connected figure, I was in a position to observe and learn much that occurred during this period, and to attend meetings of the Commonwealth Committee on Southern Africa that sat in parallel session to the negotiations at Lancaster House. I have written about this elsewhere.[1]

When, however, that Committee and the Lancaster House process both coincided on the need for a Commonwealth Observer Group to monitor the freeness and fairness of the election campaign and the elections that were to give independent Zimbabwe its first government, I was seconded to the staff of that group and, as a result, spent the best part of January to March 1980 in what was then officially Southern Rhodesia. I was part of that small detachment of staff members that arrived before the remainder of what was called the Group's Secretariat, and the Observer Group itself. In one week we had to establish an operational base and complete a reconnaissance of the country. This latter task fell to Peter Snelson and myself. I covered both the Matabelelands and Manicaland, and later, with Emmanuel Apea, headed the group's operations in Matabelelands North and South. I have also written about that time elsewhere,[2] but it had a curious echo in 2000, when a belea-guered Robert Mugabe sanctioned the farm invasions by 'war veterans';

watching BBC News 24 at the very beginning of the invasions, I saw a leader of the war veterans addressing his supporters, and recognised at once the street urchin I had hired to clean the vehicles of the Commonwealth Observer Group outside what was then the Southern Sun Hotel in Bulawayo. No veteran he, and no *mujiba* or juvenile messenger for the guerillas either; for we covered several hundred kilometres a day in those vehicles, usually on dirt roads or no roads at all, and there was extensive daily need for his services. If this was a very minor circle, then the great circles Robert Mugabe has looped and spun deserve much more comment, and hence this book.

I did not desert Zimbabwe after its independence, but was back later in 1980 to advise Teurai Ropa, the first Minister of Youth, Sport and Recreation, on policy formulation within her new ministry. Her name means 'spill blood' and was occasioned by her very rare feat of shooting down a Rhodesian helicopter. Post-independence novels have sometimes cheapened her feat by recounting its everyday occurrence. It was rare because it was almost impossible and, among other things, demands that a person stand her ground, armed with only an AK47 as Teurai Ropa was, and fire back at a looming vehicle armed to the teeth, armoured and full of fighting men who would kill all those who had not run. I had the heartiest respect for the young minister and heard many other legends about her. However, she was also very naive and was clearly feeling her way in her portfolio. Those first two years of naivety and real idealism, a real effort at reconciliation and development, were Zimbabwe's honeymoon. Then, Mugabe seemed a moral statesman and, indeed, then he was.

I was also in Zimbabwe in 1982, however, conducting the staff training of a ministry when the first arms caches were uncovered and televised in Matabeleland. This discovery, if that is what it was, acted as the harbinger of persecution and atrocity in the Matabelelands, culminating in the depredations of the North-Korean-trained Fifth Brigade. These should have overshadowed the first elections after independence in 1985, but the world was still determined to respect Mugabe, and it took some years to develop a full appreciation of what had happened.

Since independence, I have visited Zimbabwe every year and, since 1983, in a private capacity, not contenting myself with the metropolitan street grid and hotels of central Harare. I hope that I have developed some feel for the politics of the country and come to discern the outrageous from the possible in the capital's incessant rumour mill. I have spoken to scores of people in ministries, embassies, news organisations, political parties of all persuasions, universities, streets and the countryside. I have also kept up to date with the literature on Zimbabwe, both written by Zimbabwean academics and those outside, and have tried modestly to add to the latter. What follows is a summation and a judgement, for after 22 years of Robert Mugabe a judgement is necessary.

What do I not propose to do? I do not propose to demonise him. If, as headline writers shouted in the early 2000s, he is mad, then there is method in it. There are high stakes here and steps are calculated with appalling rationality. I want to iterate his method or methods. Moreover, I do not propose to say that he has simply sought to hang onto power. He has certainly done that, but, however bizarre or misplaced, there is a policy at work that was described to me, by one of his own ambassadors, as akin to Chairman Mao's – reminding me that Mugabe's party and fighting force were, before independence, Chinese-supported and often Chinese-trained. I had more than one meal with his guerilla cadres where we all sat down to eat with chopsticks.

Nor do I propose a casual armchair psychological portrait. No one has the clinical evidence for a psychological portrait, and there are precious few coherent accounts of his private life. Moreover, I am not going to trace Mugabe back to his liberation days, when his rise to the leadership was crafted by deceits and treacheries. Many would see a pattern repeated from those days, but running a state is very different from clawing a path in an exile movement. Moreover, even while exhibiting unsavoury tendencies, Mugabe has continued to have his triumphs as a statesman. He did play some role in Commonwealth and Non-Aligned affairs, in the movement towards pluralism in South Africa, and in the negotiations towards peace in Mozambique. These sit alongside his more publicised aberrations in policy, but also mean that there is neither a straight line of descent from his exile days nor a one-dimensional character who is both a demon and mad.

I do propose to say that Mugabe has been bad for Zimbabwe. This is the summation of the judgement towards which, in this book, I shall argue.

I hope that this argument, proceeding chronologically, will build in an organic manner. The book seeks to present an argument, but not to do so in a dry manner. It is peppered with anecdotes from my visits. The 'colour' of Zimbabwe is, I hope, captured here. However, despite this effort to give an impression, I hope the central argument and the arguments building towards it remain clear and within the realm afforded by evidence. In short, I hope the evidence underlying this book is as rigorous as that required for a purely academic text. I have tried to write it in such a manner, however, that non–specialist readers will find much of interest and illumination; because, frankly, why should one return to a country year after year if that country were not much loved? I have had my own love affair with Zimbabwe, not just because the physical geography is beautiful, but because many important people in my life have been Zimbabwean. This, finally, is a book for them as well as for its wider readership. I hope I have created a just picture of their country.

Many people have helped me over the years, knowing that the inform-ation they supplied would be used by me in my writings. I do not think I have extracted information from anybody under false pretences. Given the situation in Zimbabwe as I write, and the enduring closeness of political society, it is itself politic not to reveal their names. When, in my various source notes, I refer to those who were well-placed to speak to me authori-tatively, I hope my readers will accept on trust that they were indeed so placed and that I have sought to invent no evidence. If, sometimes, my anecdotes and 'colour' seem a trifle exaggerated, well perhaps sometimes they are. I have, over more than two decades, surely developed the habit of embroidery. That dusty old pub in the wilds never did have cold beer. It had beer though. What may be here embroidered has also not been, in the first place, invented. However, I have tried my best to censor myself in this book, and I am sure that not too many tallish tales have slipped through the net.

Some acknowledgements can be public. Both the University of Kent and Nottingham Trent University have given time and money for my research. Parts of it have been accomplished under grants from the US Institute of Peace, the ESRC (Economic and Social Science Research Council) and the Nuffield Foundation. It is not often feasible, or wise, to carry laptops on the sorts of journey I make. In any case, laptops weren't invented when I first visited Zimbabwe. I must thank several secretaries who have put up with notes and drafts written under unusual circum-stances. Most recently, at Nottingham Trent, Janet Elkington has either typed with unremitting patience such notes and drafts, or has sat down to reformat those computer drafts I have dashed off without too much regard for decent typography.

I thank my publishers, I.B. Tauris, in particular Dr Lester Crook, who has been badgering me for this book since my 1992 volume on Kenneth

Kaunda and Zambia.[3] Well, Lester, here it is, a mere ten years later. It is a fuller and less contingent history now. I must also thank my previous Vice-Chancellor, Professor Ray Cowell, who hired me to be the Dean of a promising but then problematic faculty. He gave me the sabbatical the writing of this book required, and I thank Professor Marianne Howarth, who ran the faculty in my absence.

Finally, reserving a primary debt to the end, I wish to thank Ranka Primorac, whose deep knowledge and familiarity with Zimbabwe was always instrumental to the better thinking and writing of this book.

It would be intemperate and insensitive to dedicate this book to any one of my Zimbabwean friends. They will each remember a time (or several times) when they had to care for a derelict soul. This is for them all, and for the hope of a better country in which they live, and which, Robert Mugabe permitting, I propose to continue visiting.

Stephen Chan
The Lace Market
Nottingham

NOTES ON PREFACE

1   Stephen Chan, *The Commonwealth in World Politics: A Study of International Action, 1965–1985*, London: Lester Crook, 1988.
2   Stephen Chan, *The Commonwealth Observer Group in Zimbabwe*, Gweru, Zimbabwe: Mambo Press, 1985.
3   Stephen Chan, *Kaunda and Southern Africa: Image and Reality in Foreign Policy*, London: I.B.Tauris, 1992.

A Moment in the New Millennium

Saturday night at the Italian Bakery, a cafe bar just a short ride up Second Street in Harare, not far from the main university. The tables are too small, the service is friendly but random, and the pasta is distinctly uninspired. But the clientele is multiracial, whites, blacks, coloureds, Asian, and mostly young; and mostly well-heeled. The girls dress as clones of their fashionable counterparts in London, and the boys affect the louche habits also of a faraway metropolis. The car park is full of limousines that would not be out of place in quite a rich part of that metropolis.

There is something endearingly innocent about the atmosphere. It is easy to have a good time and, in somewhat better times, one would say that this was the Zimbabwe of dreams: buoyant, mixed, cosmopolitan, young enough to be idealistic. But the talk at more than one table is about farm invasions, losses among the opposition activists – meaning activists killed – and the spiralling-downwards economy. One pays the bill in large denomination notes, and this would suggest another affinity with Italy, except that few people in Zimbabwe earn too many large denomination notes. The crowd at the Italian Bakery may be exceptions, but even they are feeling the pinch.

Nevertheless, one senses a seriousness under the laughter. This always emerges in times of siege: not so much a gallows humour as its close cousin, siege jokes. The farm invasions have reached a new phase. Enough have taken place for a curious *politesse* to have emerged. The 'veterans' appear in delegation. The farmer or farm manager offers them tea and cakes. The talks about appropriation of the farm are perhaps tense but cordial. Sometimes, rarely, bargains are struck and the otherwise hapless farmer is left with a token of what was his. So that, in August 2001, at the Italian Bakery, there could be gossip about how Mrs So-and-so was overheard saying to Mrs What's-her-name that her veterans were so much nicer than those who had seized Mrs Down-the-road's farm nearby. Siege jokes. And, as with all improvised *politesse*, each month can bring variations or returns to earlier savageries. No one expects that the cups of tea approach can last.

Many at the Italian Bakery are card-carrying members of the Movement for Democratic Change (MDC), the major opposition party, headed by Morgan Tsvangirai, and as with all political discussion enlarged intimacies are claimed, so that people talked of 'Morgan', as if he were a familiar; which, given the relative smallness of Zimbabwean political circles, he could be. The intimacy seems more credible than the beer-claims on the fringes of British party conferences. In any case, party politics have their own *politesse* and the unusual realisation about a night at the Italian Bakery is that, notwithstanding the headlines, the overall atmosphere and restrained composures of discussion could have located the scene anywhere: amidst the fires, some sangfroid on the edge of down-town Harare. Not too far away, blood might be significantly more heated.

PART ONE

BY FAIR MEANS OR VERY FOUL

ONE

As it Was in
the Beginning

As 2001 entered its last quarter, farmers began the ritual wait for the return of rains. In South Africa, the repatriation – deportation – of 20,000 Zimbabwean workers began on 16 October; and, in Harare, President Mugabe began applying price cuts and price freezes on basic commodities. 'That socialism we wanted can start again,' said the President, adding angrily that recalcitrant companies would be dealt with severely. 'Let no one on this front expect mercy.' He went on to say that the state would 'take over any businesses that are closed'.[1] However, companies began closing anyway, since production had now become unprofitable, and the state, already beleaguered, had neither funds nor organisational capacity to take them over.

Much of Mugabe's proclamation was for rhetorical effect. Whether the rhetoric indeed had effect is something of which his lieutenants may or may not have advised him. By now, the President was not much given to contrary advice and would have seemed, like Hitler in his bunker, to be moving phantom regiments. However, Mugabe was not moving phantom regiments without certain precisions. The short-term logistics of any application of rhetoric were very well put together. In retrospect, the farm invasions by 'war veterans' was a well-crafted and well-supplied series of phased operations. It was the longer-term consequences of rhetoric and its related policies that Mugabe seemed determined to brazen out. Here, it was not Soviet troops at the gates of Berlin, but Commonwealth pressures, first thinkings aloud of EU sanctions and, crucially for a man setting about a form of autarky – Africa for Africans

– the increasing disdain of African presidents, particularly the nearby Presidents of Malawi and South Africa, the involvement of Nigeria in the Commonwealth pressures, and economic squeezes from South Africa – manifest in the repatriation of the senders-home of remittances for 20,000 families in Zimbabwe.

In Zimbabwe itself, the barons of Mugabe's own ZANU-PF party were restless. In parliamentary elections, the MDC opposition had swept all the major cities and all of the Matabelelands to the west of the country. Mugabe's powerbase was now provincial, eastern and central rural, policed by the 'veterans', and extremely well organised. Somehow this was reminiscent of the powerbase provided for his ZANLA liberation army guerillas from 1976 to 1980 and, back then, the idea of a peasant base was very much in accord with the Maoism that, again rhetorically, Mugabe occasionally espoused. Certainly those guerillas were Chinese-trained. There were Chinese military advisers in Tanzania and elsewhere. However, as one of his senior party loyalists put it in a private conversation, Mugabe was seeing the endgame of his presidential term, before scheduled elections in early 2002, not as a rerun of the original liberation of Zimbabwe – official history accords more weight to the guerilla struggle than to the Commonwealth and Lancaster House negotiations – not as a rerun of a Maoist guerilla war, but as a form of Mao's later cultural revolution. The pure socialist Zimbabwean man was to stand against the world's whites, their international power centres, and those of their black friends as well.

After the initial clumsy violence of the farm invasions, it might have been tempting to use the analogy of the Khymer Rouge, with their Year Zero in Cambodia. However, both analogies are somewhat strained. The countryside is not being laid waste, nor are urban populations, nor even a generation of youths, being shipped into that countryside. The young people are not waving red books but, in the universities and city suburbs, form core memberships of the opposition. However, it remains a provocative thought that the man, characterised by many British newspapers as a mad dictator, may be instead some sort of ruthless romantic. Romantic, ruthless, well organised in operational issues, given to rhetoric: this is a preliminary list. This book's intention is to explore Mugabe in all these and other aspects. No simple dictator this.

AS IT WAS IN THE BEGINNING

The crafting of Mugabe from a form of socialist purity dates from 1975. Then, the first glimmerings of a negotiated settlement to the dispute in Rhodesia began to appear and were taken seriously, not least by President Kaunda of Zambia, whose ramshackle defiance of the white south, combined with astute (if intuitive) diplomacy, had made him a key player in the metropolitan schemes of the US and Britain to safeguard the northern borders of South Africa from significant threat. No one thought then that a guerilla war could lead to guerilla victory, but grinding low-level violence would, over time, strain the nerve of Pretoria, and its response or intervention would ruin Western diplomacy with the entire rest of the continent.

However, the intermittent (and unsuccessful) talks, beginning in Geneva that year, demanded a guerilla voice. Joshua Nkomo was then the pre-eminent external nationalist leader, and he commanded a guerilla army of sorts – although, with its parades in Zambia, its host country, its own visual rhetoric completed by a few tanks and MIG fighters, it was more often a show army than a militarily active one. President Kaunda needed to send signals, but he would not risk Pretoria's military reaction within his own country.

The other guerilla faction was, if not led by Mugabe, emerging from an internal power struggle in which Mugabe had secured a strategic position. That he was, even if disliked by frontline presidents such as Kaunda, their preferred choice to partner Nkomo in the new international talks is illustrated by Kaunda's releasing him from detention in order that he might participate in negotiations. Similarly, when Mugabe later joined up with the ZANLA guerillas who had transferred their operational bases from Zambia to newly independent Mozambique, President Machel favoured Mugabe in the power struggles that followed. In a very real sense, Mugabe attended the series of negotiations by default – presidents chose him – but in a more intimate sense of *realpolitik*, Mugabe became one of the two voices for a new Zimbabwe by sheer intrigue and power-play. Even now, it is not hard to find, in Zimbabwe, real veterans who are anxious to relate the ruthlessness of events that took place in the politics of exile and militarisation. It is almost impossible to substantiate these stories, but it would seem certain that Mugabe, who never himself fought in the field (but did spend many years in prison), was never a leader chosen by his troops.

Mugabe did not take to Nkomo with great kindness. Reliable enough legend has it that once, when both men were summoned to President Nyerere of Tanzania – who wanted increased cooperation between them – and they saw the President separately and by turn, that Mugabe, when it was his turn, marched into Nyerere's office and scorned the gestured offer of a chair with the words, 'If you're expecting me to sit where that fat bastard just sat, you'll have to think again'.[2]

Mugabe, whether or not a pure socialist, was a purist. For him, Nkomo had made and was capable of making too many compromises. Both men were past masters of the political arts, but Mugabe practised treacheries 'at home' in his own party; he would have to be drawn, as if teeth were being extracted, to compromise with his Rhodesian enemies. The frontline presidents would have to begin the patient task of drawing his teeth.

THE FRONTLINE, THE COMMONWEALTH AND THE BRITISH AT THE BEGINNING

It could not be said, today's official histories notwithstanding, that – even as late as 1979 – the Zimbabwean guerillas were winning. They were certainly causing the Rhodesian Government and forces to plan for a long war of attrition, and the drain on the Rhodesian economy and white manpower was immense. However, even if under armed convoy, all major roads were in use; transport and communications had not been undermined by the guerillas. The Rhodesians were in fact able to strike, by means of commando raids and aerial bombardment, at guerilla rear bases in both Zambia and Mozambique, and Lusaka imposed blackout conditions every night. By day, within Rhodesia itself, helicopter reconnaissance and manoeuvrability meant that guerillas, once spotted, were in grave danger. The Rhodesians organised themselves militarily in a series of provincial Joint Operational Commands (JOCs) each led by a Brigadier – with several sub-JOCs attached to them. With both road and aerial manoeuvrability, nationwide centres of command, and Vietnam-style 'protected villages' under both enclosure and guard in particularly sensitive areas, the military machine, in itself, was extremely strong. For years afterwards, again Vietnam style, Rhodesian veterans lamented that they were, in fact, never defeated militarily; and this was, in its narrow sense, true.

By contrast, it has to be said that the guerillas, while often amazingly brave, were split. The ZIPRA forces, attached to Nkomo's political wing (still headquartered in Zambia), fought far less often than the ZANLA forces, attached to Mugabe's Mozambique-based ZANU wing. Indeed, there were times when elements of the two guerilla forces fought each other, and ZIPRA forces in the Matabelelands were not completely averse to informing the Rhodesian JOC as to the whereabouts of ZANLA troops transgressing 'their' turf.

The operational tactics, particularly of the ZANLA forces, underwent a long process of extemporaneous trial and error. Chinese training notwithstanding, platoons and patrols were often sent to their deaths so that their higher (and safer) commanders could learn about Rhodesian response rates and response times. Strategy, however, never deviated far from its central focus of destabilisation. This had two broad targets: the first was certainly the white rural economy and civilian infrastructure (not the military headquarters or the major cities); the second was the destabilisation of any possible collaboration with the Rhodesians within the black rural infrastructures of villages and village leaders. Only in very recent times has it become emotionally possible for novelists such as Alexander Kanengoni to write about the often arbitrary terror (and arbitrary mercies) that became sustained features of guerilla operations in the black rural heartlands.[3] Of course, sustained efforts were made as well to reinforce the ethos of oneness with the rural people. There has been a great deal of writing on the use of spirit mediums to give authen-ticity and spiritual enhancement of the liberation cause.[4] There is no doubt that the liberation struggle was genuinely popular and supported. Black Zimbabweans, after all, were then deprived of equal rights and were economically marginalised and socially ostracised by white society. There was also a particular condescension in the Rhodesian demeanour, both Boerish and simply boorish, towards the black majority that was, to even the casual observer, let alone the sufferer of it, extensively offensive. Insofar as this was felt, also extensively, in the rural areas – at the hands of white farmers who also controlled both most and the best of the land, under licence of historical legislation and appropriation[5] – there remains a residual resentment among many black people. The farm invasions may be abhorred by most, but land redistribution is clearly supported. None of this, however, means that the guerillas fought a pure war. Far from it. Nor, even if they were not being defeated, were the Rhodesian forces noticeably winning. Ian Smith, faced with the drain on his resources by a lengthy war of attrition, hoped to shorten its length by 'mixing' his government a little with black faces – most notably that of Bishop Muzorewa – and, thereby, winning a measure of black popular support away from the guerillas. A series of contradictions were being set into play by the beginning of 1979, building on other, older contradictions (a great deal of the Rhodesian military was composed of black soldiers, including crack undercover units such as the Selous Scouts); and both sides were essentially digging in for both a war of attrition and a war of denying the other position. What changed all this was the advent of Margaret Thatcher.

The recently elected Thatcher was dynamic and determined to lead her country into a new era. Whatever one's opinion about her domestic agenda, she was, in foreign policy, given to naiveties. Nevertheless, she appointed as her Foreign and Commonwealth Secretary, Lord Carrington, an urbane and worldly man, able to take counsel and with the instinct of recognising when it was good. For Thatcher, however, to establish her new domestic era, she had first to cut loose millstones from the past; and she, in her enthusiasm, did not distinguish easily between internal and external millstones. Rhodesia was one such external stone. Ever since Ian Smith's unilateral declaration of independence in 1965, successive British governments had been weighed down by international pressures – not least through the Commonwealth – to bring the rebellious and illegal regime to heel. Thatcher reasoned to herself that a legalised Rhodesia, however controversially come to legality, would remove Britain from further responsibility; that is, a legally independent Rhodesia – under whatever name – and, thence, a recognised state, accountable in its own right in international affairs, no longer part of Britain's accountability. The Ian Smith and Bishop Muzorewa axis seemed to her sufficient foundation to drive this project forward. Britain would have to take the risk of recognising the hybrid government and its state, expect and diplomatically court other Western states to follow suit and, at the very least, the criticisms of Britain would have to become diffuse. African governments would have to criticise a growing number of state recognitions and, in time, would have, themselves, to recognise Smith and Muzorewa under the achieved reality of her *realpolitik*.

This was a very neat formulation, and the British Prime Minister was evidently so taken by it, and so enthusiastic about the rubric of taking risks to enter the future, if not cleanly then quickly, that she, on the spur of the enthusiastic moment, announced it without further consultation. She did this on a late-winter tour of Australia, then under the conservative prime ministership of Malcolm Fraser. Both Fraser and Carrington are very tall men. They framed Thatcher on her television appearance, and their jaws dropped simultaneously when she announced the possibility of British recognition for Smith and Muzorewa. If this became a cherished television moment, it also set into motion two strands of a 'rescue' mission. Mrs Thatcher had clearly to be rescued from herself, but Carrington knew she could not now be satisfied until, sooner rather than later, Britain was rid of Rhodesia, and that meant bringing Rhodesia to a genuinely recognised independence; so he and his Foreign and Commonwealth Office had a clear enough, and difficult enough, mission. The other strand was taken up by Malcolm Fraser, a Commonwealth leader. The Commonwealth, through which so much criticism of Britain had been channelled, was always going to be involved. Now, however, it would not be only the African Commonwealth states – many of the 'frontline' states, confronting Rhodesia and South Africa, were Commonwealth members – but even a distant and conservative Prime Minister of Australia who saw the simple Thatcherite strategy of cutting the Gordian knot as simplistic. Not even Thatcher's new Britain could live without African and other third-world friends, allies and trading partners. There was to be the biennial Commonwealth Heads of Government Meeting (CHOGM, but CHOGM is a most unlovely acronym so I shall use 'summit' throughout) in August that year, to be held in Lusaka, capital of a key frontline state and host to ZIPRA guerilla forces, and presided over by Kenneth Kaunda, then at the height of his reputation as a rare moral statesman. His colleague moral statesman, Julius Nyerere of Tanzania, would certainly attend and thus Lusaka would be the stage where Britain, the frontline and the Commonwealth would either come together or come to blows over Rhodesia. Failure in Lusaka could, among other things, permanently disable the Commonwealth and, at a stroke, Britain would have lost a problematic but traditional means of access to third-world international affairs and influence. Carrington thus set August and Lusaka as a deadline and target. He and the British Foreign and Commonwealth Office set about a summer of hectic shuttle diplomacy.

There were other key Commonwealth actors apart from Kaunda and Nyerere of the African frontline; there were Fraser in the old 'white'

Commonwealth; and Jamaica's Michael Manley, cricket-playing and LSE-trained, the white Prime Minister of a black nation who had flown Hurricanes for Britain against the Nazi Blitz. There was one other Caribbean statesman, from Guyana but now Commonwealth Secretary General, Shridath Ramphal. A sophisticated and accomplished statesman, he had been a key figure in negotiating the Lome Convention between Europe and a great part of the third world. English-educated, like Manley (only at King's, on the other side of Aldwych from the LSE), and Anglophiliac, he and Carrington were destined not to get along and, ever since the negotiations of 1979, debate has raged as to which of the two men did most to make them work. Two camps have produced two literatures (these are surveyed in the bibliographic essay at the end of this book). However, it is fair to say that the symbiosis between the two was essential to bind Britain and the Commonwealth to the negotiations that grew out of the Lusaka summit of August 1979. Britain negotiated to redress and discharge an historical responsibility. The majority of the remainder of the Commonwealth (all except New Zealand) stood behind the guerilla parties, and this meant, once again, that Robert Mugabe had to be got to the negotiating table, and taught how to negotiate and to compromise. The Commonwealth knew that if these talks failed, the guerilla position would be seriously endangered, especially if the guerilla parties were seen to be causing their failure. Thatcher would return to a version of her earlier plan, and its chances of success would have grown in relation to how much the guerilla parties were seen as having left Britain no other alternative. First, however, there was the small matter of how to achieve progress in Lusaka. Britain, the frontline and the rest of the Commonwealth all prepared. It is fair to say that those conspicuously not preparing were the guerilla parties. They were to play no part in Lusaka and, after Lusaka, were essentially given a *demarche* to appear at the negotiations others had prepared.

Leading up to Lusaka, Carrington had to maintain a dual agenda. The first part was keeping Thatcher on-side. She had not to be recidivist to her own inclination. The second was a far-ranging diplomacy. Lord Harlech spent much time cultivating US support for Carrington's approach, and Sir Antony Duff shuttled among African capitals, essentially sounding out the least gains with which African presidents could live. Here, Carrington had to rely, to an extent, upon Ramphal, who was in turn sounding out African presidents, especially Kaunda and Nyerere.

Kaunda was to be the summit host and, therefore, its chairman; and both he and Nyerere hosted, or had hosted, the guerilla factions. On their soil, the guerillas had been trained; and, from Zambian soil still, ZIPRA guerillas, in the manner of speaking described above, moved forth. And, even though Mugabe's faction was now headquartered in Mozambique, Nyerere could still call Mugabe forth to negotiations, as Kaunda could Nkomo. If not in the same seat, Mugabe and Nkomo might well have to sit beside each other again, learn to cooperate with each other, and learn – not only how to negotiate as a team – but to negotiate. Kaunda and Nyerere, and the non-Commonwealth President Machel were key. Not quite puppeteers, they had to become sponsors who drew lines in the sand and stand behind those lines with drawn sabres. Meanwhile, as Ramphal and his allies delivered Mugabe and Nkomo, Carrington, with US and South African help, worked to ensure that, come the negotiations, Ian Smith and Muzorewa would also be delivered. For South Africa, the prospect of continuing guerilla war on its northern borders was highly unattractive. All Lusaka had to do was to agree that negotiations begin, and agree a broad framework for those negotiations. The Commonwealth wanted to keep it tight for the British, but not so tight that Mrs Thatcher would chafe. Keeping it tight, giving less room for British manoeuvre than Britain might wish, meant cultivating and charming Thatcher at Lusaka.

LUSAKA AND LANCASTER HOUSE

That is exactly what Commonwealth leaders did at Lusaka. In consultation with Ramphal, Kaunda kept the issue of Rhodesia way down the agenda. It was not to arise until the summit's third day. By then, cooperation and progress would have been achieved on many smaller items and a constructive mood was meant to have emerged. As it was, it did; but not without these plans being jeopardised by the spectacularly clumsy and unilateral action of the Nigerians, nationalising BP on the eve of the summit. Thatcher and Carrington were furious – in contemporary political vocabulary, incandescent. For different reasons, so was Ramphal. However, all were wise enough to approach Lusaka as if they had everything still to play for. The Queen blessed the summit with her own high (and sincere) words, already seeing eye-to-eye more with Ramphal than

Thatcher, partly because she had a genuine concern and felt a genuine responsibility for the Commonwealth, and partly because the worldly Ramphal knew perfectly the manners of paying court. If, however, Thatcher did not know how to pay it, she knew how to receive it; and the conversion – or beguiling – of her was accomplished through nakedly ancient technique. At the summit's carefully crafted break, all the leaders residing in a specially constructed 'village', a line of the carefully chosen came calling, one by one, at her villa: Fraser, Manley, Nyerere, all at their simultaneously most authoritative and lubricous best. To be sure, they reinforced what Carrington had also been advising: that negotiations, involving the guerilla parties, therefore Nkomo and Mugabe, were essential. No 'settlement', otherwise founded, could attain diplomatic recognition or political blessing. At the same time, the Commonwealth leaders sought and attained various safeguards as to the nature of these negotiations. The summit, which had lasted from 1–7 August, agreed that the British would convene all-party talks. These were held before the year's end in London, at Lancaster House. Carrington chaired them. The South Africans duly obliged Smith and Muzorewa to attend; Zambia prompted Nkomo; and Tanzania and Mozambique performed the task of sending Mugabe.

Once in London, Nkomo and Mugabe liaised regularly with Ramphal who, in turn, consulted regularly with Kaunda, Nyerere and Machel. At the same time, the Commonwealth High Commissioners in London met regularly in the guise of the Commonwealth Committee on Southern Africa, and these meetings were convened in Marlborough House, Ramphal's Pall Mall headquarters, a stone's throw from Lancaster House, with only St. James's Palace between. At least Mugabe never had to share the Marlborough House elevator with Nkomo. It was too small. (To my astonishment, I once witnessed Nkomo entering the lift, filling it, and then watched as his two aides raced up the stairs to be able to greet him on Ramphal's floor. What the ghost of Queen Mary, still said to walk the stairs and landings, made of all this, we shall never know.)

Carrington duly had the telephones of all parties tapped, set out on a chairmanship of alternating iron bluff and gentle persuasion, and was given Thatcher's trust. He wished for either a genuine settlement or – and the debate still exists as to whether this was his fallback or first option – the collapse of the talks with the guerilla parties at least divided, at best blamed for their collapse. The guerilla parties negotiated under the common banner of the Patriotic Front, with Ramphal crafted their own iron and gentle responses to Carrington, refused to be divided, and were advised, and negotiated. It was Ian Smith who broke first, unable to bear the direction which the talks began to take. Carrington's dislike of Ramphal and his interventions turned to a studied distaste, but his admiration for Mugabe grew. Once, exhausted and withdrawn to White's (his club in St James's), Carrington was caught musing, addressing no one in particular, that some day Mugabe would be the one to be offered membership of this exclusive retreat.[6] The hard-edged intellectual brilliance of Mugabe, once celebrated by the European left and admired by Carrington, always emerged in fits and starts; but it was clearly on display at Lancaster House.

The negotiations at Lancaster House lasted from 10 September to 21 December 1979. The discernible early British attitude was one of tolerance for Nkomo, contempt for Smith, faint contempt but some support for Muzorewa, some respect and great distrust of Mugabe. On-the-spot punditry, reading inflections, was of the opinion that the British might even look to an exercise of double detachment: detaching Nkomo from Mugabe, and Muzorewa from Smith, and crafting an amenable enough, moderate enough, perhaps controllable enough coalition of their own. Whether this was ever anything more than a passing whim, it certainly became a whisper; but it seemed as if a hundred whispers surrounded the talks, and a great many of them warned of a reborn Perfidious Albion. Carrington would never have owned to that, but he was studied enough in his determination to chair the negotiations with tenacity, brinks-manship and sheer strength – and so he did.

The first real brinksmanship on his part took place on 15 October when, tired and annoyed at the recalcitrance of Mugabe and Nkomo, he threatened to continue negotiations with Muzorewa alone. He won that one, as the guerilla parties gave ground and the rejoined negotiations continued. Round Two probably came over 10–11 November when, with the help of Ramphal and Kaunda, the guerilla parties managed to secure Carrington's consent to a military Commonwealth Monitoring Force. This was to help guarantee any ceasefire. Carrington's original and, for a time, stubborn proposal had been for Rhodesian forces to police the ceasefire – effectively giving them a superior hand to that of the other highly interested and militarised parties. By the end of November, it was honours even between the British and the Patriotic Front. The Muzorewa position was marginalised, and December began with the draft of a partial accord. Looking back over this period, it all seems rather bald and episodic. It was not so at the time. The Patriotic Front was placed under great pressure, and Carrington was unrelenting in applying it. Not only that, the frontline and Ramphal also applied pressure on the Front. The British and the frontline all stood to gain if the negotiations succeeded. For the frontline, a period of stability was essential to staunch various economic haemorrhages, a number caused directly by the Rhodesian war. The Zimbabwean guerillas were becoming as Palestinians to their Arab neighbours: a cause to be supported, and a problem. The frontline and Commonwealth applied pressures on Carrington as well, sometimes very successfully; but it is fair to say that Mugabe and Nkomo weathered a storm of pressures and seldom lost their individual composures or public unity. It was this display of dignity under stress that began to temper Carrington's view, particularly of Mugabe. In any case, Carrington had himself been a soldier, and knew very well that his and the other pressures on the Front, particularly Mugabe's ZANLA army, meant the risking of an uncertain, perhaps eventual, but perfectly possible military victory. After all, even if the Rhodesians were later to complain that they had not been defeated in the field, they could not say that they were defeating the guerillas in that same field. In fact, the Rhodesian field was sustainable through protracted mobilisation and turning as much of the field as possible into a fortress. The sheer scale of Rhodesian deployment meant that the guerillas were achieving some progress in their fight. To give up that progress, however slight, was to be asked much; so when, on 4 December, Carrington's draft partial accord on the table, Mugabe and Nkomo present in Ramphal's office, mid-winter cold and dark outside, Ramphal spoke by phone and at length with Nyerere. The upshot of this conversation was agreement between the four men that the partial accord placed the Patriotic Front forces at risk – but not at extreme risk. It was time, with great misgivings nevertheless, for that risk to be taken. And this was the time that Carrington was found musing in White's, amazed that he had done it, amazed that Mugabe with his armed strength had done it. If any man left Lancaster House transformed in the eyes of Western statesmen, it was Mugabe.

CHRISTMAS AFTER ALL

If Mugabe had begun the acquisition of a different hue abroad, within Rhodesia he was still a black man (but even the most rabid Rhodesian was creating mental space for black, preferably moderate, majority rule), but also irredeemably red. The Lancaster House Agreement had Britain reacquire authority over what became, again officially, Southern Rhodesia; Lord Soames was despatched to be Governor; the Rhodesian forces were to confine themselves to barracks, and the Guerilla forces were to be confined to Assembly Points watched over by the Commonwealth Monitoring Force – British, New Zealand, Fijian and Kenyan troops invited by Carrington. A somewhat more independent Commonwealth Observer Group, convened by Ramphal's Commonwealth Secretariat, was to make a show of monitoring everything; and all political parties – including those of Mugabe (ZANU) and Nkomo (ZAPU) – were to be allowed to campaign, ahead of elections to commence at the end of February 1980. Even so, it was to be the Rhodesian civil service that organised the elections. Whatever the popular vote, a set number of white seats were guaranteed under transitional constitutional provisions – sufficient to hold any balance of power in a hung parliament – and, outside the Lancaster House Agreement itself but in keeping with Carrington's already legendary reputation during the Lancaster House talks, Soames was determined also to be a man of steel, and he paid particular attention to any reported violations of the ceasefire by the guerilla factions – especially Mugabe's faction. Despite such safeguards, representing the significant compromises accepted by Mugabe and Nkomo, Rhodesian opinion was willfully full of trepidation. On the eve of Mugabe's return to Southern Rhodesia, in order to launch ZANU's election campaign, the largest newspaper, the *Herald*, ran a front-page banner headline that, if elected, Mugabe would ban Christmas. His Marxist reputation ran before him although, astoundingly, this Marxism had neither any exceptionalisms (to explain his patient moderateness at Lancaster House), nor any descriptors (Maoist, Stalinist, it didn't matter, red was red and Santa Claus was to be a first casualty of political redness). The same newspaper, on 28 January, did have the decency to cover its front page with a huge aerial photograph of Mugabe's homecoming rally. Probably a quarter of a million people attended – although the ZANU claim was for some 1,600,000 – and the entire evening preceding the 27 January rally witnessed busloads of singing ZANU supporters, chugging and chorusing through the streets of Salisbury. It was a remarkably peaceful rally and, for the first time, newly enfranchised citizens and international observers alike began to sense the possibility that Mugabe might actually win this thing outright. That didn't stop the shadow games in political circles. Rumours abounded of possible coalitions to stop Mugabe. Either Nkomo or Muzorewa might team up with the guaranteed white parliamentarians to deny ZANU a majority. Thankfully, few rumours were to the effect that Nkomo and Muzorewa might enter power together; and the unsentimental realists were, in fact, looking to a coalition between Nkomo and Mugabe, hoping that Nkomo would win sufficient seats (if only because Mugabe had lost sufficient seats to Muzorewa) to dominate the coalition. But, Santa Claus or no, majority or minority partner, the possibilities of Mugabe being at least part of an independent government loomed large and for the first time only one month before the elections began.

In that month, there were sufficient violations of the ceasefire for Soames to consider, very seriously, the prospect of banning Mugabe and ZANU from the elections. He was encouraged in this view by the Rhodesians, and his personal staff – Eurocrats drawn from Brussels – seemed more at home in this white society than with the guerilla politicians. It took a delegation of Soames's own fieldstaff, somewhat less cloistered than those at his headquarters – led by a local council official, Ron Turton, seconded from Chester – to persuade him, in rather blunt (if not rude) terms, that he was being ill-advised. At times, it seemed that the future of the elections was on a knife-edge, and that the country would re-enter, very chaotically and swiftly, the war from which it had so recently and unexpectedly escaped. A year earlier, no one would have thought it possible. If Mrs Thatcher's instinctualism produced no other result, it instigated a process that led to the independence of Zimbabwe. Her outburst in Australia, however, required much legwork and fancy footwork by Carrington, Ramphal and the frontline presidents; and very great patience, compromise and risk-taking on the parts of Nkomo and Mugabe. Throughout the election campaign, Mugabe barely rattled a sabre, and worked the stump like any other, perhaps slightly and occasionally shrill, normal politician.

Mugabe won the elections outright. He did not need to enter a coalition with anyone, but elected, in any case, informally to form one with Nkomo. All of Southern Rhodesia, about to become Zimbabwe, was shocked by the scale of the victory. Nkomo took all but one of the seats in his Matabelelands stronghold but, elsewhere, it seemed almost as if no contest between equal players had taken place. Mugabe won just about everywhere else, and Muzorewa was reduced to the holder of three seats. All the South African money that had clandestinely helped finance his campaign came to nothing in the face of a genuine desire for change, and a desire to recognise those who had been bold enough to fight for change. The guaranteed white seats aside, it was a rout in favour of those who had gone to war and, even if that war had not been as well fought as later propagandists would claim, and even though the guerillas had conducted atrocities against their own people, the war for independence had been won. But even the guerilla parties, even ZANU, could scarcely believe the scale of it all. And if they could not, nor could the white Rhodesians, who had hoped till the last for some coalition that would keep Mugabe out. To them, he was still the man who would, if no longer end, then contemplate ending Christmas. Amidst the celebrations and disbelief, not to mention relief in the frontline, there were private if gracious fears among the British, and foreboding among the Rhodesians. It was amidst these contrary responses that Mugabe's 4 March acceptance speech, nationally televised, seemed epochal. As if suddenly, even the residual warrior was – in one broadcast – transformed into a statesman of gravitas and generosity. Mugabe spoke of peace and, above all, of reconciliation. Without doubt, it was a masterpiece of a speech; and, whatever the later view of Mugabe, there was not an unimpressed person in Whitehall and the dying Rhodesia at that moment in March 1980.

FROM ONE BEGINNING TO ANOTHER

The winning of the elections was a triumph; and the speech won Mugabe many new friends internationally. Even the South Africans were, momentarily, a little relieved – and even impressed. The Rhodesian general Peter Walls was retained in post; the Rhodesian security chief Ken Flowers likewise. Mugabe made a consistent point of including a white minister in his cabinets, often in the agricultural portfolio; and all these symbolisms were enough to render Zimbabwe a new byword for reconciliation, not least as a prospect for South Africa. Certainly, the actual beginning of running a state – particularly such a mixed state – was impressive enough

for even Zimbabweans to glide over questions that might otherwise have
lingered, or been raised, about the mysterious death in exile of Mugabe's
predecessor, Herbert Chitepo, and the equally mysterious death of the
liberation general Josiah Tongogara on the eve of independence. It was
time for all to bless the new beginning and to seek a forgetfulness of
various roughshod pasts. The new beginning was portrayed, in the international press at least, in a beguiling and almost arcadian way. One British
broadsheet featured the new, very young Minister of Youth, Sport and
Recreation, Teurai Ropa, at home with her husband, the former ZANLA
and now Zimbabwean general Rex Nhongo. A once fighting duo, they
were described as seeking no great material reward in their new roles
(something about which today's Zimbabweans might wax lyrically ironic),
and their modest house – something to which they were modestly unused
– was unceremoniously host also to a litter of chewed corn cobs, an
evidence that the couple still ate traditional fare and were not seduced by
ministerial and diplomatic cuisine.

Ropa did not serve as minister long. She went back to school, took a
BA degree, and wrote a brief novel. Nhongo became head of the armed
forces after Walls's eventual departure, and prospered. Ropa had been a
genuine war hero, having singlehandedly shot down a Rhodesian helicopter
(one of the very few, if not the only one, who managed this). At the battle
of Chimoio, after Rhodesian commandos had staged an audacious and
devastating attack on a ZANLA base inside Mozambique, Ropa was seen
– having helped lead such counterattack as the ZANLA forces could
muster – seated on a rock, her AK47 still smouldering at her side. She
was eight months pregnant, and was knitting bootees for the child-to-be.
In a way, she seemed truly to represent what appeared to be happening:
a new birth out of the turmoil of war. But the new birth came into very
new challenges, and with its own old and very smouldering baggage.

NOTES ON CHAPTER 1

1   *Guardian* (London), 16 October 2001.
2   There are many versions of this story, differing only in how pejorative was the
     language used. My version was related to me by an aide to President Nyerere,
     who claimed to have been present.
3   See, for example, Alexander Kanengoni, *Effortless Tears*, Harare: Baobab, 1993.

4   The finest of these, each with a somewhat different emphasis, are: Terence
     Ranger, *Peasant Consciousness and Guerilla War in Zimbabwe*, London: James
     Currey, 1985; David Lan, *Guns and Rain: Guerillas and Spirit Mediums in
     Zimbabwe*, London: James Currey, 1985; Norma J. Kriger, *Zimbabwe's Guerilla
     War: Peasant Voices*, Cambridge: Cambridge University Press, 1992.
5   See the first two chapters of Ranger, op. cit.
6   As reported in John Newhouse, 'Profiles – A Sense of Duty: Lord Carrington',
     New Yorker, 14 February 1983.

TWO

The Pursuit of New Wars

Of all the new ministries, that of Youth, Sport, and Recreation betrayed two impulses. The first impulse it shared with some others, in that the cabinet disposition was in two parts, and the newly returned and better-educated exiles were given the technocratic portfolios, and the veterans – who had stayed and fought – were given those to do with social development. No wonder Ropa, seeing this, took herself back to school. The second impulse was unique among the Zimbabwean ministries. In Africa at that time, ministries of youth were frequently used as mobilisation agencies. National service, as a paramilitary but agriculturally develop-mental arm of government, would conscript youngsters at school-leaving age. No one entered the workforce without some, even if minor, skill. And all would have been subjected to nation-building doctrines in keeping with official rubrics. The most extreme (misused and abused) example of this was the Malawian Young Pioneers. President Hastings Banda had slaughtered some 6000 Jehovah's Witnesses with his cadres of impressionable youth. In Zimbabwe, it was Ropa's ministry that was meant to perform a sort of youth mobilisation service. The ministry never did create a conscript force but, nevertheless, had a real problem on its hands as to what might be done with the thousands of youngsters who had fought in the war, had been excluded from the new national army, and had best be given a rural vocation – even though there was no spare rural land. The ministry was spectacularly, if quietly, unsuccessful; but, in their troubles of the new millennium, Mugabe's people once again turned to the idea of a national service for youth. Again it was unpopular with the youthful population, and unsuccessful. In some part it was an effort that, in 1980, merely echoed what had been attempted by Zimbabwe's neighbours. In other part, it had overtones of European socialist experiments and, of course, of Maoist doctrine during the Cultural Revolution. Somewhere, at the rear-end of policy, was an echo of a means to, if not a fully socialist end, a peasant rural economy. Mugabe promised land reform and redistribution, but as the 1980s wore on no great programmes of redistribution took place. Even if the Ministry of Youth, Sport and Recreation had been very successful, the rurally mobilised, trained and indoctrinated youth would have had nowhere to go.

Nevertheless, the euphoria, relief and general goodwill that greeted Zimbabwe's independence continued – even though it was never matched by inward investment, and even though, from 1981, South Africa inaugurated a regional 'Total Strategy' to destabilise its northern neighbours, particularly those deemed Marxist, such as Angola and Mozambique. Zimbabwe was not a primary target, but the region became a deeply uneasy one. From 1980 to 1982, it may be said that the government of Robert Mugabe sustained its idealism and the independence and reconciliation credentials with which it had been invested. 1982, however, saw the beginnings of an international banking crisis, with a consequent tightening of liquidity for African countries. Almost overnight, as commercial banks withdrew facilities, the IMF became the lender of first resort to Africa. In Southern Africa, three years of mild but sustained drought began. The Zimbabwean Government began a series of prudent fiscal adjustments and, amidst the new stringencies, the first whiffs of corruption began to appear.

What was the financial situation in 1983? Drought reduced the earning power of those in the countryside. Inflation and new taxation measures reduced the financial capacity of those in the cities, and this further affected the countryside, as remittances to rural families declined. The 'communal areas' – renamed from the Rhodesian appellation of 'tribal trust lands' – now survived only because of government handouts; and the budget for 1983/4 deliberately and dramatically inaugurated a slow-down in the purchase of land for black resettlement. What had been little now became less. Rural or urban, the budget's fiscal prudence affected particularly those already of low income. This budget, drawn up between the Ministry of Finance and Mugabe's own Prime Minister's office, was shielded from public debate until its formal announcement. It incorporated many standard IMF austerity measures – although it was claimed that these were voluntarily adopted, rather than imposed. They were probably indeed voluntarily adopted, but in the sense of seeking to shield an inevitable blow by padding it slightly in one's own terms. Given what was to be unleashed upon Africa at large, this was wise; but it softened, it did not necessarily reduce, the normally prescribed range of austerities.

The Zimbabwe dollar was devalued by 17 per cent, although in real market terms this was closer to 25 per cent. The price of imports rose correspondingly, but exports did not rise. After all, the entire world was entering an economic downturn, and the world market was depressed. Not only that, but as a post-independence measure designed to encourage inward investment the Zimbabwean Government had allowed foreign firms the right to repatriate 50 per cent of total profits. At a certain point, this allowed an outflow of funds unmatched by inflow. Meanwhile, the Government did not dare raise company tax, but by 1983/4 the 25 per cent of total revenue that company tax had provided had declined.

The Government's response was to raise sales tax (15 per cent before independence, 10 per cent after independence) to 15 per cent, then 18 per cent, then 23 per cent on selected items. Essential commodities, such as staple foods, were spared. The 1983/4 budget introduced a 2 per cent tax on all income above Zim.$100 a month. The average worker, as a result, now paid Zim.$10–12 in additional taxes than had been the case at independence. As mentioned above, funds for land purchase were slashed, leaving the prospect of considerable unfinished business. It seemed as if the division of land ownership might remain fixed, with its obvious actual and historical inequities; but the Government would not then contemplate land nationalisation with no or low compensation.

In addition, the general ambience of an external security situation – South Africa beginning to run rampant in the region – was greatly exacerbated by the 'discovery' of a possible internal counterpart. In 1982, the first arms caches were uncovered in strategic locations in the Matabelelands. Perhaps they were left over from the war, but the Government took them – or at least advertised them – as an evidence of internal security risk; as an evidence that disgruntled ZIPRA fighters were preparing a western insurrection, that Nkomo's ZAPU party was untrustworthy and had withheld knowledge in bad faith, and that it was now necessary to stamp out the internal enemy. In the midst of drought, financial slow-down, retrenchment of land redistribution, and external war, the Zimbabwe Government now geared up to fight, once again, within Zimbabwe. In doing so, it applied lessons it had learned from the most atrocious of Rhodesian tactics, and added to them by a peculiar North Korean savagery.

It should be pointed out that although the North Korean influence in Zimbabwe was internationally noted, this was only one manifestation of North Korean influence in Southern Africa at that time. In Lesotho, for instance, the hitherto moribund National Youth League – exactly that sort of youth mobilisation and development scheme described above – was revitalised by North Korean training and some limited access to arms. As early as 1982, South Africa launched a cross-border raid into Lesotho, alarmed by the advent of a North Korean – hence Communist – embassy within its traditional sphere of influence. The South Africans not only then held an ideological aversion to Communism but, in 1976, had seen its own forward columns repulsed by Cuban units in Angola. Much has been written about the Cubans but, albeit on a smaller scale, the North Korean entry meant that there were two Communist regimes with military force, or military advisers, in Southern Africa. In Lesotho, the National Youth League began calling for even greater diplomatic contact with Communist states and, although this reflected a struggle among internal Lesotho factions, South Africa raided Lesotho again in December 1985, then closed the borders. The Lesotho army launched a successful coup in January 1986, and the Prime Minister, Leabua Jonathan, long a minor thorn in Pretoria's side, fell.

The Lesotho example, seemingly a self-contained scenario of a small, fractious elite in a small country surrounded by South Africa, was nonetheless instructive. The model held out for the National Youth League was the Malawi Young Pioneers. Disciplined, organised, capable of a real contribution to developmental work in the Malawian country-side – their Youth Farms were, in production terms, exemplary – they had been used, all the same, as a blunt political instrument. The persecution and slaughter of Jehovah's Witnesses was appalling – although it drew scant protest in the West – as was the lesser slaughter of Hastings Banda's political enemies. The ruthless crushing of opposition, without scruples or any moral reflections – the ruthless devastation of any possible (not necessarily actual) support network for opposition – was a hallmark of Banda's years. This was not visited upon Lesotho, but the model was an ominous one. Its ruthless content was indeed visited upon the Matabelelands in the west of Zimbabwe, throughout the mid-1980s. If not scant protest, such protest as emerged in the West or the region was understated in the extreme. This is partly because, at the time, no one knew or believed the scale of repression. Still basking in its independence glow, and the lingering accolades about reconciliation, the Zimbabwe Government hid its policies well. In 1985, after the first post-independence elections, academic commentary conspicuously played down what it seemed to suggest was a minor 'dissident problem',[1] and, even years later at the 1991 Commonwealth summit, this time held in Harare as a ten year celebration of the independence the Commonwealth had helped bring about, international human rights groups concentrated their criticisms on abuses in the 1990 elections, mentioning not at all the depredations of the mid-1980s.[2] The 1991 summit was, of course, concerned with the high ideals of human rights, and this book will return to that summit, as well as to the 1985 and 1990 elections. There were, however, no human rights accorded the victims of the war against 'dissidents' in the Matabelelands.

The war against them was waged by Zimbabwe National Army regular units, and a specially organised, North-Korean-trained 'Fifth Brigade'. The regular units engaged such dissidents as could be found, but the Fifth Brigade fought little and terrorised much. Its primary function was to deny any possible base in the Matabelelands to the dissidents, and this denial was accomplished by scorched earth policies and plain murder of citizens in suspected locales of dissident activity. For years, even Zimbabweans in the Matabelelands found it traumatically impossible to speak, particularly speak politically, of these events. The description that follows owes a little to my own fieldwork interviews in the late 1980s and early 1990s – in which the respondents seemed to talk almost in a foreshortened code – and more to the immense work of uncovering and recovery undertaken by Richard Werbner, Jocelyn Alexander and Terence Ranger and their colleagues both in Zimbabwe and abroad, which began to be published in the 1990s, particularly towards the end of that decade and in the early new millennium.[3] I do remember, however, footage of the first march-past of the Fifth Brigade, fresh from its training. This was no ordinary parade march. The Fifth Brigaders jogged in formation, performed the high Korean Tae Kwon Do kicks in formation, and smashed their fists through tiles in formation, all the while singing about death to the nation's enemies. Mugabe took the march-past, and I remember thinking, having witnessed many military and martial events, that these were not soldiers in the normal sense. These were officially trained and legitimised terrorists, not special forces or commando units. These would kill, and not just in battle. These had that North Korean trait of a complete lack of sentimentality, although others might put their lack more strongly.

THE WHIRLWIND, THE STORM, GUKURAHUNDI

The two large provinces that constitute the west of Zimbabwe are Matabeleland North and Matabeleland South. The majority population there are Ndebele, of Zulu ancestry (although this is debatable in its pure form, exact differentiations now being hard to make between those of Zulu blood descent and those of historical political affiliation to the Zulu regional 'superpower' of Shaka). Near the provincial capital, Bulawayo, Zimbabwe's second city, lie the Matopos Hills, an area of great spiritual significance and sweeping beauty. Here, there are natural columns of great boulders, sitting on top of one another; rhino still roam the plain below; Rhodes asked to be buried there, and rainbow lizards dance on his grave to this day. Lobengula, the last great king of the Ndebele, was deceived and defeated by Rhodes, despite his ambassadors being kindly received by Queen Victoria. Once a generation, a female shaman is meant to appear at Matopos to anoint the spiritual heir of Lobengula, the one who would restore his reign and extend it over all Zimbabwe. Every year Nkomo would go to the great rock columns, hoping to be greeted by the shaman – who never came for him. At independence, the city of Bulawayo seemed divided at Lobengula Street: one side was white, and the other not. That white part boasted huge boulevards lined with tall Jacaranda trees. Rhodes, it seems, was determined to be able to wheel a team of oxen in each of the main streets. The other major towns of the Matabelelands were less grand. Plumtree, near the Botswana border, was tiny. At independence, only a dirt road linked the two countries. To the north lay Hwange National Park (Wankie back then) and Victoria Falls on the Zambian border, and, to the south of Bulawayo (one highway linking them all like a necklace), were Gwanda and Beitbridge. Gwanda was also tiny, boasting a small hotel called Hardy's Inn, which in turn boasted life-size portraits of Smuts and Rhodes. This was Rhodesian heartland and on the South African border, on one side of the Limpopo River, stood Beitbridge. South African soldiers used to stand on that bridge, deliberately just on the Rhodesian side of the border, to taunt the process leading to independence in 1980. The entire stretch of land between Victoria Falls and Beitbridge, with minority exceptions of denser wooded hills, was reasonably accessible and thinly covered with scrub and trees: not the best possible guerilla territory. Guerillas would have to rely on tiny support units scattered over many villages.

Who were the guerillas of the 1980s? They were not, in the first instance, an invention of Mugabe and his ZANU colleagues – although the campaign of ruthless persecution created support and some new recruits for them. Nor were they a unified group. There were at least two, if not more, factions; and, although they advertised their loyalty to the Ndebele party, ZAPU, and its former military wing, ZIPRA, the factions were autonomous from the ZAPU leadership. It was almost certainly the case that Nkomo and his lieutenants had no command over them or instigation of them.

During the liberation war, as noted above, ZIPRA and ZANLA were not given to cooperation, and were sometimes nakedly antagonistic to each other. Some units on both sides retained their hostile attitudes, both during the electoral process that led to independence, and afterwards. Especially for those who had been placed together in the camps, or assembly points, that had been a feature of the truce during the electoral period, and which lingered afterwards, hostilities could become venomous. The assembly points were part of the Lancaster House Agreement, and were policed by the Commonwealth Monitoring Force. The guerillas were permitted to retain their arms but, by being gathered together, were meant to provide a visible signal that the war was suspended. Those assembly points populated by only one of the two guerilla factions usually gave few problems to the Monitoring Force. The Kenyan units were able to fly in Tusker Beer, and shared it with their guerilla counterparts. The Fijian units, not so tastily provisioned, had beer nevertheless, and in their quarters, bravely but necessarily positioned between assembled ZANLA and ZIPRA forces, would lie on the floor at night, calmly drinking their beer while feuding rifle fire whistled overhead. They would emerge the next morning to 'clear up the mess'. This is to make light of a very difficult series of situations from Assembly Point to

Assembly Point. Many guerillas, not trusting the electoral process, left the camps and were labelled 'dissidents' by the eventually elected government. At the very least, having taken their weapons with them, they added to the huge numbers of armaments still at large in the country.

Those guerillas who remained in each assembly point had been meant to assemble from the adjacent area, that is from their area of operations. However, when the Lancaster House Agreement became known, and before its timetable of implementation, both ZANLA and ZIPRA units crossed the Mozambican and Zambian borders into Rhodesia in order to stake a claim to various parts of the country. This was particularly true of ZIPRA guerillas, who often deployed themselves in this short time precisely to deny or counterbalance ZANLA territorial predominance. The ZANLA rank and file, who had borne the brunt of the fighting, were understandably unimpressed by this opportunism.

So it was that after the war, independence being celebrated elsewhere in the country, large numbers of guerillas remained encamped. Many had nowhere left to go, some hoped for enlistment in the new army of unity; the Government did not have clear ideas what to do with them; the schemes within the Ministry of Youth, Sport and Recreation were not even first conceived; when they eventually came, they were too little and too late, and depended on too little land. Towards the end of 1980, the first year of independence, a decision was taken to relocate guerillas from the rural assembly points to special locations in the cities – in particular Chitungwiza, near metropolitan Harare, and Entumbane, near Bulawayo. At a stroke, the new authorities compounded the problems of military men without a purpose, and military men engaged in inter-factional quarrelling, with the problem of cohabitation in urban civilian environments. The result was not only explosive in itself, but exploited by ZANU politicians, themselves unable to forgive grudges incurred during the war, and both ZAPU and ZIPRA began to be accused of fresh crimes of dissidence. Gun battles broke out in Chitungwiza, but a full-scale, two-day fire-fight took place in Entumbane. Nkomo, the ZAPU leader, had entered Robert Mugabe's government as Minister of Home Affairs – itself a disappointing position, but one he could not turn down since Mugabe, with an absolute majority of his own, was being seen to proffer a magnanimous unity – and he was now in a precarious position. As Minister of Home Affairs, he had some responsibility for law and order (though not demobilisation), and his own ZIPRA combatants were being accused of breaking law and order. If they had indeed initiated the fighting – and this is not clear – they had almost certainly been goaded into doing so by inflammatory remarks from senior ZANU politicians; but now they, along with Nkomo, were on the defensive. The government raided Nkomo's farm, searching for weapons, and arrested nine senior ZAPU figures in Bulawayo. Perhaps both Nkomo and ZIPRA had been neatly set-up. Perhaps it was far too neat for a set up. Either way, some ZIPRA elements made the decision there and then that, for them, for ZAPU and – more ominously – the Ndebele people, there could never be trust and equity under Robert Mugabe's ZANU. The seeds of true dissidence had thus been sown.

Although Nkomo and senior ZANU figures rehearsed words of moderation and conciliation at year's end, fighting erupted again in February 1981. Independence was not yet a year old. Abroad, the Zimbabwean Government basked in the warmth of its cooperation with the white settlers; but the world was not investing economically in Zimbabwe; and, at home, the reconciliation between blacks and whites was not being mirrored between ZANU and ZAPU. Nkomo was demoted to Minister without Portfolio. In August 1981, 106 North Korean military advisers quietly slipped into the country and, in February 1982, the arms caches were discovered.

Alexander Kanengoni, the Zimbabwean novelist, has written movingly of the liberation war, and of the new war that, shortly afterwards, started.

> Another war?
>
> Once on a visit to Dzivareskwa along the road to Bulawayo, he had seen huge armoured personnel carriers rumble west towards Matabeleland: another war that threatened to tear the country apart had broken out. ZANU versus ZAPU, the Shonas versus the Ndebeles: a civil war!
>
> Munashe clearly remembered how the problem had begun: the discovery, at former ZIPRA assembly points, of huge arms caches, allegedly to topple the government. He was returning from the uncompleted journey to Chimanda and moving distractedly across the barren plains, the surrounding villages watching him curiously, when news of the discovery had broken out. Unlike much other news, the situation in Matabeleland disturbed him. Was this the first sign of another war? As he watched the convoy roll by and saw the sweating faces of the young troopers at the back of the armoured vehicles holding their rifles loosely, arrogantly, at the ready, he noticed a familiar madness in the pupils of their eyes, their pursed lips and felt the air explode with the sickening smell of gunpowder, he quickly turned and walked away. And he thought: war is the greatest scourge of mankind.[4]

The war that followed was indeed terrible. However, apart from ZANU and ZAPU and their respective merits and blames, there was a third major player in what it regarded as a (highly serious) strategic game. This was South Africa. In August 1981, about the time that the North Koreans arrived, South Africa – then just setting about its Total Strategy of military and economic destabilisation of the region (of which, more below) – sent a first signal in Zimbabwe. The Inkomo Barracks were sabotaged, and thereafter South Africa sought to fan the flames of rivalries between ZANU and ZAPU. In July 1982, in a superbly planned and executed commando raid, South Africa destroyed most of the Zimbabwe airforce. The white air command in Zimbabwe, retained as part of the post-war reconciliation, were courtmartialed (although later acquitted of any collaboration) and, if nothing else, the South African action effectively determined a first movement towards a ZANU autarky, without either ZAPU or white initiators. At the end of 1982, South Africa began organising, training and recruiting a several-hundred-strong dissident group, comprised mostly of former ZIPRA fighters. These called themselves Super-ZAPU, believing their political leaders in ZAPU proper could no longer help their people. In a way, they were analogous to the Real IRA since, despite South African prompting, they saw their foundation principles being undermined. There is, after all, an Ndebele strand of autarky too, and both Super-ZAPU and the other former-ZIPRA forces who took to the countryside were not immune to this. Throughout 1982, the government purged the Zimbabwe National Army. ZIPRA personnel were transferred, demoted or simply killed. Many, in the face of this, deserted; some joined the guerillas. However, this meant a certain historical sociology among the guerillas. Those from 1980 were joined by those 'created' by government persecution in 1982. Then there was Super-ZAPU, created by South Africa. Now, in December 1982, came the passing-out parade of the Fifth Brigade. The Brigade flag, conferred by Robert Mugabe, bore the slogan 'Gukurahundi'. It means 'storm'.

This term was also used by ZANU and ZANLA towards the end of the liberation war. If it was, to any extent, a return to that war, then it was with new twists. In large (but not total) part, it was not a return to that war, but a carrying of it forward under the purist and most chauvinist of rubrics. New external factors had fed into the situation but, even without South Africa, the entire first handling and subsequent inflammation of

Ndebele dissatisfaction was an internal failure of great magnitude for the new government. Insofar as the old war was recognisable, it was because the government soldiers, especially the Fifth Brigade, used many of the old guerilla tactics they had pioneered only recently: the sudden descent upon a village, the mass mobilisation of the villagers, the requiring of villagers to sing songs of solidarity with what was now the government, the exemplary beatings, the forced confessions, and both selective and arbitrary killings. What, even now, most external supporters of the liberation war do not realise is the extent to which the guerillas were, so often, terrorists to their own people. It is realised, but not talked loudly about, in Zimbabwe. It has crept into various novels and short stories; and it is Kanengoni again who, in a collection of his short stories, described one of these events under the title, 'Things We'd Rather Not Talk About'.[5] This time, however, it was not a case of Shona guerillas terrorising Shona villagers. Then, there were mediating and compensating devices. The guerillas needed support and provisions. They needed spiritual endorsement and blessing – legitimation – from the mystical healers, mediums and shamans. Shona soldiers let loose upon Matabeleland – and the Fifth Brigade was entirely stripped of Ndebele membership – meant a lack of such compensation; and its replacement by cultural difference writ into a political antipathy. The enforced village gatherings became, under the Gukurahundi, savage occasions. It left a scar upon the nation. When, in the late 1980s and early 1990s, with an officialised reconciliation between the two sides, I sought to talk to Ndebele figures about what had happened I was given only cursory, coded and curt comments. It had been something too recently traumatic to talk about. The detailed knowledge of all this has only recently entered the public domain, although Richard Werbner's account of 1991 lay unappreciated for some time by most Africanists; more recently, Jocelyn Alexander, in particular, has published a moving series of interview statements with those who had first-hand experience of the Gukurahundi.[6]

The twist comes in that the government soldiers also used the techniques practised in the war – only it was in the war against liberation – by the Rhodesian army. Much more highly mobile and with far heavier ordinance than that of the guerillas, the Rhodesian military machine, once deployed – that is once guerilla units had been found – was formidable. If Teurai Ropa became legendary for shooting down a Rhodesian heli-copter, no Ndebele 'dissident' in the 1980s managed a repetition of the feat. Aerial visibility and manoeuvrability are devastating advantages, and were particularly so in the sparsely shrubbed Matabelelands. Added to this was the range of the Rhodesians' own sense of pointed (and sometimes pointless) atrocity.

And added to this again was the gratuitous cruelty inculcated into the Fifth Brigade by the North Koreans. There was little subtlety about it all, and 'ways of torturing a person' might be left as a brief indication of what was learnt for use in this grotesquely monopolitical but multi-cultural war. Apart from torture, arbitrary murder and destruction were common. 'The Gukurahundi could never discuss, only shoot you,' said one of Alexander's respondents. A favourite was to shoot people in their toilets, an indication of filth joining filth, and the killing of families was not sufficient if only done cleanly. The Gukurahundi liked to herd people in their huts, then fire bazookas into them. The idea was not only to leave bodies, but pieces of bodies, as a warning to others. But a warning against what? For all the research on 'dissidents', whether former ZIPRA or Super-ZAPU, it is highly unlikely whether they ever numbered more than a few hundred. They never denied the government anything in the rural areas. Governability was not threatened. They raised a question of governance, certainly. But 'the Gukurahundi could never discuss', so the question of governance could never be made into a national discourse. All Mugabe's Government had to do was to wait till the elections of 1985 – in which no major challenge was either expected or materialised – declare a renewed mandate, and rely upon the 'above-ground' ZAPU leadership to persuade the 'dissidents' to return from their awkward but, inevitably, fruitless mission in the bush. For, if the crushing response to them was uncalled for, their entry into 'dissidence' was also uncalled for. Firefights in camps, and opportunistic rhetoric by a small number of politicians, do not mean that a people-at-large are ready for insurrection. However, it is government, by virtue of being government, that must bear responsibility for the way it governs; and for the treatment of those governed. The citizens of the rural Matabelelands were treated with sustained casual cruelties that never reached levels of genocide; but there were parallels with Nazi atrocities in the occupied territories of the Second World War. And, if an analogy is made to the Nazis, then the Fifth Brigade was a Gestapo. In the late 1990s and early 2000s, a political figure would arise in Zimbabwe with self-declared Nazi nomenclature. And there is a mixture of labels now: Maoist, Nazi, perhaps an inflection of Stalinism. The remainder of this chapter will ensure a wider perspective. Mugabe's mistakes at home may at least be contextualised by events around his home, and impinging upon the Zimbabwean hearth. A blowing up of an entire airforce (never mind how many planes were second-hand and antique Vampires, somehow purchased from derelict New Zealand stock) is, after all, a declaration of intent on the part of those responsible – and those responsible were not internal 'dissidents'.

By 1988, the storm within Zimbabwe was over. An amnesty was declared. Preceding it, in 1987, another effort at political reconciliation took place. ZANU and ZAPU achieved a national unity – somewhat on ZANU's terms – and the name chosen for the cojoint party both emphasised that ZANU had set the terms and echoed the days before independence, when Mugabe and Nkomo's people had negotiated as one 'Patriotic Front'. The party of government was now called ZANU-PF. Nkomo became one of two vice-presidents. The commander of the Fifth Brigade was promoted to head such airforce as had been rebuilt. No official report was released about the actions and atrocities in the Matabelelands. Such apologies as have been forthcoming have been as if teeth were being slowly extracted – or somewhat like Japanese apologies for its war in China, and its atrocities against both civilians and Allied prisoners. It was white activists – later members of parliament for the new opposition of the late 1990s and early 2000s – who first sought to reveal some of the detail of government action in the Matabelelands. In November 2001, Mugabe, hard pressed by both internal opposition and external pressure, called these (popularly elected) MPs (without irony) 'terrorists'.[7] During the state terrorism of the 1980s, however, it has been estimated that as many as 18,000 died.

Why was the storm over in 1988? With such loss of life and depredation, why did the 'dissidents' come in from the bush? Since it all began, Mugabe had won an election in 1985. Although the Matabelelands clung to Nkomo, it was clear that nationally Mugabe was 'the only show in town'. More significantly, it became clearer that there was a genuine external enemy on the rampage. If South Africa had served some regional notice in 1982, by destroying the Zimbabwean airforce and then sponsoring Super-ZAPU, these came to be seen as minor actions when compared to the sweep of its actions elsewhere, particularly in Angola and Mozambique. The ZAPU leadership knew that something much larger than what the 'dissidents' claimed to represent was at stake.

They pleaded with the fighters to end their rebellion. The international community was also grinding towards a showdown with South Africa. By 1986, still seeking to persuade Margaret Thatcher that her policies towards Southern Africa were wrong (with Geoffrey Howe, as Foreign Secretary, having somewhat less influence on her than Carrington), the Commonwealth and Europe were moving towards sanctions against South Africa. In 1986, Mugabe sent Zimbabwean forces into Mozambique, to help rescue that country's transport links (particularly the Beira Corridor, which linked Zimbabwe to the sea) from attack by South-African-sponsored Mozambican rebels. Mugabe, in fact, toyed with the idea of taking the military fight to South Africa itself. Nyerere, in Tanzania, was saying the same thing. Mugabe never did this. It would have been a very uneven contest. But what it meant was that Mugabe had now a 'real' war to fight, and a wider war at least to contemplate. The Gukurahundi suddenly seemed a sideshow. After all, majority rule had been the animating rubric. In the region, it was still not fully achieved. It was more important than how the majority fought and quarrelled within their rule.

THE WAR FOR TOTALITY IN SOUTHERN AFRICA

Total Strategy was the South African response to what the apartheid regime saw as Total Onslaught. With the independence of Zimbabwe, and the electoral triumph not of Muzorewa but of Mugabe, there was no longer a northern zone of buffer states. Once, not long before, Botswana, Lesotho and Swaziland had been tame neighbours. The South Africans had placed their bets on a similarly tame and moderate Zimbabwe. Mugabe had not been their preference. In a way, a buffer or cordon of moderate states was a second choice. The first choice had been for a *cordon sanitaire* exactly – a white zone – but Angola and Mozambique had unexpectedly lost white rule in 1975; and now Zimbabwe had also lost white dominance, and not even the second-order choice of moderation seemed reflected in Mugabe. Notwithstanding his immediate overtures towards racial reconciliation, Mugabe's image in South Africa was still – if not that of the man who would forbid Christmas – that of the Marxist rebel. If that seems a reading lacking the nuance one might expect a formidable state apparatus like South Africa's to have, then it is well to

remember that no official African research unit existed in the South
African Government until after 1976. In any case, the Marxist fear seemed
real enough to the state's security and military men. The army still
smarted from having to withdraw from Angola, in the face of Cuban
encirclement of its forward lines at the end of 1975. It was not the great
Cuban and African victory sung in the frontline states, but it had been
the result of South African over-confidence and military error. Ever
after, the generals itched for a 'payback time'.

Total Strategy was adopted from the writings of the French General
Andre Beaufre on the Algerian war. It proposed the use of a totality of
available instruments, so that war was not only military but political,
economic, psychological and cast within consistent diplomatic justifiability.
For the South Africans, the aim was not to win. South Africa did not
want the trouble of governing the region. What it wanted, and began to
get, was the destabilisation of the surrounding regimes, the denial to
them of the ability to rule. Thus destabilised and denied, preferably
divided and at odds within themselves, they could not concentrate on
spreading their contamination of majority rule further southwards. The
South Africans supported UNITA guerillas against Angola's Marxist
government, RENAMO guerillas against Mozambique's and, somewhat
half-heartedly by comparison, Super-ZAPU in Zimbabwe.

The new doctrine was adopted when P.W. Botha became South
African Prime Minister in 1978, and its application began in 1981. He
established government structures that could bypass even his own cabinet,
and concentrated decisive power in the hands of his State Security
Council. Its members came to be known in Pretoria's shorthand slang as
the 'Securocrats', and many spoke of the securitisation of the state. The
minority regime became an even more minority regime. Repression at
home mirrored the increased intervention away from home. As well as
support for rebel guerilla groups, South African armoured columns
frequently invaded Angola. There was a special grudge there on account
of the Cubans, and it is fair to say that the war in the Angolan theatre
became not only a guerilla war but a conventional one of tanks, artillery
duels and aircraft. South Africa maintained air superiority until 1988.

The havoc played by South Africa in the region was astronomical. In
addition to the world banking crisis of 1982, and the consequent
difficulties in securing liquidity, came the local destabilisation that war
caused. The Commonwealth and EU campaign to launch sanctions

against South Africa applied, finally, little unabsorbable pressure on Pretoria. Total Strategy had meant a total preparation at home as well – although the increasing withdrawal of multinational operations did start to hurt; but these were largely independent withdrawals, and not the result of official sanctions. Besides, the outside world could not impose full-throttled sanctions on South Africa, for Pretoria had a capacity, via the regional transport and trading routes it controlled, to pass these on to its neighbours. 'And here's destabilisation from us, and here's destabilisation from your Commonwealth and European friends.' This is why Zimbabwe sought to make an intervention of its own. The Beira Corridor linked Zimbabwe, through Mozambique, to the sea – to a port capable, if with difficulty, of handling Zimbabwe's exports and imports, which was not South African. The deployment of Zimbabwean troops – without air cover – was a rash but bold challenge to South Africa's securocrats. It was Mugabe, without much of a fall-back plan, taking Pretoria on at its own game of military muscle and economic prizes. While the rest of Africa talked about making a stand, while the Non-Aligned Movement, India loudly within it, talked of making a military stand, Mugabe showed the other side of his face to that balefully seen in the Matabelelands, and made a stand.

The Zimbabwean intervention is outlined below. It did not end South African destabilisation, or even dent it. It was a stand that said that it would not go unchallenged. But it did not destroy RENAMO, Pretoria's proxy in Mozambique. If anything, as will be seen in a later chapter, it revealed a face of RENAMO to the Zimbabweans that the Mozambican Government had sought to hide from the world: that, South African sponsorship, training and equipment aside, countless atrocities aside, some core part of RENAMO seemed to be fighting for something that was not South African, but had something to do with governance and government in Mozambique. The Zimbabweans were at first puzzled that government troops would run and hide as battle began, but RENAMO would stand and fight.

What accounted finally for Total Strategy was the prelude to 'Glasnost' in the Soviet Union. In parlous economic condition, the Soviets, who had been bankrolling the Cubans (and by this time Soviet officers were acting as advisers) in Angola, needed to cut their losses. The Soviet high command pleaded for one last, properly provisioned throw of the dice – and Gorbachev gave it to them. A squadron of latest-generation MIG fighters, with latest-generation avionics, and Soviet pilots, arrived in Angola. Faster, more manoeuvrable, and better armed than the South African Mirages, Cheetahs and Jaguars, the MIGs meant that the owner-ship of air superiority had suddenly shifted. With a final showdown clearly looming, both Pretoria and Luanda (and Havana and Moscow) invested much in preparing for a decisive battle over the city of Cuito Cuanavale in 1988. Held by Angolan Government troops, and Cubans, its fall to UNITA and the South Africans would signal who had won the last dice game. If the South Africans won, and Gorbachev withdrew his MIGs and financial support, and the Cubans had to leave, Total Strategy would have won its landmark victory. Cuito Cuanavale was, in preparation, ringed like something out of a Warsaw Pact manual: layered mine fields surrounded it; phalanxed banks of surface-to-air missiles were deployed within it. Whichever way the South Africans and UNITA troops came, they could only come by sustaining huge casualties. If they had come, UNITA soldiers would have taken the brunt of the landmines, and the South African armoured columns would have followed them in. It was not to be. In the manoeuvring for position outside the city, Cuban forces once again surrounded and trapped a significant number of South African units, and the call once again went to Pretoria – as it had in 1975 – that it should withdraw, or its sons would return numerously home in body bags.

1989 saw the fall of the Berlin Wall, the coming to power in South Africa of F.W. De Klerk. The world was suddenly changing. How it changed, and did not change Zimbabwe, will be seen later. For now, let us see how Zimbabwe fared in Mozambique.

THE ZIMBABWEAN WAR IN MOZAMBIQUE

Total Strategy could involve duplicity as well. In 1984, after a sustained programme of destabilisation, South Africa forced Mozambique to sign the Nkomati Accord. Under this Accord, South Africa was to suspend its help to RENAMO rebels, and Mozambique was to expel the South African fighters and representatives of the ANC (African National Congress) from its territory. In short, South Africa required the literal distancing of its ANC enemies from itself – Mozambique was one country too close. This was a terrible humiliation for Mozambique, and its president, Samora Machel. He had fought a war of liberation himself, had offered a new front for the Zimbabwean fighters, and a headquarters for Robert Mugabe to refurbish ZANU-in-exile in his own image. Now he was being required to expel those who represented the last great liberation struggle in Southern Africa – that in South Africa itself. Mozambique duly expelled the ANC; but Pretoria did not cease its support of RENAMO.

In June 1985, in a summit involving Machel, Mugabe and Nyerere, both Zimbabwe and Tanzania agreed to support Mozambique militarily. The Tanzanian support was never as extensive as that of the Zimbabweans. 5000 Zimbabwean troops entered Mozambique in the first instance; but this soon swelled to 10,000. Ostensibly, they were there to guard the Beira Corridor. As noted above, this was very much in Zimbabwe's own interests, but it was also in the interests of several multinational firms who had invested in the refurbishment of the rail link at the Corridor's heart, and in port facilities at Beira, and in the interests of both bilateral and multilateral donors. However, it was not simply a defence of the Corridor against RENAMO attack, but a clear military action against RENAMO's overall operational capacity. The Corridor cut Mozambique in half. A secure Corridor would force RENAMO to devise two self-contained operational strategies, prevent or hinder reinforcement of operations in one zone from another and, particularly, help protect the capital, Maputo, in the southern zone. As it was, the Zimbabweans soon realised that they could not fight a successful defensive war from within the Corridor. In an almost South African military strategy, they decided to 'defend forward', take the fight to the enemy, not wait for the enemy to come. Zimbabwean forces took the RENAMO headquarters of Casa Banana, and there discovered documents proving that South Africa, despite the Nkomati Accord, had remained a most active supporter, provisioner and adviser of RENAMO. Although by 1989 the Corridor was, by and large, 'safe', and the Zimbabwean force reduced to 3000, RENAMO was far from destroyed. A superb radio communications network meant it could mobilise a national operation much more easily than the government could.[8] And, although it always denied its responsibility, the South African Government exacted a terrible and personal revenge for Mugabe's help to Mozambique and Machel. For Mugabe and Machel were not only liberation-leaders-turned-government-leaders, they were close friends. On 19 October 1986, flying home from a frontline summit,

Machel's plane – with Soviet pilots – was mysteriously destroyed. It would seem that someone had repositioned a homing beacon – in front of a mountain.

If Machel's death had been a personal rebuke, and warning, to Mugabe, the later romance between Machel's widow and Nelson Mandela seems an apt rejoinder. But Machel, for all the mistakes and blunders of his government, had remained an idealist. No one will write books about him and say that he was a wicked man.

The timing of Machel's death, and the wider signal it sent, could not have been blunter or more immediate. The Non-Aligned summit had taken place in Harare from 28 August to 7 September 1986. Mugabe had become Chairman of the Non-Aligned Movement, and the movement – in its Harare Declaration on South Africa – had waxed long and urgently on the need for sanctions against South Africa. It was in Harare that Rajiv Ghandi, himself to be assassinated in his turn, spoke of a Non-Allied Movement military force, an army, that would come to Southern Africa. The rhetoric seemed to suggest that it would march on Pretoria itself, and finish the business. Those who rattle such sabres, Machel's death seemed to say, would find their heads cut off.

But it was not just a war played out by great, blunt gestures. In securing the Beira Corridor, the Zimbabwean army did indeed inflict defeats upon RENAMO that the Mozambican army had never achieved. RENAMO units did stand and fight, but those who fought were not always 'regular' combatants; it was very much the case that child soldiers were used in this war.

> Right now, the war is a series of ritualised contacts. RENAMO sends a FRELIMO garrison written notice of its imminent attack. FRELIMO withdraws; RENAMO attacks; RENAMO withdraws; FRELIMO reoccupies. RENAMO don't send written notices to the Zimbabweans. They won't withdraw. But this means that FRELIMO can't win.[9]

> [FRELIMO] are cowardly, incompetent, lazy, and badly-officered. The Zimbabweans don't even coordinate with FRELIMO forces. The Zimbabweans run their own show in Mozambique.[10]

> Recently, a Zimbabwean force received one of the RENAMO warnings of attack and decided to hold its ground. RENAMO clearly thought it was a FRELIMO group it was attacking. The Zimbabweans held the attack, then countered. Then spent hours weeping over the boy soldiers they had killed. It's come to the slaughter of children now.[11]

One of the Zimbabwean letters home, which was shown to me, summed up encounters of that sort: 'I feel disgusting'. And yet such encounters began a quiet mood change in Harare, and within Mugabe. If even children fought better than the soldiers of the Mozambique Government – even if those children had been press-ganged and atrociously blooded – what was going on? Was it just that the children had been brutalised and had nowhere else to go? Was it just that South Africa sponsored the rebels? And, in the search for what motivated RENAMO there began also a search for what, in fact, animated FRELIMO. Was it indeed the best government for Mozambique? The intellectual left in Zimbabwe was the first to start questioning in this manner.[12] This was to have profound effects for the region in the early 1990s, as we shall see; for now, the Zimbabweans had a vital transport corridor to secure – and they did. With some radical truncation of ambition (there never was a Non-Aligned army that marched on Pretoria), with some radical rethinking of political correctness (the Mozambican Government might not have been fully correct), and with personal loss (the death of Machel), Mugabe had nevertheless, on a minor front compared with that in Angola, tweaked the nose of Pretoria. In any case, this was enough war for him. With defeat at Cuito Cuanavale in Angola in 1988, it had also been enough war and Total Strategy for the South Africans. By 1989, the Beira Corridor was safe, the war in the Matabelelands was over, and South Africa had been dragged to the conference table over both Angola and its southern neighbour, South Africa's last minority-ruled territory, Namibia. Mugabe had not begun his reign with the intention of carrying forward militarised liberation to South Africa and its cross-border interests. To an extent, those interests did cross Zimbabwean borders. However, despite some South African involvement in the Matabelelands, it would seem that Mugabe's war within his own borders was wholly concerned with a bringing to heel of the last man who could also stand as a liberation leader within Zimbabwe – the fat man who had once sat in the chair Nyerere had offered Mugabe – defeating his followers and humiliating the man himself. Zimbabweans paid a terrible price for that ambition. It was not just the slaughter of children in Mozambique that offered appalling food for thought. Those slaughtered by the Gukurahundi, and their families, were never destined to receive full official explanation, redress or untempered apology. In years to come, at the ballot boxes, all the Matabeleland constituencies would reject Mugabe. At the elections in 1985, and for those in later years, Mugabe's government won sweeping majorities. In that curious Zimbabwean game of patience and silent memory – an interiorised resistance – the Matabelelands would wait, and not as fruitlessly as Nkomo awaiting the spirit medium of the Matopos.

It was in a curious respect for electoral mandate that saw Mugabe launch forth into Mozambique only after the 1985 elections.

THE 1985 ELECTIONS

These elections were, given the circumstances, remarkably free and fair (on the polling days at least). The drought had broken and a record maize harvest was predicted – much grown on African peasant land. Bernard Chidzero had returned from his position with the UN and, as Finance Minister, had introduced a modest but visible float of economic improvements. There had been a huge growth in the number of schools; less, but still visible, growth in health care facilities. All this lead to Mugabe's ZANU party securing another absolute majority, with 77 per cent of the vote (compared to 63 per cent in 1980). The interesting aspect was that, although nowhere close to threatening Nkomo's ZAPU domination of the Matabelelands, ZANU actually increased its percentage vote in both Matabeleland North and South. Intimidation may have helped this trend, but the Fifth Brigade had operated in rural areas, away from the critical mass of voters. Some of it may have been due to Ndebele disenchantment with Nkomo. In any case, many of his best lieutenants were in jail, and Nkomo himself was toying with the idea of an opposition coalition involving ZAPU and the minority parties – but the minority parties were wiped out. The white seats – still reserved under the Lancaster House Agreement until 1987 – were split (and four white MPs had joined Mugabe), but the black minority parties picked up only one seat. Muzorewa lost everything in these polls. Whatever the trauma in the Matabelelands, Mugabe had won the trust of the remainder of Zimbabwe. He even appointed a former Ian Smith minister, Chris Anderson, to his new cabinet. A number of ZAPU politicians, including former ministers, crossed over to Mugabe. If he had called a referendum then for a one-party state, he would have won it. But even firebrand political figures, themselves highly active in the struggle for liberation, such as Edgar Tekere, went on record to say that a one-party state might best be achieved by total electoral domination, and not by decree or legislation. As he licked his wounds after 1985, Nkomo seemed to sense that this was a tide he could not resist. The irony, at the 1990 elections, would be the reprise of Tekere's reputation as an independent firebrand and, if the 1985 elections were free enough and fair enough, those of 1990 were more often held not to be. In 1985, Mugabe had won a new mandate and would go on to challenge South African hegemony in the region and become, his domestic record notwithstanding, an international statesman. At home, the Matabelelands were subdued but, derived from the key figures of ZANU itself, a challenger would step forth again to embitter the intolerant side of Mugabe.

NOTES ON CHAPTER 2

1   For example Luke Trainor, 'A Triumph for Mugabe', *New Zealand International Review*, X:5, 1985.
2   For example Human Rights Watch, *Abdication of Responsibility: The Commonwealth and Human Rights*, New York: Human Rights Watch, 1991.
3   Richard Werbner, *Tears of the Dead*, Edinburgh: Edinburgh University Press, 1991; Richard Werbner, 'In Memory: A Heritage of War in Southwestern Zimbabwe', in Ngwabi Bhebe and Terence Ranger (eds), *Society in Zimbabwe's Liberation War*, vol. 2, Harare: University of Zimbabwe Publications, 1995; Terence Ranger, *Voices from the Rocks: Nature, Culture and History in the Matopos Hills of Zimbabwe*, Oxford: James Currey, 1999; Jocelyn Alexander, JoAnn McGregor and Terence Ranger, *Violence and Memory: One Hundred Years in the 'Dark Forests' of Matabeleland*, Oxford: James Currey, 2000.
4   Alexander Kanengoni, *Echoing Silences*, Harare: Baobab, 1997, p. 62.
5   In his collection: Alexander Kanengoni, *Effortless Tears*, Harare: Baobab, 1993.
6   Richard Werbner, op. cit. (1991), esp. Ch. 5; Jocelyn Alexander, 'Dissident Perspectives on Zimbabwe's Post-Independence War', *Africa*, 68:2, 1998.
7   *Independent* (London), 19 November 2001.
8   Military and intelligence sources to the author, Harare, 1990.
9   Military source to the author, Harare, 1989.
10 Diplomatic source to the author, Harare, 1989.
11 Ministry source to the author, Harare, 1989.
12 Lloyd M. Sachikonye, 'Unita and Renamo: "Bandit" Social Movements?' *Southern African Political and Economic Monthly*, 3:7, 1990.

THREE

An Unlikely Champion Arises

1989 saw huge changes in the world. Eastern Europe changed in a kaleidoscope of falling governments and Berlin walls. In Southern Africa too, the last outpost of apartheid South African rule, Namibia, conducted its own independence elections. The process leading up to these had been fraught – not least when the South African army began a search and destroy operation for SWAPO liberation fighters who had, brazenly or mistakenly, crossed the border from Angola during what was meant to be a truce. There are stories of Australian UN peacekeeping units preventing the slaughter of outgunned SWAPO forces by simply parking their vehicles in front of the South African columns. It was not without drama and, even in Zimbabwe – in the midst of formal coalition finally between Mugabe and Nkomo – a pot was simmering and threatening to boil over. Not an Ndebele insurrection this time, but a challenge to Mugabe from within his own liberation circle, from an old comrade-in-arms and leading figure in ZANU.

It had been Edgar Tekere who had called for any one-party state to be achieved only at the polls. Now he himself would challenge Mugabe at the 1990 polls. But Tekere was an unlikely champion of pluralism. Always a firebrand, his penchant for intolerance was well known; and it had been Tekere who, notoriously in the first ten years of post-independence Zimbabwe, had staged his own farm invasion, in the course of which a white farmer had been killed. In an echoing sense, this was a sign of things to come later; but in 1989 Tekere was indeed reinventing himself as a champion both of pluralism and, particularly, against corruption.

For corruption had by now come to Zimbabwe, and had come at high levels – although, almost as a residual revolutionary modesty, some of the early corruption had concerned not fleets of Mercedes or BMW cars, but Toyotas. Before majority rule was established in South Africa, and South-African-manufactured BMWs came on tap, the Mercedes was the elite car of choice; in Kenya, those who owned them were called the Wa Benzi – the Benz tribe – a euphemism for corrupt people. From the recently established Toyota factory in Zimbabwe, ministers seemed to provide for their extended families against all official quotas and, in a new-model-hungry Zimbabwe – still somewhat used to refurbishing Peugeot 404s and 504s from the sanctions culture – many were sold on for huge profits. Compared to what corruption would become, it was small cheese, and even slightly pathetic; but there was still some sense of shame in Zimbabwe, and seven ministers and one deputy minister resigned over this and other uncovered issues in 1989, and one committed suicide. If the Ndebele people had been disillusioned by the Fifth Brigade's atrocities, a murmur now ran through Zimbabwe about corruption at the top. For, at the end of the 1980s, despite tight economic times, a police-man stopping a motorist really did just want to check the registration or certificate of roadworthiness. Now, if the poor were seeking to remain honest, but the rich were not, and the powerful were becoming rich, there seemed a moment for a champion to emerge.

Besides, not only were world currents moving in favour of pluralism, Southern African currents were too. These were not only to do with the independence of Namibia as a free state – now there was not a single part of South Africa's old *cordon sanitaire* left – but to do with movements within states; not only within South Africa itself, but soon within that very pillar of one-party-state stability, Zimbabwe's northern neighbour, Zambia. At the end of the 1980s, there seemed an intangible mood – not at all amenable to formal analysis – which could be felt by those in Southern Africa. The intellectuals of Zimbabwe felt it and felt also the mood of Eastern Europe. Not Marxist in any antiquarian sense, they were developing a curious neo-Marxism which combined some of the world systems theory of Immanuel Wallerstein, whereby the world of capital had its historical ebbs and flows – it was flowing now in Europe – and the critique of collaboration with the global centres of capital, developed by André Gunder Frank. This was allied with a certain African essentialism: if the South, and Africa in the South, could delink itself from the capitalist North, it could set about achieving an autonomous development and an autochthonous vision of development. The Egyptian writer Samir Amin, working out of Senegal, would have an important influence here – and a research and publishing link between Senegal and Zimbabwe would flourish.[1] It seemed in 1989 an exciting time for both historical movement and for intellectuals – as in Eastern Europe – to be involved in political change. The hybrid neo-Marxism certainly saw corruption among the already rich as a subscription to and collaboration with global capital; it thought that the ebbs and flows of history might visit Zimbabwe too; and, still idealistically – even nine years after independence – it thought that Zimbabwe could be an African leader in self-solutions. Many who had been disaffected or disillusioned by ZANU and Mugabe, and many intellectuals, declared themselves for Tekere – who could not, himself, be mistaken for an intellectual; but he did seem to be fervent and sincere in his sense of mission and change. Expelled from ZANU, he established the Zimbabwe Unity Movement – ZUM – as his political party in 1989, and set about his campaign for the parliamentary and presidential elections of 1990, the elections at the end of the first decade of independence.

Not all who joined Tekere were idealistic, or had any sense of future history. There was a sort of ZANU-essentialism as well. Some saw the coalition, the Unity Accord, between Mugabe and Nkomo as a betrayal of ZANU as it once was. Some ZANU chauvinists took up ZUM colours; so with the disillusioned, the poor, the intellectuals and the chauvinists, ZUM was a motley party – and none of its parts was organised and big enough to give ZUM a real powerbase. That which was big enough – the poor – went unorganised, for ZUM was not noted for organisation. Any sense of powerbase was regional: Manicaland, on the eastern border with Mozambique, was Tekere's home base and it became his only real power-base. Even so, ZANU (or ZANU-PF as the coalition was now called) retained its own strong links with Manicaland, and the battle for supremacy there would become bloody. Mugabe called on Tekere to rejoin the ruling party because – intellectuals and others aside – it was the fact that ZANU chauvinists had joined ZUM that made Mugabe take it very seriously. They would know how the government functioned, and how it might fight an election. As it was, the election took on a bloody hue, not just because ZANU-PF sought to crush ZUM at the polls, but because each side saw the other as traitors to ZANU or the vision of ZANU.

Curiously, the ZANU-PF election manifesto led with the declaration that it would establish a socialist society on Marxist-Leninist principles (curious given the fact that Bernard Chidzero's policies as finance minister were closely geared to anticipating IMF demands). The preamble to the ZUM manifesto led by denouncing corruption. Again, as a portent, the third plank of the ZANU-PF platform was to amend the constitution in order to acquire land for resettlement, 'wherever and whenever required'. Although the ZUM manifesto mentioned land under its tenth point, it was very much an urban manifesto, concerned with corruption, unemployment, urban housing, investment, taxation, prices, the freedom of the judiciary and the power of parliament against Mugabe as – by now – the executive president. ZUM campaigned against a one-party state. ZANU-PF suggested that democracy could only be firmer under one-party rule.

OTHER POLITICIANS AND THE ELECTIONS THEMSELVES

Of course, part of the ZANU-PF reversion to a rhetorical Marxist-Leninism was to do with the perceived battle for the soul of a true ZANU – the nationalist ZANU that had fought for independence. To that extent, Manicaland was not only an electoral battleground, but a spiritual one as well. Both Muzorewa – of the corrupted nationalism and ill-fated alliance with Ian Smith, admired at least by Margaret Thatcher – and Ndabaningi Sithole – a veteran nationalist politician who predated Mugabe, and who won the only non-Mugabe or Nkomo seat in 1985, and called his small party ZANU-Ndonga – were from the region. Not only that, so had been Herbert Chitepo, the ZANU leader who had been assassinated in Zambia in 1975; many still laid a finger of blame against Mugabe or his close lieutenants. Chitepo had been a legendary figure and, as time passed after his death, his probity, indeed purity, became part of the legend. In 1990, he represented an earlier ZANU that had been uncorrupt. This is the Chitepo of whom the novelist Alexander Kanengoni wrote so movingly. Kanengoni's demented protagonist – a former guerilla driven mad by visions of the war – has finally died and (in what I perceive to be a take on Stanlake Samkange's pioneering novel, 30 years earlier, and its scenes of an afterlife of great, learned councils of elders and leaders[2]) entered a heaven in which all those who remained

pure, true to the early promise of nationalism and freedom, are gathered
to hear Chitepo speak.

> He saw him at last, the Chairman, on the raised platform: grey hair and fiery
> eyes...And then the Chairman talked angrily of a series of monumental
> historical betrayals and he said that he and a few others were the living
> examples of such betrayals...and Chitepo continued:
>   'It's shocking to see the reluctance that we have to tell even the smallest
> truth. Ours shall soon become a nation of liars. We lie to our wives. We lie to
> our husbands. We lie at work. We lie in parliament. We lie in cabinet. We lie
> to each other. And what is worst is that we have begun to believe our lies...
>   'We owe the people an explanation. The struggle continues.'[3]

Elsewhere in the same passage, another legendary liberation figure, Jason
Moyo, speaks of corruption: 'and he asked how in such circumstances the
struggle could not be said to have lost its way'.

Part of the savagery of the 1990 elections, and that savagery was centred
in Manicaland, was to do not just with democracy or its lack, one-party
statism or pluralism, land ownership or redistribution, even Mugabe or
Tekere, but to do with another form of ownership – with who owned
Zimbabwe's soul.

To the Ndebele in the Matabelelands, those who had supported
Nkomo's ZAPU and its ZIPRA army, this was not a battle intimate to
them; but they had had some soul terrorised out of them by the whirlwind of the Fifth Brigade and, although still supporting Nkomo, even
in his coalition with Mugabe, rebuked him gently but discernibly at
the 1990 polls. These polls, as has tended to be the case in Mugabe's
Zimbabwe, were reasonably peaceful. But the events leading up to election
day were marked by violence, intimidation and death.

Knowing that he lacked a powerbase, Tekere sought to build his own
coalitions or even alliances. In particular, he hoped that the prominent,
freely spoken senior ZANU-PF figure, Edison Zvogbo, would ally himself
with ZUM; but Zvogbo is simply freely spoken, and would remain so for
years afterwards, himself spreading rumours of his opposition to Mugabe
but never quite leaving the president. He hoped also that the prominent
ZAPU politician, Dumiso Dabengwa, would join him. Dabengwa had
been imprisoned during the government's campaign against dissidence
in the Matabelelands, and would have given Tekere an extremely valuable
Ndebele ally. Dabengwa had made a public statement against a one-party
state. The rumour mills suggested that a Tekere–Zvogbo–Dabengwa axis

could rival, or even eclipse, the axis of Mugabe and Nkomo. But Dabengwa remained loyal to Nkomo and, as did Zvogbo, campaigned vigorously for the government.

Unable to secure such senior support, ZUM began finding its own support being cut away – almost literally. A few days before the elections, the ZUM national organising secretary, Patrick Kombayi, was shot, as was the ZUM election director, Jerry Nyambuya (Kombayi later recovered). The day before polling, five ZUM parliamentary candidates withdrew – it is thought because of intimidation. All this and other intimidations and highhanded actions led many Zimbabwean commentators, including John Makumbe, to declare the elections unfree and unfair.[4] Makumbe has become a most distinguished and courageous critic of government practice in Zimbabwe. However, on this occasion, although marked by violence and threats of violence, of savage acts and savage threats (including television advertisements by ZANU-PF in which opponents and coffins appeared) the elections were won by Mugabe handsomely, and would have been so won even without the campaign of violence – a campaign, as suggested above, to win not just the elections but a certain ownership of validation over and above the people's validation.

RESULTS AND REASONS

ZAPU, as part of the Unity Accord, fought and won the Matabelelands seats in the parliamentary election. Despite the bad blood caused by the Fifth Brigade, the message to its constituents was not, as in 1985, to contemplate parliamentary opposition, but to enter governmental power. Mugabe, having it a little both ways, awarded only three cabinet seats to Nkomo's people, and this certainly (but quietly) rankled.

But Nkomo himself was rebuked, not so much by Mugabe but by his own constituency. Although there was some confusion, and controversy, over the delimitation of his seat – because of boundary changes – the result was nevertheless revealing. Only 24·6 per cent of the registered voters turned out in Nkomo's Lobengula constituency. Although Nkomo defeated his challenger by 8706 votes to 1706, many interpreted the tiny turnout – not even a quarter of those eligible – as a protest note to the old man about his Unity Accord with Mugabe. Given the ZUM vote, some five eighths of the voters in the area named after the last great Ndebele

King, did not give their support to the man who had waited in the Matopos Hills for the mythical spirit medium to declare him Lobengula's heir. However, ZAPU did lay down an important condition for fighting the election alongside Mugabe, and this will be outlined below.

As it was, this was the only conditionality Mugabe was given in the 1990 elections. ZUM did win portions of the vote everywhere, but these were not enough to overturn ZANU or ZAPU majorities. In a very rough-and-ready sense, its share of the popular vote made it a Zimbabwean equivalent of the Liberal Democrats in Britain. However, these votes did not translate into seats. Some of this was certainly due to the significant intimidation mounted by ZANU, and some to ZUM's own organisational ineptitude. How much was due to intimidation is also discussed below. In the meantime, of the 120 elective seats, ZUM won only two; Sithole won a single seat; and ZANU and ZAPU, or ZANU-PF, won everything else. It was a major defeat, and even the great city constituencies – courted by the ZUM urban manifesto and supported by urban intellectuals and professionals – stayed aloof. The scale of the defeat was mirrored also in the presidential race, where Mugabe defeated Tekere by 2,026,976 votes to 413,840 – more than four to one. During my fieldwork in Zimbabwe in 1990, I undertook my own statistical analysis of the parliamentary results. The figurework is shorn from the conclusions outlined here.[5]

1 When calculated, as the government has done, on the basis of legitimate votes cast, the percentage vote to the government appears larger than would be suggested by a cautious analysis.
2 When calculated on the basis of all votes cast, including spoilt ballots, the government share, while still sizeable, is not quite as impressive.
3 There were a very great number of spoilt ballots and exactly what constitutes a spoilt ballot might be opened to question. In this, the third election since 1980, one might have supposed greater voter knowledge on how to fill a voting slip. This supposition cannot always be sustained, however, in the face of rural and even sizeable urban illiteracy and poor education. It would appear that, in addition to ballots spoilt by incorrect voting procedure, correctly filled in ballots were also disallowed if they contained additional comments – such as protest slogans. There is no way, except by anecdotal evidence, to suppose the number of 'protest' ballots. Many, faced with a choice

between the parties of Mugabe and Tekere, would not have brought
themselves to vote for either.

4   Having said this, there is no sustainable evidence to suggest that the
    number of spoilt ballots was significantly greater than those of the
    1980 and 1985 elections. Despite boundary changes, some patterns
    can still be traced and, on a nationwide basis, I did not feel that the
    'deliberately spoilt' or 'protest' ballot scenario detracted from the
    impressive size of the ZANU-PF victory.

5   Again, having said this, there were occasions in Manicaland when
    spoilt ballots, and how they were counted, could have materially
    altered if not overturned the final result. Manicaland was also the
    setting for some of the worst pre-election violence and intimidation.
    In public relations terms, it would have been better for ZANU-PF if
    ZUM had won something like ten seats. The result could still have
    been portrayed as an overwhelming victory in Western terms while
    suggesting fair play accorded an unpopular opposition. However, the
    number of seats where ZUM votes and all spoilt votes added together
    would have unseated a ZANU-PF candidate still do not reach ten. So,
    even if localised rigging or miscounting can be demonstrated, and it
    has not been demonstrated – ZUM did not enter a legal challenge
    over any single result – it could not have significantly damaged the
    scale of the ZANU-PF victory. There is no evidence at all of nationally
    coordinated rigging.

6   I heard anecdotal evidence of irregularities in the counting of postal
    ballots, and some amusing anecdotes about minor irregularities in some
    polling stations, but did not feel these could have materially altered
    the nationwide results.

7   The interesting factor was how few people voted, despite the election
    being extended to a third day of polling. By official register figures, 54
    per cent of the electorate cast votes – although the register is probably
    wrong and the percentage could have been higher. If there was an
    element of protest in absenteeism, some element – not to be exaggerated
    – of protest in the spoilt ballots, then these together with the ZUM
    vote and the votes cast for smaller parties suggest that, despite a huge
    ZANU-PF victory in terms of seats, there was a significant though
    minor interest in favour of political pluralism.

The ZUM support did not cease being restless after the elections – although ZUM in its 1990 form never contested another. Many professional groups went on strike – teachers, nurses, junior doctors – but the issues here were to do with pay rather than alternative government. Even these did not often venture to protest in streets outside the central grid – for the ZANU party apparatus remained formidable in what had become known as the medium- and high- density suburbs ('townships' in the old Rhodesian parlance), and party activists were not above violent interventions. Having said that, many party activists who had applied their own vigilante violence against ZUM campaigners during the election and had been arrested found themselves abandoned by ZANU on their days in court. The lessons learnt here would return a decade later in the initially autonomous organisation of the farm-invading 'war veterans' – with their later bargain with the government and ZANU-PF that no police would bring them to court. For now, the activity of vigilantes remained urban-based; for the rural areas were far less problematically behind – or, at least, not demonstrably against – the government. Although still not enjoying land reform and redistribution, these areas also remained those of the worst education, and a simplistic appeal to them won the day for the government. There was dissatisfaction to be sure – it would take a crisis in 1992 for the government to recognise this and act decisively, if not to provide an answer – but it went unarticulated and unchampioned. For the rural areas, the ZUM message had been, by and large, too urban and too intellectual. As for those intellectuals, they did not fail to have any impact at all on ZANU-PF.

The government did have a sensitivity, not to protest necessarily, but to the articulation of protest in terms that could be appreciated – even if only eventually – by others. In short, debate and discourse would mean that even ZANU-PF, with its own intellectual and technocratic wing, might absorb critical doctrine. Given the relatively self-contained size of the educated elite, debate and new doctrine could spread rapidly. The government's response was clumsy. In 1989, the university was closed for the first time. This and several closures paralleled the Zambian techniques of simply teargassing the campus and then herding the students – after some appropriate beatings – onto buses to disperse them homewards. Zimbabwe later developed its own teargas manufacturing capacity. On the early occasions of campus closure the authorities used a particularly virulent North Korean formula. The Fifth Brigade may have gone, but its style and origin of training had left behind a nasty artefact. In 1990, the government circulated leaflets to the effect that all civil servants should be members of the ruling party. This was an unsuccessful campaign and the government did not press it unduly, since Zimbabwe had a relatively well-educated civil service and even ZANU-PF saw the merits of a body of servants for the public administration of the state.

Although some intellectuals did see multi-party pluralism in terms of their preference for liberal democracy, others viewed it through the lens of 'historical stages', whereby every developing state had to go through a period of liberal bourgeois government. This was the 'socialism is reached by stages' argument, meaning that the liberal and multi-party stage could not be jumped. This did have a resonance within the intellectual wing of ZANU, and it is fair to say that this wing did ameliorate the ZANU-essentialism of an otherwise unchecked preference for one-party rule.

The other probably more significant check was, of course, ZAPU. The MPs from the Matabelelands had extracted a promise from Mugabe at the December 1989 ZANU-PF congress that the one-party state should not be raised as an election issue and, not withstanding the implication in the manifesto, this was observed. In 1990, beginning 29 June, the ZANU–ZAPU coalition central committee met against the backdrop of a landmark statement by Julius Nyerere of Tanzania. Nyerere said that the one-party state could not be an indefinite institution in Africa and that the time was ripe for it to face challenge.[6] Even within Zimbabwe itself, the local press (and there were no opposition papers as such in those days) for the first time published lengthy articles calling into question the viability of a one-party state.[7]

The day after the coalition central committee finished its business, the National Consultative Assembly met. This was comprised of the previously separate central committees of ZANU and ZAPU. In a very short period, the coalition central committee and the two formerly separate central committees had met. There could have been no more representative opinion within the dominant political discourse. Both bodies came out against the one-party state – and this was both ZAPU's bride-price and the electorally defeated but still influential voice of the intellectuals. Among other things, however, it meant that, one day, however distant, a free ZAPU could rise again. And it meant that, almost a decade later, Mugabe would again face an opposition party at the polls, not called ZUM this time and far more potent a threat.

ZIMBABWE AND THE GULF WAR

Zimbabwe is not insulated from the world. Ian Smith's Rhodesia learnt
this to its cost. Moreover, the Commonwealth had helped bring about
the very independence of Zimbabwe, and Mugabe had been chairman of
the Non-Aligned Movement. Kuwait, also a recognised member of the
movement, was invaded and annexed by Iraq in 1990. Zimbabwe's was
not the response of Zambia, where a Saddam Hussein Boulevard existed
in Lusaka. Mugabe did not attempt the sentimental feat of securing the
freedom of the British nurse Daphne Parrish from an Iraqi jail, thereby
seeking to demonstrate that, after all, Saddam had a human face – after
Saddam had first hanged her lover. (Kaunda managed her release but
secured her a roundabout journey to Britain, via Lusaka, where he used
her in a press conference of astonishing banality.) Nor did Mugabe, again
like Kaunda, wander the streets of Baghdad arm-in-arm with Saddam on
the eve of allied bombing. However, in Zimbabwe, particularly among
the intellectuals and almost the entire political class – whether ZAPU
and Soviet-schooled, or ZANU and Chinese-schooled, or contemporary
neo-Marxist – there was widespread sympathy, even admiration, for
Saddam; he was seen as someone who was in the midst of challenging the
hegemony of the North. If ever there was to be a third-world essentialism
brought to life, a delinking from the North, the Iraqis would be vital
members of the South.

Mugabe himself bemoaned the fact that the Non-Aligned Movement
had been able to play no role in mediating or ameliorating the conflict.[8]
However, Zimbabwe had earlier bemoaned the invasion of Angola by
South Africa (and Grenada by the US, Panama by the US, Lebanon by
Israel), the bombing of Libya by the US, and the occupation of Palestine
by Israel. The Zimbabwean diplomatic position had consistently been
against smaller or weaker states being invaded by those stronger. Moreover,
as a member of the UN and the Non-Aligned Movement, Kuwait's
international recognition and personality were long established – notwithstanding Iraqi refusals since 1973 to accept them. As a former
chairman of the Non-Aligned Movement, Mugabe had himself recognised
Kuwait by chairing summits to which the small state had been invited.
Accordingly, on 2 August 1990, the Zimbabwean Foreign Minister
denounced Iraq, and on 7 August Zimbabwe joined the UN-imposed
sanctions.

For Zimbabwe, there was a more pragmatic consideration as well. The government calculated that whereas before the Gulf war its imported fuel bill was Zim.$450 million per annum, it would now double.[9]

However it is noteworthy that, whereas the Foreign Minister spoke and acted on 2 and 7 August 1990, Mugabe did not himself make any detailed public and presidential statement until January 1991, some five months later. Even then, although it was reported in the then major Zimbabwean newspaper on 7 January, he had actually first made it to a Nigerian newspaper some three days earlier. The habit of letting others shoulder the policies and public relations of actions he himself found unpalatable would, from this moment, be seen more often.

It should not be thought, however, that just because unpalatable Mugabe did not at this time seek to exercise privately what influence he could.[10] He and President George Bush exchanged several letters on the Gulf issue. Meanwhile, Zimbabwe took its turn chairing the UN Security Council, and the US was well pleased with its performance (though it did not help Zimbabwean Finance Minister, Bernard Chidzero, to become UN Secretary General; he and Kofi Annan were the two African 'finalists'). Less joyful were the correspondence and exchanges between Foreign Minister Nathan Shamuyarira and US Secretary of State George Baker. Shamuyarira had been a staunch supporter of the Palestinians and told Baker that had Saddam invaded Israel and not Kuwait Zimbabwe's position would have been very different. Through all of this, Mugabe made it clear that, in his view, Saddam had gone much too far, particularly in his refusal to compromise; but he was also anxious that the Non-Aligned Movement broker a sort of disengagement, making known his displeasure with the ineffectualness of the Yugoslavian chairmanship that had succeeded his own. Mugabe worked to foster what he thought to be a stronger Non-Aligned Movement position, and visited west African states in seeking to accomplish this.

What all this did do, however, was to refurbish any stains or dents on his international reputation that the Fifth Brigade might have caused. As it was, the international community was then scarcely aware of what had happened in the Matabelelands. Insofar as some parts of that community had been critical of Mugabe, it was at that time more to do with the harassment of ZUM during the 1990 elections. However, Mugabe won a crushing victory at those polls and had, moreover, entered coalition with Nkomo's ZAPU. If ever the world discovered more about the Matabelelands, then he could maintain that he had consigned what happened there to a history that had led, once again, to reconciliation. Two more events would soon occur to bolster even further his international credentials; and a more local event would allow him to act in such a way that he could trade off his performance to win the 1995 elections as well. But these would, in a way, be overshadowed by his personal tragedy, in the wake of which many would see the decline of Mugabe from a character of contradictions – international statesmanship and bravery on the one hand, and sheer domestic emotion-free ruthlessness on the other – to a character of evil and merely personal ambition. That is for the rest of this book to uncover and ponder. For now, the first of the international interventions mentioned above should be introduced. This was the second phase of Zimbabwe's involvement in Mozambique, before the third phase of breakthrough talks in Rome. Behind the scenes, now fully persuaded by his military officers and analysts that RENAMO could not, and perhaps should not, be defeated in the Mozambican war, Mugabe conducted an astonishing diplomatic exercise.

TOWARDS A MOZAMBICAN ENDGAME[11]

It was not only Mugabe and the Zimbabweans who considered the war in Mozambique unwinnable. Machel's successor, the technocratic and moderate Chissano, had also begun to consider some way if not to end the conflict then to ameliorate it. His announcement, in December 1990, of a partial ceasefire, agreed between both the Mozambican Government and RENAMO, took most of Zimbabwean opinion by surprise. It seemed to have taken most of Mozambican governmental opinion by surprise too. Under this agreement, the Zimbabwean military forces that had remained in Mozambique were restricted to the Beira Corridor and the more southerly Limpopo Corridor. The first was by far the more important, having been the centrepiece of Zimbabwean objectives upon first entering Mozambique. The unwritten fine print of the agreement seemed to allow RENAMO a quid pro quo, by which it reoccupied the northern Tete Corridor. Those claiming closeness to Mugabe said that he had been incandescent over these arrangements, and that he had not been consulted.

This line of narrative maintained that Chissano had not consulted Mugabe precisely because of the Zimbabwean view of FRELIMO's fighting capacity, described earlier. To the Mozambicans, this was arrogance and condescension. There was also the feeling that, notwithstanding its military presence, Zimbabwe had never fully repaid the years of Mozambican sacrifice from 1976 to 1980, when ZANLA troops were stationed on its soil and the country attracted repeated Rhodesian and, from time to time, direct South African attacks. Moreover, after Mugabe's chairmanship of the Non-Aligned Movement had ended, it was said that Chissano viewed Mugabe as no longer internationally politically important – 'in a political Sargasso Sea,' was one description ascribed to him – and, at least, no longer essential.

This is probably untrue. It is the case that there was less love between Mugabe and Chissano than there had been between Mugabe and Machel but the ceasefire of December 1990 has to be seen against the backdrop of considerable church and other diplomacies in the region. This had begun with Roman Catholic activity. It was said that a Catholic priest, captured then released by RENAMO, had begun protagonising its cause to both his church and the Italian Government. It was probably not the case that he approached the Italian Government directly, but that the government began taking some interest after, first, the Mozambican-based Bishops of Chimoio and Beira began making individual efforts to mediate in the conflict. It would seem that the Bishop of Chimoio became particularly active, and courageously so, in a one-party state that had been at war for some two decades, against the Portuguese, then resisting Rhodesia and South Africa, then in conflict with RENAMO. Many in FRELIMO were in no mood to listen or tolerate a discourse of negotiation. However, the Italian monastic community of Santo Egidio took up the themes of mediation and negotiation and, through this community, the Vatican and Italian Government gave a first formal acknowledgement to RENAMO by inviting its delegations to Rome, and greatly facilitating their travel and other logistical problems.[12]

Nor was this all. The Zimbabwean foreign affairs official Elleck Mashingaidze had – on behalf of the Zimbabweans, that is with Mugabe's full knowledge – been conducting his own incessant shuttle diplomacy as a mediator between FRELIMO and RENAMO. He also travelled to Rome, as did a senior Kenyan official. Here, the game assumed its full dimensions, for the Kenyans, to the north of Mozambique, had considerable sympathy for RENAMO – although they had never actively assisted the rebel group militarily. What happened next would seem to have been like this (although I have had no Kenyan account to balance the first sentence of what follows):

Unsure of how to proceed, both RENAMO and the Kenyans sought delays; so, as a ploy to neutralise the Kenyans, it was the Zimbabwean party that proposed the withdrawal of both Zimbabwean and Kenyan mediators to allow, for the first time, face-to-face negotiations between RENAMO and FRELIMO, unhindered but also unadvised. What emerged certainly surprised the Zimbabweans, and probably the FRELIMO leadership in Maputo. Perhaps it was a concession made from RENAMO negotiating naivety; perhaps RENAMO, too, wanted to wind down the war. Perhaps it was Roman Catholic pressure playing its own role, but RENAMO offered a truce, or at least, a partial ceasefire, if the Zimbabweans confined their activities to the Beira and Limpopo Corridors. RENAMO would not attack them there. They would also continue to talk in Rome.

When the Zimbabweans heard of the offer, they were indeed taken aback. The FRELIMO negotiators wondered what it was that they had done. But after it was done, the entire FRELIMO delegation came from Rome to Harare – apparently 'even the typists'[13] – to explain the situation directly to Mugabe. They seemed to have gone home to Maputo only afterwards. (This may not have been so politically prioritised as it might seem at first sight. There may have been no direct flights from Rome to Mozambique.) In any case, on reflection, the Zimbabweans decided the agreement was indeed a breakthrough and a good idea. They were tired of the war and its expense and, with the two corridors safe from attack, their own exports would also be safe.

The sacrifice was, as noted above, the northerly Tete Corridor. There, the Zimbabweans had never so much controlled the Corridor as cleared as much bush as possible from either side of the road, then escorted traffic through in heavily-armed convoys. They now withdrew from guarding these convoys. RENAMO 'couldn't believe the Zimbabweans had actually gone. They waited and watched for two weeks, then decided – whoopee – all their Christmases had come at once.'[14]

It took only a short time for FRELIMO, realising what it had sacrificed, to ask the Zimbabweans back into Tete; but by now, anxious to retrench their expenditure and to prosecute some progress in negotiations, the Zimbabweans were none too anxious, and refused.

Having said that, it was not as if the Tete Corridor was completely abandoned to RENAMO. Malawian troops provided some convoy protection – deploying their Israeli-trained paratroop units. In any case, northern RENAMO – often calling itself UNAMO to indicate some semi-autonomy – seemed prepared to deal with Chissano and restrained its attacks. Unlike the Zimbabweans, the Malawians deployed a 'hearts and minds' policy and, although it is an exaggeration to say that Malawian and UNAMO troops got on famously, their encounters did assume a ritualised demeanour.

The Italian Government, anxious to facilitate Roman negotiations, removed one RENAMO delaying tactic – expressed as the need to return home for consultations and instructions – by installing a large telecommunications satellite dish for RENAMO on the Malawian side of the border with Mozambique. In 1991, such dishes were not as readily installed as now, and it was a considerable provision. It also meant that RENAMO/UNAMO had no great wish to antagonise the Malawians. The Italians also provided RENAMO with a 12-seat executive plane. There was no excuse not to attend the talks in Rome. And, with the South African-supplied radio-communications system, RENAMO was now able to confer within itself as to a true national RENAMO political strategy.

The emerging strategy seemed to be directed towards a coalition government – some 60 per cent FRELIMO and 40 per cent RENAMO – to be installed for some five years, in order to give RENAMO time to develop a true political identity for electoral purposes. Chissano worked to deny them this – but did appreciate RENAMO's own assessment of its national appeal. He and the Zimbabweans were then confident that FRELIMO would win an election, and even if the RENAMO percentages proved correct it would allow FRELIMO government to continue without a coalition with RENAMO. Here, both Mugabe and Chissano certainly coincided. It was to take RENAMO out of the bush but maintain FRELIMO in power. But it was a high-risk strategy, and its twists and turns meant that it could never be a simple Machiavellian one.

Meanwhile, RENAMO changed its emblem. Previously based on the Portuguese Special Forces or 'Flechas' emblem of stars surrounded by five arrows, and the motto 'War and death to enemies of the fatherland', it now had fewer arrows and a less sanguinary motto, 'Victory is certain'. Perhaps RENAMO was already consulting a public-relations company.

The attitude of the Zimbabwean and Mozambican leaderships was slow to filter through to their own national media. In Harare, the *Herald* newspaper continued to refer to RENAMO as 'the bandits', and news of the slowly continuing Roman talks were relegated to small and brief columns.

The difference between these slow negotiations and the even slower ones over Angola was that the latter were facilitated and mediated by great powers, including the US.[15] The former were largely an Italian/ Vatican and Zimbabwean triumph. But they were indeed slow. All of 1991 seemed almost to waste away with tiny, incremental senses of progress, or no progress at all. It would be Mugabe who would accomplish the decisive breakthroughs, beginning in January 1992. Before then, fresh from his election triumph a year before, respected for his role thus far in Mozambique – both in war and towards peace – he would reap what would later seem an ironic accolade from the 1991 Commonwealth summit, to be hosted in Harare.

NOTES ON CHAPTER 3

1   See Samir Amin, *Delinking*, London: Zed, 1990.
2   Stanlake Samkange, *On Trial for My Country*, Oxford: Heinemann, 1967.
3   Alexander Kanengoni, *Echoing Silences*, Harare: Baobab, 1997, pp. 87–8.
4   John Makumbe, 'The 1990 Zimbabwe Elections: Implications for Democracy', in Ibbo Mandaza and Lloyd Sachikoyne (eds), *The One Party State and Democracy*, Harare: SAPES, 1991; but see the extensive and dispassionate account by Jonathan N. Moyo, *Voting for Democracy: Electoral Politics in Zimbabwe*, Harare: University of Zimbabwe Publications, 1992. This was before Moyo's more recent incarnation as a particularly passionate pro-Mugabe cabinet minister.
5   These have been previously rehearsed in Stephen Chan, 'Democracy in Southern Africa: the 1990 Elections in Zimbabwe and 1991 Elections in Zambia', *The Round Table*, 322, 1992.
6   *Herald* (Harare), 29 June 1990.
7   Charles Samupindi, 'One Party System has Failed in Africa', *Herald*, 26 June 1990; Charles Samupindi, 'The One Party State and Some Economic Effects', *Herald*, 27 June 1990.
8   *Herald*, 7 January 1991.
9   For a carefully balanced account and weighing of balances, see Hasu Patel, 'Zimbabwe's Foreign Policy and the Gulf Crisis', *The Journal of Social Change and Development* (Harare), 25, First Quarter 1991, from which these figures are taken.

10 The following account was derived from US diplomatic sources to the author, April 1991.

11 The following account is the author's own distillation and interpretation of conflicting accounts received, in Harare in 1991, from two Ministry of Foreign Affairs sources, Western diplomatic sources, and various academic and intellectual sources. The final interpretation owed much to military sources.

12 There is still no full-length work in English on the work of Santo Egidio. For an interview with its monastic leadership, see Riccardo Chatroux's contribution to Stephen Chan and Moises Venancio, *War and Peace in Mozambique*, London: Macmillan, 1998, pp. 30–33.

13 Zimbabwean Foreign Ministry source to the author, Harare, 1991.

14 Military source to the author, Harare, 1991.

15 For a concise but thorough account, see Moises Venancio and Stephen Chan, *Portuguese Foreign Policy in Southern Africa*, Johannesburg: South African Institute of International Affairs, 1996.

PART TWO

BRILLIANCE AND OPPORTUNISM'S BRIEF THEN FADING MOMENT

FOUR

Human Rights, Personal Tragedy, and Drought

At last Margaret Thatcher had gone; and, in her place, sat the lacklustre John Major – who had been humiliated by her at the last Commonwealth summit of 1989, in Kuala Lumpur – desperate, in his understatement, to make a mark upon the Harare summit and, if not for himself, to carry forward the sense of British mission that his country had obliged itself to bear in, finally, helping to ensure independence for Zimbabwe just over a decade earlier. The Commonwealth summits are held every two years, so 1991 was as close to a decade's anniversary as was possible, and there was never any other contender for the summit's host city.

At the last host city, Kuala Lumpur, however, Major had been Thatcher's Foreign Secretary – a position not always greatly to be esteemed after what she had done to an earlier incumbent, Geoffrey Howe, over the 1986 issue of sanctions against South Africa. Howe had been sent on fruitless delaying missions – to which he objected, and which all knew to be fruitless – to provide Thatcher with delay in the face of Commonwealth pressures that Britain, too, should subscribe to an otherwise agreed package of sanctions. When Howe protested to his mistress, she told him in no uncertain – and colourful – terms to follow her instructions. So it was again at Kuala Lumpur that the latest Foreign Secretary laboured mightily to negotiate and agree a communiqué with other Commonwealth foreign ministers, only to have the document – and implicitly his part in it – repudiated by an obdurate Thatcher. It was almost as if she delighted in this and, whatever one might think of the mild-mannered Major, he was decently determined never to treat his own ministers in this fashion.

If Major had replaced Thatcher, the career Commonwealth servant Emeka Anyaoku had replaced Ramphal as Commonwealth Secretary General. A Nigerian who – apart from 100 days as foreign minister in the ill-fated second government of Shagari (before yet another Nigerian military coup) – had known no other service than that of the Commonwealth Secretariat and, having worked his way up to the position of Ramphal's deputy, knew very well, both by nature and necessity, the arts of quietude and how much grease at any one time lay upon a greasy pole. Lugubrious, therefore, and (or thereby) a master of the diplomatic arts, he was also African. Mugabe and he cut immaculate figures – chairman and chief executive – on the podium at Harare, and there is no doubt that Mugabe relished the summit in itself, and himself in its chair, and the company he kept which, apart from Anyaoku, included the released and now worker-of-rooms Nelson Mandela – who, as if a past master himself, somehow shook the hands only of the most important possible actors in his own and South Africa's case.

Major not only had his hand shaken but seemed caught up in the Africanness of the summit. He signalled that Britain would support the candidature of the Zimbabwean Finance Minister, Bernard Chidzero, for UN Secretary General. There was, after all, an African Commonwealth Secretary General, and the UN variety would make a set. Of such cynicisms is diplomatic horse-trading made. Certainly, Chidzero's elevation would have been a considerable feather in both Zimbabwe's and Mugabe's hat. It would have been an ultimate accolade: just after ten years since he was a rebel leader, and as a recognition of how well (even if with blind spots) the country he had led was regarded, those powers that had once sought to deny him would now elect as their own senior-most international civil servant a minister in Mugabe's own cabinet. To be sure, Chidzero had been a fine minister. Such financial stability as had been possible had been of his crafting, and Mugabe had the good sense to accept his advice. During the summit, Zimbabwean newspapers carried lengthy reports of interviews given by Chidzero as to how he would act as UN Secretary General. Many purposes were being cultivated among the world leaders assembled in Harare.

The Sunday paper which would have been delivered to each of the leaders contained a particularly revealing interview by Chidzero. It contained three major themes, and each related to an aspect of the summit, or to something Mugabe himself would seek to implement. The first theme was to do with the historical shift to liberal democracy, and this echoed the key debate at the summit and its conclusions in what was called the Harare Declaration – discussed below.

> I think it is fair to say that the political and economic changes taking place in Eastern Europe and the USSR are profound and they converge in the direction of a shift from the centralised or command economies to market economies of one kind or another. And from a centralised authoritarian political system to a more democratic, more open society.[1]

The second theme was something that, shortly after the summit – again as discussed below – Mugabe would seek to put into a very direct practice. This was to do with conflict resolution.

And the third theme was something that echoed Major's effort to provide respectability for Britain's summit role – something lacking in the Thatcher era: 'This calls for a greater sense of vision on the part of nations but we are on one globe and one earth and we cannot indefinitely have prosperity in some and continuing poverty in others'.

What Major did was to suggest that Britain would write off the debts of selected third-world states with good records in human rights. This was both by way of refurbishing Britain's image among its Commonwealth compatriots, and introducing – in the aspect of human rights – the great British initiative at this summit. Certainly, however, Major made his mark in the final communiqué, the British Prime Minister being – very unusually for any leader – thanked twice for his economic gesture.[2]

But Major was anxious also to make a mark that was characteristic of his sense and image of decency and the tolerances associated with it. He was a genuine believer in democratic values and human rights – even if British political life did not always allow him to reveal such commitments; but international life did. So it was that he brought – to a studiously unenthusiastic but accepting cadre of world leaders, who were conscious of what had happened in Eastern Europe – a drive to make the Harare summit an historical beacon of human rights. And, since some of these had only come to Zimbabwe at independence, the decade's anniversary seemed an appropriate moment – certainly an undeniable enough moment – to consecrate those rights at the core of Commonwealth beliefs; and in a lingering Zimbabwean political consciousness. Mugabe, a decade after this summit, could never deny the document to which he had put his name. There is even some evidence that, in 1991 the President of Zimbabwe – momentarily at least – really seemed to believe in pluralism and rights.

There was at least a rhetoric and enthusiasm in the air, sweeping in from Europe, and from the prospect of Mandela in the south; and Mandela himself was in Harare as a beacon.

Having said that, the final Harare Declaration was a typical Commonwealth understatement – when it came to means and penalties. The rhetoric was indeed present, but Major's senior civil servant Lord Armstrong, later notorious for his economy with truth, here measured the mood of leaders – many of whom were within a 'needs must' school, that is one of resigned but highly tempered necessity – and drafted a Declaration that was economical in its modes of application and enforcement.

There were, it seems, two drafts. A rival draft had been prepared by the Commonwealth Secretariat's Moni Malhoutra – Ramphal's right-hand adviser – but he was not an Anyaoku favourite, leaving the Secretariat soon afterwards, and Major in any case pushed for the Armstrong draft that was, finally, more in keeping with the Commonwealth mood. Mugabe would have regretted even more the Malhoutra version, but it has disappeared without trace. This is a shame, as Malhoutra had been a real friend of Zimbabwe. He had been director of the Secretariat of the Commonwealth Observer Group in Zimbabwe in 1980, had directed its work with great clarity and decisiveness, and was among the first visitors to purchase many fine pieces of Shona sculpture, to which his eye, and his sense of psychological depth, were immediately attracted. Perhaps it was all as well – since psychological depth has, perhaps, no place in diplomatic communiqués.

As was usual with summit declarations, the Harare Declaration was prefixed to the communiqué proper and consisted in 13 paragraphs, paragraph 9 having 11 sections, one of which had a further eight sub-sections. These sub-sections were almost a paean to liberal international economics, including 'the central role of the market economy', 'the freest possible flow of multilateral trade', with a specific genuflection towards 'effective population policies and programmes'.

Paragraph 9 also touched upon 'the fundamental political values of the Commonwealth', including a range of democratic processes – 'which reflect national circumstances' (Armstrong reflecting the caution particularly of some African presidents here) – but, having qualified democracy, the paragraph seemed to make 'the rule of law and the independence of the judiciary' an absolute.

Other parts dealt with human rights, and seemed to associate these with levels of sustainable development – so that, finally and as with all such masterly written documents – the declaration could be given flexible interpretation.

Having said that, the binding nature of the declaration lay in paragraph 4, often taken as part of an extended preamble, but which traced a line of descent, and a line of commitment, to all previous Commonwealth declarations from 1971 onwards. These were described as 'a commitment to certain fundamental principles' and, although Anyaoku never sought to cultivate these 'fundamental principles' in any coherent manner, for example as some sort of extended treaty among members, there was till then a small but definite body of opinion that these declarations and their principles were a constitutional foundation for the Commonwealth.[3] Because Anyaoku never saw them as such – being far too pragmatic by inclination to seek inviolable foundations – the interpretation of them as constitutional never gained political endorsement. However, although not taken as a foundational constitution in terms of principles and beliefs, the collection of declarations – and the Harare summary of them in particular – did come to be regarded as a delineator of membership. They were thus narrowly constitutive: they defined a member in good standing but, as many non-governmental groups present at Harare lamented, they did not and could not sanction any defiler of principle[4] – except to remove such a state from the Commonwealth's constituted membership. Since Harare, such removal has been exceedingly slow and reluctant – but it has been done and, as 2002 began, with Mugabe running rampant over many rights, the independence of the judiciary, and agreements mediated by Commonwealth ministers, it was thought aloud that the Harare Declaration might finally be invoked to exclude Harare itself from Commonwealth membership.[5]

Thus, the key points in the Declaration – that may be 'adjudicated', are not so much within paragraph 9, as in paragraph 4, where the fundamental 'liberty of the individual under law' and that individual's 'inalienable right to participate by means of free and democratic processes in framing the society in which he or she lives' become the litmus test of whether a state might be adjudged still a member in good standing. It is not completely right to say that the Harare Declaration has had no lingering resonance in Mugabe's mind. Its residue may be seen, I feel, in his determined path towards elections, that is that these elections are the 'democratic processes' to which all citizens are inalienably entitled. Mugabe will say he has always provided such elections and that, generally, the narrow, on-polling-day conduct of the elections has been proper. It is an exceedingly narrow defence, of course, since the days (months, years) leading up to polling have been – with the exception of 1995 (outlined below) – violent and traducing of the rights of a great number of citizens. Mugabe had proved determined, however, to hold even the 2002 elections with which this book ends.

The interesting moment of retrospective reflection here is that, at the moment of the Harare Declaration in 1991, Mugabe – satisfied with his accomplishments, bathed in a new international glow, flattered by an African Commonwealth Secretary General and happy with the prospects of a Zimbabwean UN Secretary General – might actually have believed all that the declaration contained. Perhaps it was only the stages-of-history view of the world but, even as late as 1993, on a visit to Beijing, Mugabe pointedly and, in diplomatic terms unnecessarily, lectured his Chinese hosts: 'The question of opposition to a system is necessary and the acceptance of that is necessary for our systems to work … the party that is in power should ensure that the elections are as transparent as they can be.'[6]

Back at the 1991 summit itself, the Zimbabwean papers carried front-page headlines on how Commonwealth 'leaders back monitoring of polls'[7] and, again as late as 1993, long newspaper lead articles reminded readers approvingly that poll monitoring 'all began with Zimbabwe's 1980 elections'.[8] As well as many photographs of Mugabe meeting the Queen, Mugabe farewelling the Queen (she looking delighted, he looking proud), the summit ended with Mugabe's closing address. 'Let the Common-wealth live and live forever,' he said, and reinforced the democratic values of the Harare Declaration.[9]

All of this is poignant now and if, in early 2002, there is any residue at all of the Harare Declaration, it can only be within the narrow hair-splitting of legal apologists, or within an arch and grim irony. Yet, as suggested above, Mugabe led for a few short years an officialised discourse of democracy and openness. A senior minister, Dumiso Dabengwa – though once imprisoned as an Ndebele political figure during the repression of the Matabelelands – opened an international academic conference in 1991, one that would explore, among other things, exactly that repression, with the words:

We urge the emergence of a class of scholars capable of withstanding threats and intimidation and rising above racial, ethnic and tribal considerations ... The new breed of Zimbabwean social scientists ought to stand up against the supp-ression of any information and should develop an ever-critical mind with respect to the facts, especially purported facts, and actions of political leaders. Anything short of cultivating a tradition of selfless enquiry and exposure of the truth will certainly lead to a nation of sycophants and robots without the necessary powers of independent thought which we should all cherish.[10]

The Commonwealth summit did transact one other item of business. Reporting of its animation was buried in small columns, amidst the other small columns of international news – alongside reports of shortlived ceasefires in the Balkan wars – and concerned the now protracted negotiations in Rome between FRELIMO and RENAMO. The summit communiqué accorded two paragraphs (31 and 32) to Mozambique (giving it slightly more prominence than paragraph 41 gave to Afghanistan), but they endorsed the Rome process and, more particularly, 'urged an immediate end to all external assistance, material and otherwise' to RENAMO – giving Zimbabwe what it wanted: a shot across the bows of, among others, the Kenyans, leaving the Rome process open to regionally unfettered Zimbabwean interventions. This will be discussed at length in the next chapter. For now, it is enough to record briefly the first, particularly powerful intervention, shortly after the Commonwealth summit, with Mugabe in a full conflict-resolving and democratic flight. It is also to be noted how compressed and condensed was the last great batch of Mugabe's positive accomplishments. It is almost as if he had sprung from a winter of his imposing then crushing discontents – all largely unnecessary – to a new lease of internationally commended life. It is also to be noted how, in the midst of endeavours and triumphs, tragedy struck him like a thunderbolt.

A CONDENSED PERIOD

Mugabe had not been given to international diplomacy before the Commonwealth summit. Even as chairman of the Non-Aligned Movement, after his initial flurry – based again upon that organisation's summit in Harare – he was, even as the normally antipathetic Americans complained, a chairman 'who did nothing for NAM. He was a most inactive chairman until right towards the end.'[11]

The region's diplomatic crown had usually been worn by Zambia's Kaunda; but Kaunda had fallen from power in an astonishing multi-party election at the end of 1991, and the title of region's peacemaker, all other things aside, was vacant.

The Mozambican peace process will be discussed in detail in the next chapter. For now, Mugabe inaugurated 1992 with a sudden visit to Malawi. The Americans knew of it, but his own Foreign Ministry did not. The Rome negotiations had been stopping, starting and stalling in their progress – pointed concentration on details slowing them down. A decisive slash through the Gordian Knot was required, and Mugabe provided it by meeting, in Malawi, the leader of RENAMO himself, Afonso Dhlakama, a shadowy man, unknown to the West and to Zimbabwe, but who, from a first published photograph as late as 1990,[12] looked amazingly like the young Mugabe. The twinning of appearances apart, there was an apparent twinning of minds. It was a stunning diplomatic coup and, by itself, a major step in the tortuous processes of conflict resolution.

That was 10 January. On 27 January, Mugabe's wife, Sally, unexpectedly died. This was a terrible blow to Mugabe. Theirs was hardly a normal relationship. She was Ghanaian, they having met when the young Robert was a student and teacher in Ghana – the pioneer of African nationalism. They apparently never had children (and scandalous Rhodesian political gossip during the liberation war spoke, graphically, about his inability), and she led, as first lady, not only a very independent existence but one in which she performed far more than the routine and ritual number of public and charitable services. The Zimbabwean populace genuinely loved her, and it is the case that her president husband loved her too – though she was not without her own controversies. Mugabe took her death very badly, and seemed to freeze in his presidential duties. I do not think he froze, although many did, as recorded below. Forced by events, perhaps, but he set out upon a slow-motion chess game with South Africa and, having lost his queen, installed a fat pawn to act as king. This pawn had his own view of the chessboard as well. It was March, and by March drought and famine were in the air; and the question of land was playing out a game of its own.

DROUGHT AND SOUTH AFRICA

Although after the 1990 elections Mugabe had appointed a white minister, Denis Norman, in the transport portfolio and after the death of Sally took leave (without informing his cabinet of its length) on the Irish farm of the Heinz millionaire Tony O'Reilly,[13] he harboured still an antipathy towards what white South Africans had done to the region, and to Zimbabwe. Some have detected a streak of racism in Mugabe; if this is the case, it was, in 1992, selective. Despite De Klerk's coming to power in South Africa, with what seemed then a moderate but definite reformist programme, Mugabe did not want to meet him. This was, to an extent, irrational – but Mugabe did not wish to accord the South Africans any diplomatic or international regularity: they still had much to redeem; but they could not redeem it in isolation. Yet Mugabe accepted his turn as chairman of the frontline states reluctantly, since it might have meant, finally, the impossibility of not meeting De Klerk. Diplomacy was moving rapidly. Mugabe's own visit to see Afonso Dhlakama had helped to speed it up even more.

Two events that would force a change in Zimbabwean policy occurred in April 1992, while Mugabe was being hosted by O'Reilly and grieving for Sally. One was to do with De Klerk; for if Mugabe had been reluctant to meet him, the Nigerians certainly were not, and De Klerk arrived in Abuja on 9 April to see president Ibrahim Babangida, who was also then the chairman of the Organisation of African Unity (OAU). It was not just Mugabe who would have been unhappy. The ANC in South Africa certainly was. 'It is too early to invite De Klerk, even if it is for a good cause. It is worse in the sense that the opinion has not been sought of major players,' meaning the ANC, said a senior ANC official.[14] The Nigerians, determined to push home their advantage as the first leading African power to talk with De Klerk, angered the ANC even more when Babangida, in a rush of rhetorical blood, compared De Klerk to Steve Biko, Desmond Tutu and the ANC's own Nelson Mandela.[15] Rubbing in the salt, the South African foreign minister, Pik Botha, called Nigeria and South Africa the 'two giants in the sub-Saharan region', thereby pointedly putting Zimbabwe in its place; and his Nigerian counterpart agreed.[16]

There was some guarded Harare opinion that the Nigerian initiative, carrying an implied OAU blessing, would pave the way for a De Klerk–Mugabe visit,[17] distasteful as this might be. However, while the

Zimbabwean newspapers made headlines of what was happening in
Abuja, there was a studied playing down of (or lack of comment on)
Mugabe's absence and the fact that, during this absence, a Zimbabwean
minister had been despatched to South Africa.

Although an announcement was made on 30 March that Joshua
Nkomo would be Acting President in Mugabe's absence, this was not
reported in the *Herald* until 3 April. By that time, Nkomo had convened
the cabinet in emergency session on 31 March, Denis Norman had left
for South Africa on 1 April (the *Herald* did not report this until 4 April).
By 4 April, in fact, Norman had secured South African agreement to
deploy 15,500 rail wagons, and its own locomotives, to bring drought
relief to Zimbabwe. What was not reported was that this was not entirely
an act of humanitarian largesse or political goodwill. Privately, the South
Africans were demanding a cash downpayment (although to be fair
Zimbabwe already owed much money to South African agencies). The
size of this downpayment was such that it was thought in Zimbabwe that
what the South Africans really wanted was the visit of a more senior
minister – such as Nathan Shamuyarira, the Foreign Minister – with all
the diplomatic symbolisms that could be exploited from this, including
Mugabe's embarrassment.[18] Compared with what South Africa had done
earlier, this was minor *realpolitik*, but there is no doubt that people were
in danger of starving in Zimbabwe and other neighbouring countries.
With no one else, however, were the South Africans prepared to treat so
harshly – a white Zimbabwean minister notwithstanding – and, thereafter, Zimbabwe was determined, as a point of defiant pride, to pay for
the vast bulk of all the food aid that came streaming in. There is, in any
case, a hierarchy to aid and, in the end, even with deferred or commercial
payments little comes free.

The root of all this was the drought. Mugabe, apparently, was warned
in July 1991 that famine in early 1992 was a distinct possibility. He did
not consider the warning seriously until December, after his Commonwealth triumph had been completed (and all the preparations it had
entailed throughout 1991), but the planning systems for how to deal with
it were mishandled and operational plans shelved by an agriculture minister,
Witness Mangwende, with a PhD in international relations and no background in agriculture.[19] The regional Early Warning Unit, aided by the
FAO, had indeed warned of food shortages in July 1991, and was now
quick to say it had done so,[20] but elsewhere, as in the Agriculture Minister's

office, there was either buck-passing or denial. The normally sympathetic *Herald* lambasted the government in its reports and editorials: 'Shortages expose poor planning' ran one editorial headline.[21] Television, normally obsequious, expressed outrage at the already apparent hunger of the poor.[22]

To be fair, almost every Southern African country was affected, and few were prepared – not always because of poor planning. Zambia had anticipated record harvests from the immediate land reforms of the new democratic government. Then the weather had turned sour. Even so, even satirical Zimbabwean magazine columns now regretted having looked condescendingly at Zambian food planning in the past: 'Remember how we all laughed at those Zambian (food) riots? How we thought it amusing that people could take to the streets to toyi-toyi [dance] about the price of food? We ought, as the saying goes, to be laughing on the other side of our faces.'[23] But, even in South Africa itself – where Denis Norman had gone – 100,000 farm workers were expected to become homeless.[24]

The Zambians were much more adroit in handling the drought. The new president, Frederick Chiluba, ensured that he was reported, not only in the country but weeping as he toured the affected areas.[25] The (white) Zambian agriculture minister, Guy Scott, somewhat cheekily (repaying the sentiment of condescension in kind) invited white Zimbabwean farmers to resettle in Zambia. 'Private development companies will open up land for a mixture of foreign commercial farmers and small Zambian farmers,' he said, making it plain from which country he expected the foreign commercial farmers to come.[26] Scott knew also that these white farmers faced another threat, for on 27 February the first reading of the Zimbabwean Land Acquisition Act took place in parliament, with the third and final reading on 19 March 1992. This will be discussed below, but drought and land ownership could never be far divorced in any political mind. In any case, a first reading of production figures was revealing. Total Zimbabwean maize production for 1992 was expected to reach 513,600 tons but, of this already small amount, only 63,300 tons were sent to the Grain Marketing Board. The breakdown was as follows:[27]

Sector	Production	To Grain Marketing Board
Communal farms	200,400	25,000
Large commercial farms (mostly white)	292,000	32,300
Resettlement farms	21,000	6000
Totals	513,600	63,300

The resettlement farms (such as those attempted, years before, by the Ministry of Youth, Sport and Recreation) were negligible concerns. However, both their and the communal farms' output was used in the same way: it was retained so that people could eat. It was not distributed via the Grain Marketing Board so that non-productive areas could also eat. The white commercial farms also sent little to the board, partly so that black farm workers could eat, but also so that there would be stock feed for the expensive cattle which richer people – typecast as white people – would eat. There was thus a disproportion not only in diet but in contribution to the alleviation of national scarcity.

Not all the imported maize could come only via South Africa. Logistically, the huge amount needed would mean that some had to enter Zimbabwe via the Beira and Limpopo Corridors.

But Mozambicans would also be hungry, and RENAMO soldiers would attack and pillage the food transports – never mind peace talks in Rome. The Beira Corridor Group, a private consortium representing the multiple investment concerns within the Corridor, published a complex paper on how to operationalise drought relief via the Corridor,[28] and petitioned government – awaiting Mugabe's return – to arm more heavily and upgrade the Zimbabwean presence in the Limpopo Corridor, which had become particularly vulnerable to RENAMO incursions.[29]

In all of this, with his decisive sending of Denis Norman to South Africa after the cabinet of 31 March, a second cabinet on the issue on 7 April, and a third on 9 April, why did Nkomo act as he did? Was it the true presidentialism which had been denied him? Was it a true national concern? Perhaps it was these things, but there were other issues in his mind as well. In the Matabelelands, there continued a deep dissatisfaction with Mugabe; and if there was meant to be a unity government, the paucity of Ndebele ministers rankled in particular. There was no cabinet minister – only a deputy regional minister – from Matabeleland South; so the region to be worst affected by the drought had held no place in the Mugabe cabinet discussions that had dismissed the warnings of drought.[30]

The drought was indeed catastrophic in Nkomo's home territory. Independent journals described its impact, indicating the severity in Mberengwa.[31] It was predicted that in Bulawayo – even with heavy restrictions – running water would last only until July 1992.[32] But Harare was largely unaffected and, until his return from Ireland, Mugabe was not seen outside Harare. Unlike Zambia's Chiluba, no cameras caught him weeping in parched lands with impoverished peasants standing close by.

But perhaps Nkomo also saw – as must have Mugabe, unless blinded by the praise he had received on account of the Commonwealth summit and his actions regarding Mozambique, or by grief – the total national condition. Not without some chortling, this was reported throughout 1992 in the South African press; but the early assessment of Robin Drew was both accurate and sobering.[33] It listed five endogenous and five indigenous factors that merited serious policy consideration in Zimbabwe. The exogenous factors were: the rolling world recession; depressed commodity prices; high European interest rates; a reluctance to invest in sub-Saharan Africa; the pull of funds towards Eastern Europe. The indigenous factors were: the Zimbabwean budgetary deficit; an inflation rate of some 30 per cent; high unemployment; a sliding exchange rate which had devalued the currency by 47 per cent in 1991; a deteriorating balance of payments. Added to this was a sixth factor common to both lists, and that was the anticipated effects of compulsory land acquisition from white farmers. This had a local effect, through an anticipated impact on food production, and an external effect, in that the World Bank and others were against it.

The 60-page Land Acquisition Act of 1992 was not effective. The land issue would, however, resurface again and again, reaching – if not a climax – a considerable crescendo with the invasion of farms by 'war veterans' the better part of a decade later. The act, however, was rushed through parliament in three weeks. There was heavy international criticism – not a little of which had been orchestrated by the white farmers themselves, who certainly had a reasonable case, in that food production and security needed to be planned and safeguarded, particularly in perilous times (the Commercial Farmers Union had warned in April 1991 that Zimbabwe might have to import maize). It is true that Mugabe's government had no plan for appropriate training and production-maintenance programmes during any land redistribution. Insofar as Mugabe was engaged with the issue, it was from the point of view of social justice. 'Let us, you see, carry out this act once and for all. Those who support, support, those who will want to sabotage, let them sabotage. We will go through that path of comforts and discomforts and we will evolve measures ourselves in the process of remedying that.'[34]

Of course, the broad figures of land ownership could only support Mugabe's social-justice perspective. Since independence, the government had purchased 3.3 million hectares (8.15 million acres). In 1992, 4500 mostly white farmers owned 11.5 million hectares. This was one third of the entire country. 7 million peasants lived on 16.4 million hectares of 'communal' farmland.[35] From these figures, most of Zimbabwe was already under some form of cultivation, and the only way forward in the macro terms of equity was redistribution.

Having said that, despite the controversy surrounding it, the Land Acquisition Act proposed to purchase only another 5.5 million hectares. The status quo, certainly in productive terms, would have still been biased towards the white farmers and, politically, if this redistribution had taken place the issue would have been, for some time, finished. In a sense, and this is the value of hindsight, the protests of the white farmers were too effective. Having milked political mileage from the passing of the act, Mugabe allowed the Agriculture Minister to retain considerable flexibility – which was used immediately, essentially to postpone indefinitely any redistribution. 'Only those with the potential to be good farmers should be chosen for resettlement and proper services should be provided to ensue productive communities are established,' Mugabe said.[36]

Many commentators saw the land-acquisition issue as an example of how Mugabe made policy. From July to October 1991, all official attention was given to the Commonwealth summit – yet July to December were exactly the months of serious drought warnings. Mugabe met Dhlakama on 10 January 1992. On 27 January, Sally Mugabe died. From 27 February to 19 March, the Land Acquisition Act was being rushed through parliament. Mugabe then went on holiday to Ireland, leaving Nkomo to bring to the cabinet, finally but immediately, the question of drought. By the time Mugabe returned, drought had eclipsed redistribution as the central agricultural and rural issue. 'Mugabe is a one-issue at a time president. He gives deep meditation to these single issues, but this means another issue can only be taken up when the last is finished.'[37] This deep meditation, however, is not technically based. 'We will evolve measures,' he had said, regarding the consequences to production in any land redistribution. The meditation is simultaneously broad-based – to do with sweeping, once-and-for-all acts – and, as shall soon be noted, curiously emotionally parochial in some tactics and avoidances. In this lack of technical thinking, it is perhaps unlikely that Mugabe gave much meditative time to the complex projection of figures that led to 'stock-out' day – the day national food stocks would be exhausted – and the Agriculture Minister did not seem to do so either.

It was one of those curious exercises – the calculation of when food stocks will end. It is done with calculations of tons of rail-wagon capacities and 'leakage' to the country hosting the rail lines – not to mention the guerrilla army fighting the host – and of lead times (some eight weeks from realisation that orders need to be placed), immediate go-slow rationings and short-term airlifts (the Russians had offered cargo planes). With all the raw figures, the calculations can be done on the backs of many envelopes in a hotel room – but the reading of it is as dry as dust. 'Stock-out' day, the day of dust, was finally variously calculated and agreed to be 18 April 1992, Easter Saturday.[38]

Perhaps Mugabe understood more than seemed to be the case. But perhaps he understood that to grapple with the issue he would first have to grapple with the South Africans and with De Klerk's Government, if not De Klerk himself. 'It is too early to invite De Klerk,' the ANC official had said of the Nigerians. It was too early to invite the leader of the state that had blown up your airforce, had killed your best political friend, had caused depredation in so many neighbour countries, and was only now – painstakingly still calculating how slow and staggered the steps to change might be – emerging into an indeterminate light of sorts. No, let Nkomo do it. Let him send the white minister to deal with the white government. Mugabe would absent himself, and it would have been extraordinary if Mugabe and Nkomo had not had some understanding as to what Nkomo would, seemingly by himself, do.

Mugabe seems to do two things recurrently, whether or not the quality and detail of his technical thinking and meditation improve or decline: with the prospect of difficulty to come, he finds it opportune – even if cloaked in broad, very broad, socially just terms (so broad by 2000 that individuated moralities played no part) – to raise (or have raised) the question of land redistribution; second, if there is something he finds personally unpalatable, in his terms questionably moral, he will not be present, and someone else will do it. We shall see these things repeated some eight years later.

OPPOSITION AND RUMOURS OF OPPOSITION

In the remainder of 1992, however, Mugabe turned his blindness to the drought warnings into a ruthlessly efficient *tour de force* of calculated food distribution. In some ways, he was never more presidential and populist – and popular – as if he were, in 1992, already on the stump for the next elections in 1995. There was the almost – in such circumstances – requisite pillaging, profiteering (some closely associated with senior ZANU-PF members) and incompetence. Moreover, in the cities ZANU-PF members and officials received considerable preference in the food distribution, while others had to wait, sometimes fruitlessly, in long queues. But in the rural areas – where 70 per cent of the electorate lived and which, to be fair, the drought had hit somewhat harder than in the cities – food distribution was less nakedly biased. Opposition spokes-persons complained that 'Zimbabweans must take heed that maize does not belong to ZANU-PF, but to the state,'[39] meaning that, whether fairly distributed or not, ZANU-PF was intimately associated with, and was seen to be associated with the food distribution. There were some deaths from malnutrition in the Matabelelands, but there was no widespread starvation. Even so, given the low stocks and delivery times of maize, by November 1992 many aid recipients were being given only one third of a normal ration. Some 6000 tons of maize were arriving daily in Zimbabwe – via the Beira Corridor and South Africa – but some 8000 tons a day were required. The government had been buying food on the international market, not depending on donor largesse, but funds were running low. Despite all this, and despite the fact that it was well known that the govern-ment had not planned properly for the occasion, the 'evolving of measures ourselves' was here – for ZANU-PF at least – a brilliant extemporaneous exercise in opportunism, both in feeding enough people just enough, in rewarding its party faithful, and in refurbishing the party image. It left the opposition – itself undergoing restructuring – flabbergasted and constantly wrong-footed.

In July 1992, the opposition won some popular approval for its call that Mugabe should reduce the size of his cabinet.[40] In October 1992, the first Zimbabwean academic accusations of Fifth Brigade atrocities began to be published in popular outlets.[41] But none of this was enough to dent seriously the ZANU-PF momentum.

In March and April 1992, the perennial rumours resurfaced that Edison Zvobgo, a senior ZANU-PF figure, might challenge Mugabe – helped considerably by Zvobgo himself in scathing attacks on Mugabe over press freedom, and in a cover story in the nation's most popular magazine.[42] By June some of the opposition had regrouped itself into a coalition called the United Front, with several former ZUM officials at its helm, and by November the Forum for Democratic Reform became the latest to enter the opposition lists. There was political dissatisfaction, but it was to very little effect. In fact, the fragmentary origins of the opposition parties – many small parties and interest groups coalescing – meant that ZANU-PF could simultaneously point to an opposition as evidence of democracy, and not be afraid of its coherence and efficacy. And Mugabe sustained himself in his belief that, always, he could turn disaster into triumph – so that just as 1991 had ended in his Commonwealth triumph, so too 1992 was ending in his triumph over drought. When the President himself is seen in the countryside, handing food to a hungry family, any normal – never mind small and fractious – opposition will find its going hard.

But there was a glittering triumph of another sort as well, so it is now back to Mozambique and Rome that attention turns.

NOTES ON CHAPTER 4

1   *Sunday Mail* (Harare), 20 October 1991.
2   Commonwealth Heads of Government Meeting Harare, 16–22 October 1991, communiqué, paras 56 and 57.
3   For the first interpretation of them as such, see Sir William Dale, *The Modern Commonwealth*, London: Butterworths, 1983; for a greater insistence that these were surely constitutional, see Stephen Chan, *The Commonwealth in World Politics: A Study of International Action, 1965–1985*, London: Lester Crook, 1988
4   A joint press release to this effect was published in Harare, 21 October 1991, signed by a range of NGOs, including the British NGOs: British Refugee Council, Commonwealth Human Rights Initiative, Index on Censorship, PEN, Justice, Methodist Church Overseas, Minority Rights, Penal Reform, Rights and Humanity.
5   *Guardian* (London), 21 December 2001.
6   *Sunday Times* (Harare), 9 May 1993.
7   *Herald*, 19 October 1991.

8   A. O. Adegbola, 'Poll Monitoring is Playing an Increasingly Important Role', *Herald*, 8 June 1993.
9   *Herald*, 22 October 1991.
10 Cited in N. Bhebe and T. Ranger (eds), *Soldiers in Zimbabwe's Liberation War*, vol. 1, Harare: University of Zimbabwe Publications, 1995, p. 2.
11 US Ambassador to the author, Harare, April 1992.
12 In Paul L. Moorcraft, *African Nemesis: War and Revolution in Southern Africa 1945-2010*, London: Brasseys, 1990, p. 282.
13 See *Wall Street Journal*, 3 April 1992, for a front-page article describing the Mugabe–O'Reilly relationship.
14 *Herald*, 7 April 1992.
15 *Herald*, 11 April 1992.
16 *Herald*, 10 April 1992.
17 Foreign ministry source to the author, Harare, April 1992.
18 ZANU-PF Central Committee source to the author, Harare, April 1992.
19 *Observer* (London), 29 March 1992.
20 *Herald*, 9 April 1992.
21 *Herald*, 11 April 1992.
22 *Independent* (London), 15 April 1992.
23 *Parade* (Harare), April 1992, p. 39.
24 *Observer*, 19 April 1992.
25 *Times of Zambia* (Lusaka), 14 March 1992.
26 *Daily Telegraph* (London), 21 April 1992.
27 *Herald*, 23 March 1992.
28 Beira Corridor Group documents 9/92 of 27 March 1992; and discussion draft dated 17 March 1992/b.
29 Beira Corridor Group senior executive to the author, Harare, April 1992.
30 Senior ZAPU source to the author, Harare, April 1992.
31 *MOTO* (Gweru), March 1992, p. 11.
32 *Horizon* (Harare), March 1992, pp. 8-9.
33 Robin Drew, 'Drought chooses worst time', *Johannesburg Star*, 10 February 1992; thereafter, the South African press, both black and white, pronounced power shortages in Zimbabwe as 'the Heart of Darkness', *Sunday Times* (Johannesburg), 27 September 1992; and as 'Catastrophe for Zimbabwean Firms and the Zimbabwean Stock Market', *Citizen* (Johannesburg), 5 October 1992.
34 *Financial Gazette* (Harare), 12 March 1992.
35 *Economist* (London), 15 February 1992, pp. 51–2.
36 *Herald*, 28 March 1992.
37 Diplomatic source to the author, Harare, April 1992; this was echoed by several domestic political sources to the author.
38 The author took part in one of these exercises in calculation. When he presented his results to an informal group of parliamentarians, no one would believe it. Specialised agencies and agricultural experts soon settled on Easter Saturday, the period in which Jesus was dead.

39   *Weekly Mail* (Johannesburg), 27 November–3 December 1992.
40   *Guardian* (London), 7 July 1992.
41   *Star* (Johannesburg), 21 October 1992, reporting on articles in the Zimbabwean
     Financial Gazette.
42   *Parade*, April 1992, pp. 30–31.

FIVE

The End of War in Mozambique: Mugabe's Roman Triumph

Just as Caesars marched in triumph in Rome, so, after some twists and turns, did Mugabe. The meeting with Dhlakama had been a crossing of the Rubicon, so it is there, in Malawi, where we shall start. Or perhaps we should start with an image of 1975, when the departing Portuguese settlers, alarmed at the sudden independence caused by a military coup and new leaders in Lisbon, sought to sabotage the new Mozambican state by destroying as many flushing toilets as possible – a considerably cruder rearguard action that the Ethiopian Derg perpetrated on its withdrawal from Eritrea; there, the retreating Ethiopians simply, and more effectively they thought, took every book in the university library back to Addis Ababa with them; and the Derg leader, Mengistu, found an exile home in Zimbabwe, where, ever after, he was reported to consume two bottles of whiskey a day. In Malawi, the abstemious Mugabe and Dhlakama discussed the refurbishments of more than the toilets of Mozambique.

In Britain, normally concerned newspapers covered the event sparingly;[1] but considerable preparation and secrecy had gone into this meeting. Moreover, to give the occasion some piquancy for the early 2000s, there were both Zimbabwean and US fears that RENAMO diplomacy, unable to be as reliant on Kenyan advice as before the 1991 Commonwealth summit, had extended itself to 'play the Muslim card' – Mozambique being an Indian Ocean country with coastal Islamic communities not unlike those in Tanzania and Kenya – and had been in contact with Indonesia and Saudi Arabia, both of whom had in turn made representations to Zimbabwe.[2] Although rumours and reports were rife – many able to be discouraged – they included Libyan grain relief for Zimbabwean Muslims.[3]

In any case, the US seemed particularly unsurprised by Mugabe's visit to see Dhlakama. The State Department had a somewhat schematic view of the post-cold-war Southern Africa, and Mozambique required some 'tidying up', before South Africa was, itself, tidied up.[4] If the exact US prompting beforehand is unclear, its follow-up was decisive and open. In the wake of Mugabe's visit, Deputy Assistant Secretary of State Jeffrey Davidow went to Malawi in February, and met Dhlakama as well.[5] He also met President Chissano and urged further compromise. By April, a visit to Dhlakama was being scheduled by the Assistant Secretary of State, Herman Cohen.[6]

If the US was unsurprised – at least enough to have what seemed a prepared follow-up – the Zimbabwean Ministry of Foreign Affairs was kept uninformed and unconsulted. Having said that, there had been some high-level transfer of key personnel from Foreign Affairs to National Security before the visit to Malawi; but Mugabe went to Malawi unaccompanied by any Foreign Ministry staff. He took the Minister of State for National Security and the Acting Minister of Defence and, as well as other personnel from these ministries, members of the Central Intelligence Organisation.[7] It would seem that the initiative, however prompted, had been planned entirely by Mugabe's own office, in concert with a few chosen others.

And it may have had little or nothing to do with US prompting. Certainly, the Zimbabweans would have known what the US also knew: that Chissano's and FRELIMO's position was parlous.

> FRELIMO troops have been unpaid for months, except around Maputo; and the RENAMO offensive – compounding the drought – has reached the outskirts of Maputo. They are well-commanded by a General Garcia. FRELIMO seems to be fighting only to survive, and reliably holds only Maputo and the Beira Corridor.[8]

Moreover, FRELIMO was negotiating poorly in Rome, and by this time, in place of Kenyans, unofficial Portuguese and South African advisers were in Rome with RENAMO. International creditors were applying economic pressures on Chissano, and altogether – with drought also thrown in – Chissano had few cards left to play. He could not, of his own initiative, make more concessions in Rome: he had exhausted his stock in Maputo and FRELIMO quarters by making many to ensure that the

Rome talks achieved some preliminary progress. He needed, at least, to be able to say to his people that matters were being taken out of his hands. To this extent, Mugabe was doing a favour for Chissano and, indeed, the two men had met in December, in the Mozambican city of Beira – although it is uncertain if Mugabe had mentioned to him his plans.

The meeting with Dhlakama was hosted by Malawi's President Hastings Banda. However, Mugabe and Dhlakama soon fell to speaking to each other in Shona, thus freezing Banda out of any actual participation. 'I should say how impressed we were by how "presidential" Dhlakama was,' said one onlooker[9] (although it was likely that Dhlakama had been coached extensively by Portuguese image-builders). Mugabe's public comment was understated: 'My first reading of him is that he is a man with some ideas'.[10] But he followed this up with the clear indication that second readings of the man would be undertaken. 'The discussions with Dhlakama were for the first time and, if need be, we will be holding further discussions.'[11]

What Mugabe wanted, above all, was progress at Rome. He and Dhlakama could not settle the technical niceties of ceasefires, elections, government and demilitarisation in a summit. But he held out a carrot for Dhlakama, saying that Zimbabwean troop withdrawal 'should be a matter for the talks' in Rome.[12]

However, if Mugabe was understated in public, privately he was, if not ecstatic, well satisfied by events; and in the murky world of politics he felt that he could do business with Dhlakama. The US was also well satisfied. FRELIMO was generally astounded by the meeting, and the frontline Southern African states were also astonished. Mugabe had taken Bernard Chidzero's manifesto for the UN secretary-generalship and made conflict resolution seem like a natural talent – even if, previously, it was conflict itself that seemed his talent.

TALKING UNTIL TALKING ON TELEVISION

It was not, however, as if Zimbabwe had not been attempting conflict resolution in Mozambique before this time. It would seem that Chissano had approached Mugabe as early as 9 July 1989 to mediate the conflict, but this had been based on FRELIMO's own terms for the ceasefire. Nevertheless, although Mugabe did make some effort, most of the running fell to his foreign-affairs official Elleck Mashingaidze, who did himself meet with Dhlakama in August 1989. RENAMO duly released its own ceasefire plan that month, seeking above all equality with FRELIMO and the withdrawal of Zimbabwean troops – so there was certainly a negotiating position, and something which the Zimbabweans could themselves use as leverage. That could be used against both RENAMO and FRELIMO – RENAMO because Zimbabwean troops were fighting it, and FRELIMO because it depended increasingly on these very same troops. Nevertheless, negotiations did not race forward, and after a Zimbabwean offensive in February 1990 RENAMO announced that Mugabe was no longer acceptable as a mediator. The Zimbabwean Ministry of Foreign Affairs did remain involved, and an effort to instigate direct talks between RENAMO and FRELIMO took place in Malawi in June 1990. Dhlakama himself flew in – on Lonrho's Tiny Rowland's executive jet – but left before the talks actually began.[13] Talks did finally begin between the two sides in Rome, between 8 and 10 July 1990, at the monastery of Santo Egidio.

Tiny Rowland was himself busy with his own efforts at mediation. For him, and Lonrho, it was a matter of economics. According to Alex Vines, Lonrho arrived at an agreement directly with Dhlakama, as early as June 1982, to safeguard Lonrho's oil pipeline. The price was half a million US dollars per month.[14] For Lonrho, no matter what privileges its money bought, a peaceful region would increase its profits even more. Rowland had his fingers everywhere – including South Africa – and it was not that Mozambique was important to him only in itself, but as part of a web of projects, investments and transactions. The aim would have been to make this web both more secure and more complex still. In any case, he enjoyed intrigue and his close relationship with many African leaders. He was the last real adventurer in the multinational world.

Dhlakama was not simply a reclusive guerrilla leader. He himself visited Portugal from 5 to 11 November 1991, and held talks with the government in Lisbon. He was ready enough for Mugabe on 10 January 1992. However, what all this diplomatic traffic – official or otherwise, US, Kenyan, Malawian, Italian, Catholic, Portuguese, Lonrhodian, with the South Africans very much in all the shadows – meant was that, in a crowded field of players, the Mozambicans had very few in whom they could confidentially place their trust. If Mugabe talked directly to RENAMO, to Dhlakama himself, the one big piece on the FRELIMO side of the chessboard would be seen to be assuming not only moves of its own, but perhaps an endgame of its own. Mugabe's meeting with Dhlakama not only helped Chissano with his own hardliners in FRELIMO – the 'matters are out of my hands' move – but it also meant that Chissano had nothing else to which he could cling except the talks in Rome; and Mugabe had taken great care in his discussions with Dhlakama to privilege the talks in Rome.

There were, altogether, 12 rounds of talks in Rome, beginning in July 1990 and ending in October 1992. I do not propose here to describe these in any detail.[15] Suffice to say that the early rounds, apart from the so-called ceasefire of December 1990, were typical 'talks about talks,' and talks about who might be recognised as observers and mediators. It was only during round 8, between October and November 1991, that 'basic principles' were finally agreed. Thereafter, round 9, December 1991, saw work begin on electoral law. That work was completed in round 10 after Mugabe's meeting with Dhlakama; but the truly thorny issue of actual and verifiable ceasefire had to await round 11, held from 10 June to 10 August 1992, and these were painstakingly slow as here, finally, both sides had most to lose. The diplomatic traffic through Rome was crowded indeed and here, once again, Mugabe appeared, as if *deus ex machina*, to forge the breakthrough.

One of the key RENAMO demands was not just equivalence of military disengagement, equivalence of armed forces at ceasefire, or equivalence of numbers in any national army – but equivalence, pure and proper, between RENAMO and FRELIMO. In short, it was a political, not a military, demand; and, as a political demand, it could be satisfied by symbols. Mugabe recognised this, although Chissano and FRELIMO did not.

To be fair, at that point, FRELIMO's army stood at 80-90,000 men, whereas RENAMO's numbered only 15-20,000. In addition, FRELIMO had a huge secret service and, altogether, sufficient militarised personnel – in an economy on a war footing – to need to be able to absorb as many as possible into a post-war force. Otherwise, post-war unemployment would be a threat to peace. RENAMO was demanding a national army of no more than 30,000. On 4 July 1992, Mugabe, together with the host President, Quett Masire, met Dhlakama in Botswana. Dhlakama insisted upon a meeting with Chissano. But one other thing took place as a result of this meeting. Dhlakama secured an interview on Zimbabwean television. The man was coming in from the cold, but Mugabe was already starting to trade in symbols. He next put pressure on Chissano finally to meet directly with Dhlakama.

Dhlakama, however, wanted an African summit meeting: 'African' because he wished to be recognised among African leaders as himself an African leader; and 'summit' because he wished to be seen as a president talking to another president. Between 4 and 7 August 1992, Dhlakama and Chissano met in Rome, mediated by Mugabe and, at first, Tiny Rowland. It had been Mugabe's phraseology and persuasiveness that had bought Dhlakama to an 'African' summit that was being held in Italy. Dhlakama had wanted an African location, but Rome now being, momentarily, Africa, it was Mugabe who had to take the lead. The talks got off to a bad start. After all, it had been Chissano who had conceded most – for he knew Dhlakama would advertise the meeting as one of equals. In the early hours of 5 August, the talks were on the verge of collapse. Mugabe, with great diplomatic skill, kept them afloat. On 6 August, talks were still not advancing quickly. Dhlakama was refusing to sign a ceasefire. Mugabe took him aside for 90 minutes – made personal guarantees of his safety and that of RENAMO – and, with that stroke, the friend of Chissano and FRELIMO, the benefactor at the hands of FRELIMO during Zimbabwe's liberation war, became the protector of Dhlakama and RENAMO. It was an extraordinary flip in midair. RENAMO played the result to the hilt. In its journal, Dhlakama was described as having received 'unanimous recognition as a true political leader, democratic, understanding and humane'.[16] Not everyone who had followed the brutalities of the war would have recognised this description.

More was to follow. On 6 August, Mugabe delivered Dhlakama the second of his television instalments – only this time, and for the very first time, Dhlakama was able to speak on Mozambican public television, and give his version of the peace talks, why they were taking so long, and what he stood for. Chissano may have been choking on Mugabe's twists, but on 7 August Dhlakama signed a declaration with Chissano, agreeing to sign a peace accord by the first of October.

The days between 20 August and 4 October 1992, Round 12, were not easy. Demilitarisation and the size of a national army were still thorny issues. On 2 September, Dhlakama flew to Pretoria to enlist the help of South Africa. De Klerk and Foreign Minister Pik Botha were encouraging of the Rome talks continuing. They had, by now, their own domestic negotiations to prosecute and, like the US, wanted the Mozambican issue 'tidied up'. On 18 September, Tiny Rowland facilitated another meeting between Dhlakama and Chissano in Botswana and, finally, the two instructed their teams in Rome to prepare final texts for a peace accord.

When the two could not agree on a fitting African capital in which to sign the accord, it was again Mugabe who suggested Rome as a capital of Africa. Dhlakama, Chissano and Mugabe were all in Rome on 1 October. Dhlakama refused to meet Chissano until the draft peace accord had been analysed on a line-by-line basis. Nevertheless, the RENAMO delegation was dressed in new Italian suits – a sign, perhaps, that they were prepared for a great photo opportunity. Mediators, however, shuttled back and forth among Dhlakama and his people in the Forum Hotel, Chissano and his in the Grand Hotel, and Mugabe and his at the Majestic Hotel. The detail of civilian administration during the ceasefire was a last-minute sticking point. Anyone who knows Rome can imagine the caravans of mediators shuttling among the hotels. US Assistant Secretary of State Herman Cohen arrived to take his part in the circus. It took till 4 October before the accord could be signed. Before the two antagonists, Dhlakama and Chissano, put their pens to paper, Mugabe made the formal speech as to what was about to happen:

> This event we are going to witness now – the signing of a ceasefire and general peace agreement – is an event that will forever remain memorable in the minds and hearts of the people of Africa, especially those of Mozambique. It is an event which marks a transformation of relations amongst them, from relations of conflict to relations of peace, from war to peace …
>
> Today is not the day of Judgement. It is the day of reconciliation. Today is not the day when we should examine who was right and who was wrong. Today is the day when we must say we are all right. Both are right in being party to the process of peace. We cannot escape that process.[17]

In a sense, Mugabe has made that speech twice. The one in Rome, in 1992, was an echo, an heir, in some ways a copy, of the one he had made in the new Zimbabwe in 1980. Then, and again in Rome, he was, after many twists and turns, the great man of reconciliation.

NOT SO GREAT MEN

Alex Vines is the great chronicler (or estimator) of how much money was paid out to RENAMO to guarantee the peace process. Not all of his estimates are verifiable and, indeed, many promises of financial assistance to RENAMO never finally materialised. Much certainly did, but the US, Italy and Portugal (and Lonrho) soon learnt to meet the sometimes gratuitous demands for funds with gratuitous promises. It seems that the Italian Government did pay for the suits that the RENAMO delegation wore to the final round of talks and the spring ceremony; but it also paid for superb seats for both the FRELIMO and RENAMO delegations at the opening World Cup football match in June 1990, between Argentina and Cameroon.[18] (Both delegations cheered for Cameroon.)

It is reasonable, however, to accept the estimate of some US$20 million spent on the peace process by the Italian Government. Santo Egidio spent £185,000. The monastic community had estimated that peace might be reached by 1993, and was budgeting accordingly. Drought played a major role in advancing the time of settlement; and Mugabe's dramatic and highly personalised interventions were a seal to key moments of breakthrough and progress; 'personalised' because he came to know Dhlakama well. He never liked him, and preferred the company of Chissano; but he could appeal to him in the manner of one haughty African statesman to another. That was to flatter Dhlakama. Chissano won the post-ceasefire elections, and Dhlakama – well provisioned by at least some of the financial promises materialising in his specific direction – never became a statesman of any stripe at all.

There are stories from the peace process that cheapen both Chissano and Dhlakama, but these are probably stories that accompany all political leaders who stay in penthouse suites and drink liberally single malts at another's expense – while their men are fighting in a jungle. No such stories attached themselves to Mugabe throughout the peace process. If anyone emerged with credit from it all, it was Mugabe. He was the one who, at some considerable risk of incurring the wrath of a still staunchly apartheid South Africa, sent his soldiers into Mozambique. It was a mission mixing Zimbabwean trade self-interest and principle. While so engaged, Mugabe came to realise that RENAMO, muddied and bloodied as it was, was not itself without some (if vague and not always discernible) principle. Perhaps the Zimbabweans could not afford, economically, to stay and fight another five years; if they had, RENAMO could not have won. In time, both the US and South Africa, in a new mood of majority rule and peaceful democracy, wanted Mozambique 'tidied up'. Perhaps Mugabe responded to that mood. At the same time, if he had indeed persevered a little longer with his military expedition, not withdrawing it to the transport corridors, that same mood would have started to erode RENAMO's international support. Even its African friends, such as the Kenyans, knew RENAMO could not win outright, and wanted only for it to be taken seriously as a political actor. It was Mugabe who gave it that political room. In doing so, he had to reduce the full political space once occupied by FRELIMO, the very force that had once succoured him, and which, years later, he had come to help protect. Dhlakama changed as an obscure man, without philosophical commitments, under pressure and temptation from much wider world changes. Mugabe was the one who changed on the basis of something thoughtful and morally fraught with very public difficulties.

Yet, what was this Mugabe at the end of 1992? Even with his Roman triumph, itself well televised, and carrying his renewed message of reconciliation, his record – after 12 years in power – was mixed. In some ways it was very mixed indeed. He had fought two post-independence elections, and won them handsomely – but against the backdrop of violence, firstly on a large scale in the Matabelelands, and secondly targeted against the country's first significant and unambiguous opposition party.

He had fought two wars – the first against his own citizens in the Matabelelands, the second in Mozambique. The first used atrocity and the second was meant, among other things, to have been against atrocity. He had entered, almost totally unprepared, a devastating drought, but emerged from it electorally stronger than ever. The food distribution was often biased, but exactly targeted to combine just enough relief with maximum political gain.

He worked hard for, and enjoyed, two significant diplomatic triumphs – one in the Commonwealth and one in Mozambique. Both were international landmarks, but the first, with its emphasis on human rights, would return to haunt him; the second involved some political surgery on a still friendly former host.

All the credit side, therefore, contained debits. The debit side proper was less spectacular, although – within ten years – it would be more so. Bernard Chidzero did not become UN Secretary General and, despite his best efforts and those of others, the economy continued to worsen.

The land issue remained unresolved.

The widower had surely run out of at least international grand strokes. In South Africa, a grander man with grander strokes was growing into a much grander game; and Mugabe would soon be largely eclipsed by Mandela. Perhaps the Roman triumph was to be his last.

NOTES ON CHAPTER 5

1   *Independent on Sunday* (London), 12 January 1992, gave one-and-a-half column inches.
2   Zimbabwean political source to the author, Harare, April 1992; US embassy sources confirmed the Saudi connection, but maintained no knowledge of an Indonesian move. These US sources stressed also RENAMO's courtship of the Vatican and other Catholic powers such as Portugal. 'So there were Christian as well as Moslem cards.'
3   Cabinet Office source to the author, Harare, April 1992; this source reiterated Indonesian approaches.
4   US diplomatic source to the author, Harare, April 1992.
5   *Guardian* (London), 28 February 1992. Jeffrey Davidow was an established Africanist. He had written a book on the process leading to Zimbabwe's independence: *A Peace in Southern Africa: The Lancaster House Conference on Rhodesia, 1979*, Boulder: Westview, 1984.
6   *Herald* (Harare), 8 April 1992.
7   CIO source to the author, Harare, April 1992.
8   US diplomatic source to the author, Harare, April 1992.
9   Delegation member to the author, Harare, April 1992.
10 *Independent on Sunday*, 12 January 1992.
11 *Herald*, 11 January 1992.
12 Ibid.
13 For a comprehensive account of Zimbabwean efforts at this time, see Hasu Patel, 'Zimbabwe's Mediation in Mozambique and Angola 1989–91', in Stephen Chan and Vivienne Jabri (eds), *Mediation in Southern Africa*, London: Macmillan, 1993, esp. pp. 120–27.
14 Alex Vines, *No Democracy Without Money: The Road to Peace in Mozambique (1982–1992)*, London: Catholic Institute for International Relations, 1994, p. 27.
15 This has been done in Stephen Chan and Moises Venancio, *War and Peace in Mozambique*, London: Macmillan, 1998; see also Cameron Hume, *Ending Mozambique's War*, Washington DC: US Institute of Peace, 1994.
16 *Novos Tempos*, October–November 1992.
17 Quoted in Hume, op. cit., p. 137.
18 Alex Vines, 'The Business of Peace', *Accord Special Issue: The Mozambican Peace Process in Perspective*, London: Conciliation Resources, 1998.

SIX

Amazing Grace
and Decline

A flurry of academic literature marked the end of Zimbabwe's first decade of independence. Just as the earlier literature, commemorating independence and reconciliation, had been enthusiastic – almost euphoric – so the second wave was critical and discouraging. Some tried to establish specific theses – among them that Mugabe had retained, adapted and used the basic apparatus of repression that had been available to Ian Smith.[1] As previous chapters have indicated, however, it was the augmentation of the inherited apparatus by new techniques – North Korean, guerrilla practice, party militants – that most effectively turned the screw against real or imagined opponents of the ruling party and Robert Mugabe.

Almost all of the new literature criticised the loss or erosion of political freedoms. It is perhaps more accurate to say that political freedoms were not so much lost as exercised with risk. In moments of emergency – or even urgency – for Mugabe's party, the risk to political opponents could be very high indeed. Yet, notwithstanding the analyses of the first decade, it is necessary to point out that for the second decade of independence, the 1990s, there was always articulated and organised opposition to ZANU-PF and to the President. It was often poorly organised, or a minority and divided articulation, but it was never suppressed. It was often intimidated, and sometimes repressed. Even as the third decade lurched into being, the government stepped up the harassment, persecution and even murder of opponents – or plain unfortunate farmers – but opposition newspapers continued to be published and, gradually, the political opposition became united and, to a large extent because it was united, began winning victories and making national points. Mugabe always played a very hardball game – but he never suspended play. Even when he was both player and referee, he never blew the full-time whistle. This is a controversial statement to make, particularly at the start of the 2000s, but this chapter will seek to establish how, in the 1990s at least, the game of hardball was played.

Some of the new literature had particular points to prove in its criticism of Mugabe and the Zimbabwean Government, and this was in the South African literature of the time. No longer crudely racist and disparaging in that manner, it was still condescending and – because South-African-centric – the now liberal authors looked to a majority-rule region in which a rainbow South Africa took the lead and, among other things, either absorbed or turned to its own advantage the regional apparatus of economic cooperation the hitherto frontline states had established.[2] Part of the argument for why this had to be so lay in the analyses of how poorly Zimbabwe had performed economically.

In an extremely well-argued essay, Christopher Gregory noted that 'mounting unemployment, increasing levels of inflation, persistent shortages of consumer goods, declining real wage rates' beset Zimbabwe in 1990.[3] This was despite a growth in GNP somewhat greater than in sub-Saharan Africa generally. Gregory went on to look at Finance Minister Bernard Chidzero's 1991 five-year economic reform framework. He also noted a new sense of political endorsement and will to make work what was effectively a framework to enclose the type of structural adjustment favoured by, usually demanded by, the IMF. The theme of how the Zimbabwean economy had come to – declined to – structural adjustment was taken up by other authors.[4] However, Gregory expressed some scepticism as to how well Chidzero's framework could be implemented (Gregory's is, at heart, a sceptical essay, in a line of sceptical essays by him) because of the festering land issue in Zimbabwe. Jeffrey Herbst has pointed out, in his controversial but generally celebrated book, that by 1990 there were in fact two conflicts over land: the government and the white farmers, and the rise of squatters – unilateral takers-over of land.[5] Well over a decade before the much-publicised farm invasions by 'war veterans', the roots of the phenomenon were already dug into the soil. However, after his catalogue of Zimbabwean failures, Gregory briefly looked at the chances of any change at all – any progress at all – and concluded more dismally than sceptically that 'after a decade of avoidance behaviour and missed opportunities, Robert Mugabe's administration is now in a situation where it's damned if it does, and damned if it doesn't.'[6] However, Gregory underplays, I feel, the very real difficulties caused by the international economic environment, from 1982 onwards, in Zimbabwe: the costs of meeting and repairing South African destabilisation;[7] the costs of intervening in Mozambique. There is no doubt that the Zimbabwean economy was also battered by mismanagement and policies remaining unimplemented. Chidzero had indeed done his best, but at a certain point the costs to the Zimbabwean people would have caused any policy-maker to blink. This is perhaps what, humanely as well as dismally, Gregory may have meant – or should have meant: that those damning Mugabe would be his own people. If he went for structural adjustment at full throttle, they would indeed damn him; if he did not, the IMF and those like Gregory would damn him, and their damnation would mean a loss of liquidity that could only have led to further Zimbabwean hardships. How Mugabe navigated the squalls of damnation in the 1990s, politically as well as economically, is the subject of this chapter.

DISAFFECTIONS AND VIOLENCE

After the Rome peace accord, Mugabe made no further attempt to bring Dhlakama and Chissano closer together – even though at one stage RENAMO thought it could win the elections and the Zimbabweans also thought it a real possibility.[8] It was as if, having helped settle the Mozambican conflict, he had no interest in helping to build the peaceful nation.

He did, however, take an interest in the South African peace process and, for a time, sought to build bridges among the ANC, the Pan-Africanist Congress, and the Zulu leader Buthelezi. Certainly, he did not want De Klerk to be the one, effectively, to mediate the three. That would have given him, in Mugabe's eyes, too much leverage in the emerging process; but after his reluctance to allow Denis Norman, his Transport Minister, to visit South Africa during the drought, Mugabe now let his Foreign Minister Nathan Shamuyarira go 'down south' for the funeral of a senior ANC figure Oliver Tambo and once there to meet his counterpart, Pik Botha.

Meanwhile, as economic structural adjustment (known as ESAP) began to take hold, it was debated widely and, amazingly, quite expertly in the rural areas. Peasant farmers had been following the case for ESAP on vernacular radio, and it really was the case that a foreign visitor stopping at a rural bar for a beer could be bearded by a wizened son of the soil with the words 'and what do you think of ESAP then?' before being harangued in macro- as well as micro-budgetary terms, and stagger away knowing very well indeed what the old peasant thought about it.

Structural adjustment was hard on peasant farmers. As with many other sectors, they began to lose subsidies and facilities; and this was on top of the drought which, by some estimates, had killed some 150,000 head[9] of cattle. Insofar as some head had been in peasant ownership, these cattle had not been destined for elite tables but were tokens of wealth and security. The loss of cattle was a loss of savings, traditional bankruptcy. Despite this, even rural voters seemed prepared to give ESAP time – a testimony to the educational, and political, instrument that vernacular radio could be. In a sense, it didn't matter how many opposition newspapers sprang up in the cities, the control of vernacular radio was a key to rural votes. In June 1993, the opposition party, Forum, complained that the Zimbabwe Broadcasting Corporation's Shona radio service had refused to accept its advertising.[10] Simultaneously, behind the scenes, there was a power-struggle taking place within the corporation, between independently-minded managers and journalists and Mugabe loyalists. The loyalists eventually carried the day.

So it was that the opposition began to criticise the government as shrilly as possible, in whatever media it could find that would cover it. In May 1993, when Mugabe was lecturing the Chinese in Beijing on the merits of opposition within the system (only four years after the Tienanmen Square killings), the opposition – in this case the Forum leader, Zimbabwe's original black Chief Justice, Enoch Dumbutshena – pronounced that 'Robert Mugabe is scared and frightened out of his wits';[11] but this was said on the basis of no evidence whatsoever. The rhetoric of opposition had not matured, and its support-base was a long way short of matching its shrill self-image and *ersatz* confidence. The Forum was, above all, another urban party of intellectuals. At its national convention in Bulawayo (28 March 1993), it had elected Dumbutshena as its president. He held a PhD and headed a similarly qualified executive.

By this time, the opposition was not one party, but an array. Ndabaningi Sithole's ZANU-Ndonga and Abel Muzorewa's United African National Congress (UANC) were still in the field; there was a National Democratic Union, a Conservative Alliance of Zimbabwe (a largely white party), a National Front of Zimbabwe and a rump of what had been ZUM. The effort at a United Front of opposition parties had failed. (Ian Smith had briefly been one of its trustees.) None of these parties commanded great credibility, and before the elections of 1995 their number would swell. As it was, 'they'd have made a terrible government; so little talent in depth,' was a diplomatic comment after those elections.[12] In advance of those elections, Tekere's ZUM and Muzorewa's UANC merged. Muzorewa said that they sought 'to expose the ruling party's culture of rigging,' and Tekere said that ZUM had 'actually won the last election but, because of rigging, this was not evident'[13] – claims that, as explained in Chapter 3, could not be sustained and did not, in 1994, sustain the credibility of the opposition.

Nevertheless, the party bosses of ZANU-PF were far more frightened of the opposition than its merits deserved. Rumours were rife in Harare that Mugabe was contemplating retirement. Picking up on the theme, these rumours soon suggested that both Mugabe and Nkomo would retire. Some ambitious ZANU-PF figures, sensing change in the air, had already taken leaps into the dark, in the hope of landing in a new spotlight. Enos Nkala – once treasurer-general of ZANU-PF, and who had inflamed the situation in 1980, when disturbances first began among former combatants, leading eventually to the armed dissidence in the Matabelelands and the Firth Brigade – urged Mugabe to resign. 'There are no more miracles Mugabe is going to perform. He has exhausted them all, if he had any. His bag is now empty.' Although he had voted for Mugabe as party leader during the days of exile (and prison) in 1974, his view was now 'I regret voting him in'. In particular, he criticised the mortgaging of Zimbabwe to the international financial institutions – meaning economic structural adjustment, and called for a fresh generation of young leaders. 'We should all give way to a new generation of politicians with fresh ideas.' The electorate should 'throw out these people. Ten years is long enough.'[14]

As for that 'mortgaging', Mugabe pronounced himself cured of Marxism and a devotee of structural economic reform. In 1994, he addressed a forum of industrialists, declared he was making a 'confession', and that he was now 'liberated'.

[This] Forum was like a boxing ring. We used to say: these people, what do they think they are? They think government must do things for them. Who are they? Malcontents, exploiters, never satisfied – every dirty word you can think of.

This is the first time I have come to this conference liberated, perhaps because of the measures that we have put in place that have brought about the liberation of the economy.

I would like to believe that liberation also meant the unleashing of what were fettered energies that have cleared the air. Now we can relate to one another in a clear manner.[15]

He would say somewhat different things on the campaign trail in 1995 – particularly when addressing rural meetings. In 1994, however, he had messages to deliver to the IMF – signals of serious cooperation – while, at home, as the first squarings-off for the elections began, the talk was of violence. Sithole, responding to threats from the youth wing of ZANU-PF – often used as militants and vigilantes – said, 'if they kill us, we shall also kill them'.[16] And Dumbutshena of Forum, responding to Mugabe's call for a door-to-door campaign by this same youth wing – meaning a demand for proof of ZANU-PF membership – said that 'in self-defence and defence of their property we as leaders will be obliged to advise our people to keep axes and spears in their houses to fight back'.[17]

June 1994, with ten months yet to go before the elections, became a time of psychological warfare more than actual fighting with spears and axes. The key had indeed been Mugabe's call for a door-to-door campaign. The opposition, at a stroke, had been 'spooked'. Sithole warned of 'a lot of violence, even civil war',[18] neglecting to remember that Mugabe had entertained no earlier qualms about a civil war; and the *Herald* editorialised, with solemn condescension, 'we have heard with astonishment a former chief justice, Dr Enoch Dumbutshena, making wild statements that must fuel this violent trend'.[19]

In the next few days, ZUM insisted upon international observers at the elections, and threatened to boycott the polls;[20] a collective of opposition parties called for an international electoral commission,[21] to which the government responded with a magisterial reminder of the country's electoral maturity, and predicted that opposition parties would boycott the polls because they knew, in reality, that they could not win.

To this, Edgar Tekere of ZUM reacted with a particular shrillness: 'Let us build an opposition army of Angels with Swords to put down the Mugabe-ZANU-PF evil'.[22] All this left Mugabe as the clear victor in the opening skirmish of nerves. 'Those who live in glass houses, we all know, must please not throw any stones.'[23] He described the opposition parties as shaken by tremors, as thrown into 'sixes and sevens', and as 'sorry political smithereens'.[24] All this was said with a wry smile, and to laughter at a ZANU-PF National Consultative Assembly. The assembly was a show of strength, nerve and huge organisational prowess. Compared to what the opposition could muster, it was, even months ahead of time, a very uneven contest. And it was clear that Mugabe had deliberately begun the psychological skirmish to see – then enjoy – the response of the opposition. Angels, axes and spears, rhetoric: these would not frighten the man who had burnt the Matabelelands, marched into Mozambique; and was the hero of the Commonwealth, of Rome and the vanquisher of drought; who was even attempting to play the IMF at its own game.

Moreover, Mugabe knew that Nkomo and his people had no choice but to remain loyal to him and the coalition government.

> Matabeleland needs to talk with one voice right now, in order to secure water and investment. The Ndebele voice is split whenever there is talk of succession and, as long as he lives, only Nkomo can control them; and he knows he has no choice but to remain with Mugabe.[25]

Nor was Dumbutshena, who as Chief Justice at the time of the first Ndebele dissensions after independence and the author of a report on its causes – which Mugabe had refused to publish – going to play the Ndebele card. He was having enough trouble securing even a modest Shona vote, and he knew he could not detach people from Nkomo. Internationally, commentators were bemoaning the fact that a president 'yearning for authoritarian values' would certainly win the elections 'handsomely – even if there was official confirmation of the atrocities in Matabelelands';[26] but in Bulawayo itself, the Ndebele capital, the month before the election, only lethargy greeted the prospect of a guaranteed Mugabe victory, lethargy and 'cynical apathy'.[27] The opposition could not win, if only because it had been so disorganised that it had failed to field candidates for more than 53 seats. 120 seats were available for election; Mugabe, as president, was in the constitutional position of appointing the remaining 30 seats. It was to be a fractious contest, nonetheless.

GRACE-RIDDEN

Although the 1995 elections were parliamentary ones – owing to a constitutional amendment, parliamentary and presidential elections had been separated, meaning that Mugabe would now face re-election in 1996 – the ZANU-PF image was still intimately bound-up with Mugabe's. He campaigned strongly for his full slate of candidates. The parliamentary contest was scheduled for 8 and 9 April. On 6 April, however, almost as if calculated to add a late gloss to Mugabe's image, news began to leak out that he had remarried. 'President Robert Mugabe has recently married his former private secretary, a woman less than half his age with whom he has two children.' The report went on to say that he had paid a bride price, and that he had been encouraged by Sally 'to take a second wife who could bear him children', since illness had rendered her infertile and their first and only child had died of cerebral malaria in 1966.[28]

This was stunning news. In a society that placed a high premium on family life, a childless President had always been, in itself, unrepresentative. Not only that, the news that the President had lost a child years before independence was a revelation. Now, with the additional news that for seven years he had been father to a son, Robert Jr meaning that Mugabe, despite all the early Rhodesian jokes, had remained virile into his sixties – the 'lethargy' of the election was superseded by national gossip and an outburst of investigative journalism. As opposition protests lamented the election outcome, the newspapers continued to uncover new details of the Mugabe marriage.

'Zimbabwe's President Robert Mugabe, 71, would soon publicly declare his 1987 customary African marriage to former State House secretary, Grace Marufu, 37, with a Christian "white wedding".' This report added that he had paid the traditional, non-Christian, bride price in December 1992, ten months after Sally's death.[29]

The newspapers continued in this vein, each now anxious to outdo the others. Some reported a legal wedding and a civil ceremony, recently conducted by a judge.[30] Mugabe became incensed that the story was spinning out of control. Some of the journalists were charged (and convicted) of libel, but not before 'peeping Tom' reporters were lambasted for having delved too deeply into the President's private – and hitherto secret – life.[31] In fact, it took Mugabe until 1996 to obtain Catholic approval for his wedding, and the Zimbabwean public did not see photographs of the actual day until October 1996, which came accompanied by estimates of its cost, the state's contribution and Mugabe's statement that 'we knew there were some papers that wanted to destroy our love'.[32]

Whatever the newspaper intrusion, and whatever the original motivation for leaking the story, it seems clear that Mugabe did love Grace. Rumours and 'witnesses' insisted that every afternoon the presidential motorcade – not something easily misidentified or hard to see – would speed from State House to the outer suburban farm where Grace now resided. The independent and opposition papers, however, had now found a new target for indirect attacks against Mugabe, and that was through Grace. Certainly, compared with Sally, she was maladroit, untutored in protocols and manners and extravagant and tasteless in her clothing. She became – without the steel political demeanour – the Imelda Marcos of Zimbabwe. Muzorewa's son, Philemon, made a public bet of Zim.$100,000 that his own wife would be adjudged, by far, the better dresser of the two.[33] It was one of those tasteless challenges to apparent tastelessness that rumbled on. The speciality 'anonymous' contributions to the *Herald*'s letters page carried (or felt it had to carry) a piece of fanmail for Grace Mugabe, swooning at her 'beautiful white suit' – finished off with a Zimbabwean flag – and how she 'carried out her ceremonial duties with such ease'. The letter's writer was also sure she was not 'feigning, she was just herself'.[34]

And that last line was the giveaway. For all her efforts, Grace was not a natural. She was *nouveau riche* and behaved like an Arkansas farmgirl in Parisian society. As it is, not many of the Harare elite would look polished in Parisian society, and Grace was more like one of them than they could care to admit. She was a target because of her husband and, being graceless while being extravagant, she soon gained the nickname Amazing Grace. Stories of her extravagance, and its wherewithal, became favourite party-circuit fare – both parties proper and parties political. No one in the ZANU-PF hierarchy took her seriously – whereas Sally had been acknowledged as a heavyweight, crossed at peril.

By 2001, the tone of the reports had changed. Grace was now something of a political liability, and had been confined – perhaps held virtual prisoner, according to the more scandalous columns – in her own home.

> Mugabe is even suspicious of his wife. Not long after the [2000 parliamentary] elections, he decided that Grace had been planning to abscond, taking their

children with her; opinion is divided as to whether she really had been planning to leave or not. Their relationship has still not recovered from the tremendous row and Grace has been largely confined to the presidential palace ever since ... There is little sympathy for her though: 'She's had her fun – and now the bill is coming in. Tough,' said one source.[35]

Despite her mesmerising ways with the press – and she herself was a sort of barometer of press freedom, even if indirectly – the real controversy surrounding Grace was the extent to which she influenced her husband. There are many in Harare who speculate on the link between Mugabe's post-1996 political savagery and the apparent vulgarities of his newly acknowledged wife. Not politically attuned, but possessive of the hall-marks meant to lay a glamour upon first ladies, she encouraged Mugabe – who may not have needed much encouragement – to show that side of his character that was intolerant and vengeful once again. Many scholars would see Mugabe's Commonwealth and Roman triumphs as blips, and that the true man had always been essentially intolerant and vengeful. Whatever the case, the Commonwealth and Roman honeymoon had come to an end by the mid-1990s – as Mugabe's new honeymoon began.

FRACTIOUS ELECTIONS

Not even the discovering of Grace could prevent the 1995 parliamentary elections from pursuing their fractious and acrimonious course. They had been effectively won before polling even began, but the recriminations and accusations of cheating were strong nevertheless.

When counting finished, ZANU-PF had won 148 of the 150 seats. Only Sithole's ZANU-Ndonga won anything else – Chipinge North and Chipinge South in eastern Zimbabwe. Margaret Dongo, a renegade but popular ZANU-PF member, stood as an independent and lost on the night. However, there was sufficient evidence of cheating for a court to annul the result. How Dongo fared in the new contest will be recounted later. It was, however, short of a clean sweep for ZANU-PF, and was essentially the same as in 1990 – overwhelming but not complete. The Matabelelands swung in behind Nkomo and the ZANU-PF coalition. Even so, many of the ZANU-PF old guard had been challenged in the party's own primaries and, although it seemed the only show in town – even if only by comparison with the lacklustre opposition – it was not as if there was total satisfaction with ZANU-PF in itself. The remainder of 1995 would see internal battles continuing over issues of corruption.

The opposition parties fielded so few candidates because of lack of funds. By Zimbabwean law, parties of a certain size may receive state funding – meaning ZANU-PF was large enough to receive some Zim.$32 million for its campaign, and the opposition nothing. ZANU-Ndonga managed 30 candidates, there were 32 independent candidates, and four other opposition parties (including two with only one candidate each). Five parties had boycotted the polls, including ZUM. On the day, with the 53 opposition-party candidates and independents, 65 seats of the 150 were contested. 1940 polling stations were deployed in the 65 constituencies. There were no stations in constituencies without a contest – meaning that 44 per cent of the 4.8 million registered voters had no opportunity to vote. The government, anxious to fight somebody, suddenly attacked the 'elitist' white community (at 100,000 persons, less than 1 per cent of the population). On the Friday before voting, both Mugabe and Nkomo separately delivered such attacks. Nkomo did so in general terms, but Mugabe also fixed upon his old antagonist, Ian Smith. 'In many countries … (he) would have been tried or killed for political crimes. We still have him with us. In some countries, Smith would be mere bones.'[36]

It was not as if there were no issues. Apart from public concerns over corruption, structural adjustment had pushed the price of the staple food, maize, up some 60 per cent, and annual inflation was between 25 and 30 per cent. Such contest as there was, however, did finally come down to a (finally) light-hearted exchange between Smith and Mugabe.

Smith, at 76, was unable to vote because of a mistake on the register. Mugabe, told of this as he was casting his own vote, promised to intervene. 'He must vote. I'll ask the registrar-general to take action.' Smith, acknowledging this help, nevertheless wryly quipped. 'It's a waste of time, but I feel I have a certain obligation to vote. I've always voted in the past. I think they know for sure I won't be voting for Mugabe.'[37]

The election days were generally quiet, and such numbers who sought to vote were aided by light bureaucratic touches. As the voting proceeded, it was clear that the numbers were themselves light. The final claim of 61 per cent in the contested seats – 1,589,616 out of 2.6 million registered – should be revised downwards. The numbers would seem to include those who turned up to vote but were then turned away for not being properly registered or having insufficient alternative papers.

Probably some 57 per cent of those entitled finally voted in the 65 contested seats.

Although the opposition parties needed little repression from the government to maintain both their overly pluralistic array, and disarray, there was indeed a degree of repression and intimidation. Under the land reform laws, the farm of Ndabaningi Sithole – himself now 74 years old – was seized. Foreign donations to his ZANU-Ndonga party were blocked, and his supporters were threatened with eviction from state land. Nevertheless, ZANU-Ndonga doubled its representation in parliament to two.

Before the election, the opposition parties had complained about the benefits that Zimbabwean electoral law conferred upon the President's 'unlimited discretion over the electoral process',[38] and there were the usual complaints about petty harassments, such as the impounding of vehicles. The parties demanded a new constitutional conference, but had left it too late for one to be called. In any case, as the troublesome, but still loyal ZANU-PF elder statesman Edison Zvobgo said:

> All they had to do was ask [for such a conference], not to wait until two or three weeks before an election, as they have had five years within which to do that … All the opposition had realised was that they are scheduled to perish at the hands of the people or that they will be vanquished in a manner that is humiliating.[39]

And the opposition, despite some efforts, were never destined to be remotely united. When Muzorewa pulled out of the election, Sithole described him as 'a coward'. He continued, 'he has actually realised that he has no support at all' – which was Zvobgo's more general point about the entire opposition – 'anyway I would never unite with a killer who ordered the killing of Zimbabweans in Mozambique by Smith's army'. [40]

Having said that, what were those laws that gave Mugabe 'unlimited discretion over the electoral process'? The best account was by Welshman Ncube (who would later become a major figure in the opposition MDC of the new millennium). A legal academic by profession, his account was dispassionate.[41] There were five discretionary powers – the last of which was certainly sweeping, if not unlimited.

1   The Delimitation Commission was appointed by and reported to the President and, in the 1995 elections, began its work less than eight months before polling day.

2   The Electoral Supervisory Commission had its chair and two members
    approved by the President, after consultation with the Judicial Service
    Commission. Two others were appointed by the President, after con-
    sultation with the speaker of parliament.
3   The president could appoint 30 members of parliament, comprising
    8 governors, 10 chiefs and 12 direct appointments.
4   The Election Directorate – which actually ran the election – had its
    chair appointed by the President. Within this body, the registrar-
    general was meant to be a public servant, but in the 1995 elections was
    accused of bias. It was his job to keep up the electoral roll; and he was
    the frontline manager of the electoral process.

Although, when summarised in this manner, the role of the President
seems sweeping, the regulations were in fact not atypical of any system
of executive authority. It would be rare to find a system in which the
President, directly or indirectly, did not have similar powers. The question,
of course, lies in how these powers are used. Where the opposition had a
genuine cause for concern lay in section 151 of the Electoral Act.

> 151.1   Notwithstanding any other provision of the Act … the President
> may make such statutory instruments as he considers necessary or
> desirable to ensure that any election is properly and efficiently
> conducted…
> 151. 2   [such instruments may provide for]
>   a. suspending or amending any provision of this Act or any other law
>   insofar as it applies to any election…
>   c. validating anything done in connection with, arising out of or resulting
>   from any election in contravention of any provision of this Act or
>   any law.

This is, by any juristic standard, simply bad law. It is law that limits itself,
abrogates law's responsibility to executive discretion, and establishes no
checks and balances to that discretion, and provides no legal guidelines
for it. A political decision may, here, be privileged above a legal process
or legal rights; so Ncube was more than correct to indicate this section.

The problem, however, of applying these standards of critique to the
1995 election is, simply, that the President never used any of the Section
151 powers. The opposition was certainly fearful that he might (and
commentators such as Ncube were writing before the elections took
place), but he never did. To an extent, although many would see it to have

been a well-founded fear, it was also 'getting the excuses in first'. The opposition may certainly have opposed ZANU-PF and Mugabe on good grounds (or not; some opposition members were hardly political saints), but as an opposition it was simply parlous. Mugabe won these parliamentary elections because he capitalised expertly on how he had handled drought relief – and the Matabelelands were still dependent on drought relief by way of water supplies – because he had explained unpopular policies to do with structural adjustment on vernacular radio; because the opposition consisted largely of urban parties, and because opposition was poorly organised.

Although there were many incidents of harassment, the elections were largely peaceful, the days of polling certainly so; and, as the US embassy observed, any manipulations of the count were purely localised and not part of a national effort, and even the smallest parties received an hour of airtime. 'Even with every complaint by opposition and human rights groups addressed, ZANU-PF would still have won overwhelmingly'.[42]

However, there were two blemishes on Mugabe and ZANU-PF's performance. These were the seats won by Sithole, and the overturning of the result in Harare South by the judicial appeal of Margaret Dongo.

A NEW CABINET, RENEWED CORRUPTION, A NEW PERSECUTION, AND A RENEWED PRESIDENT

These, and the 1996 presidential elections, were the last full mandates Mugabe received. Thereafter, he would be pressed much more closely than ever before. To an extent, voters had returned ZANU-PF in 1995 not just because of the opposition's weakness but, even then, because they felt that the strength of ZANU-PF could still be turned to good. 'There is, on both sides of the coalition, a younger technocratic generation with extremely itchy feet, and even some ideals. They know ZANU-PF is the only game in town. They won't show themselves until Mugabe and Nkomo are gone.'[43]

As it was, Mugabe stayed on. Many of the technocrats finally deserted ZANU-PF as a better-organised opposition arose at the end of 1990s; some decided to throw their lot in with Mugabe wholesale, previous ideals be damned; and some had not waited but, like Dongo at the 1995 elections, had fought Mugabe even then.

As late as 1998, British newspapers continued to see Dongo as 'a warrior to sort out the Mugabe inheritance',[44] someone who might challenge Mugabe in the 2000s for the presidency itself. This was before Morgan Tsvangirai finally declared himself and, for the first time, presented Zimbabwe with a truly presidential alternative. Dongo was never presidential, and casting her in that light was a desperate quest. She was, however, formidable in her own right. Only 36 in 1995, she had left school at 15, walked to Mozambique and joined the ZANLA liberation army. She earned a celebrated *nom de guerre*, 'Tichaona Munhamo', 'we shall see about this on the field of battle'. After independence (and learning how to type) she became a secretary at State House, and became an MP for ZANU-PF in 1990. She was obliged to leave ZANU-PF for calling her colleagues a bunch of gangsters, and fought Harare South as an independent in 1995. Her defeat was certainly a result of localised rigging. She had been a popular MP and commanded a huge personal vote. She challenged the result and the evidence was such – the rigging was not even remotely subtle – that in August 1995 the High Court set aside the 'victory' of the ZANU-PF candidate, another woman, Vivian Mwashita, and prompted a fresh by-election. Dongo became a star. Magazines carried her on their covers, held aloft by other women in her judicial victory, under headlines such as 'Fair Play Finds a Star in Dongo'.[45] 'Beat corruption, fight oppression' had been her motto. Amidst all the jubilation, particularly among opponents of ZANU-PF, it was not well to point out that Dongo had been sparing in her own condemnation of ZANU-PF. She was against corruption within ZANU-PF, but had been forced to fight her campaign outside the party. She had not joined an opposition party, but had stood as an independent. After she had won the by-election – held in November, by a two-to-one majority – she became more identifiably anti-ZANU-PF – it would have been hard from the opposition benches (or half-bench of three) – to have been otherwise. At the time of her challenge, she was the public tip of a party iceberg that was itself deeply concerned about corruption within.

All this would surface before 1995 ended. ZANU-PF's reaction to Dongo's court victory was measured and left to the elder statesman and occasional Mugabe critic Zvobgo:

> We are going to take a very close look at the nature of polling to ensure that what happened in Harare South will not recur ... (The system) had erred in the extreme ... (Harare South) should not cast doubt about the entire

electoral process ... (but did show) our judiciary is alive and will not tolerate irregularities.[46]

In other words, 'You can have this one, but otherwise it's business as usual.'

Business as usual involved finally finding a new Finance Minister. The portfolio had effectively lain vacant almost two years because of the cancer suffered by Chidzero, and some of the drift in Zimbabwean economic management certainly derived from this. Structural adjustment, or ESAP, needed some urgent reapplication. The new Minister, Ariston Chambati, a technocratic businessman, decided to squeeze small business and increase stop-gap borrowing. Higher prices and unemployment were the inevitable by-products. But Chambati had little alternative. The rural areas, still recovering from drought (and the ZANU-PF bedrock of votes) were economically fragile. The national budget deficit was 13 per cent of GDP, almost three times the target set by ESAP.

Otherwise, the cabinet contained two women ministers, two whites – Denis Norman moved to Agriculture, showing some government affection still for the white-dominated commercial farming sector, and Dr Timothy Stamps retained Health, with an emerging HIV problem on his hands – and the Foreign Minister, Nathan Shamuyarira, bypassed in Mugabe's Mozambican initiative, dropped to Labour. In a genuflection to unity, many ZAPU MPs were made deputy ministers.

It was a tinkering, not a full-blooded effort to establish a cabinet able to grapple with the problems of government. And, although Mugabe, almost as a response to Dongo, made utterances against political corruption, the municipal elections later in 1995 showed corruption within ZANU-PF rampant. The exhausted opposition mustered few candidates. Forum did not even contest the Bulawayo mayoralty – just as it did not judicially challenge the parliamentary count in Bulawayo South, with conditions similar to those that had affected Dongo. It had neither energy nor money left. There were only about 15 people left in Forum able to do everything a party should do. Many had gone into debt to finance the parliamentary campaign, and for them the entire venture of democracy had become a personal disaster. Faced with no real prospect of challenge, the ZANU-PF selection procedures became a naked internal vote-buying exercise. Even the ZANU-PF national chairman, Joseph Msika, warned of internal damage that 'in the long-run [would] lead to the party's downfall'.[47] Mugabe himself admitted 'the existence of deceitful and dishonest tendencies within the party's provincial leadership',[48] and later bemoaned – having done little actually to stop – the fact that 'people of little stature had been appointed to lead'.[49] The *Herald* brought itself (reluctantly) to editorialise that some of the reports of vote-buying had to be true.[50] But nothing was done to halt the slide into internal corruption, the squeeze on the national budget while the state deficit increased – the defence vote, however, had been increased, despite withdrawal from Mozambique[51] – and nothing was done about land, succession or new blood in the entourage of the newly married, perpetual President.

Mugabe did find time, however, for an act of vengeance against the one man – outside ZANU-PF – who had dared to challenge and win something from him. Not only that, but the man had dared to call his party ZANU-Ndonga, claiming (as indeed was his historical right) some provenance over the foundation of ZANU itself. A veteran nationalist, he predated Mugabe and his ZANU generation, only to find no place within the party. He was jailed for six years in 1969 for plotting to kill Ian Smith, and as a result was sometimes viewed as the authentic instigator of the armed struggle. He was, however, ousted from the ZANU leadership by Mugabe, and did not join the external groups fighting for liberation. He remained in Rhodesia, but did not become a pivotal figure within the Muzorewa–Smith government either. An ordained minister with a theological doctorate, a novelist and the echo of what nationalism once was, he claimed – highly contingently – an inheritance of which Mugabe sought sole ownership. It was the 1990 question of ZANU essentialism again. The only party to have taken seats against ZANU-PF in 1995 was also called ZANU.

On 16 October 1995, Sithole was arrested on charges of plotting to murder Mugabe. Mugabe had attacked other easy targets earlier in 1995 – whites during the election campaign, homosexuals as 'worse than dogs and pigs' – but Sithole represented someone against whom Mugabe had a 'personal vendetta', according to Sithole's wife, who also accused ZANU-PF of 'pursuing a grudge'.[52] Sithole was said to have been linked to three other men, belonging to an obscure Manicaland dissident group, who had been arrested bearing arms and munitions in August near Harare stadium.[53] Their 'confessions' apparently implicated Sithole – although the munitions they had carried could not have dented Mugabe's armoured Mercedes on its way, surrounded by police and military vehicles, past the stadium to see Grace in her suburban retreat. Sithole did not come to trial till 1997 – by which time Mugabe had won the 1996 presidential election, from which Sithole eventually withdrew. He denied the charges and was eventually acquitted; but, by now, the opposition was just beginning to acquire a semblance of regularity, and Sithole was represented by Tendai Biti, who had also fought Margaret Dongo's judicial appeal against vote-rigging. Biti would become the MDC's shadow foreign minister.

Another character in the later cast of Zimbabwe in the 2000s made his first appearance at this time. In January 1996, police seized all copies and negatives of a Zimbabwean film called *Flame*. Shown widely before its seizure, it contained a scene in which female guerrillas were raped by their own male colleagues. Even though this was a frequent occurrence during the liberation war – and the heroine of Alexander Kanengoni's 1997 novel *Echoing Silences*, Kudzai, was herself raped by her own colleagues – the film evoked a furore. The chairman of the National War Veterans' Association, a certain Chenjerai Hunzvi, later to initiate the farm invasions, demanded the destruction of all copies of the film.[54] But now, the *dramatis personnae* for the future gathering into place, Mugabe fought his first but last peaceful – even if because unchallenged – presidential race. This was the first presidential race as such – separate from the parliamentary elections – arranged to stagger any possible political change in the country, and more clearly to separate legislature from executive. It was the nature of the executive that would haunt Zimbabwe's approaching new millennium.

That nature, or one side of it, went on the campaign trail in a very extensive manner. Remote areas found the President – heavily escorted – visiting. In those areas, Mugabe would speak, praising ZANU-PF for having won the liberation war, then attack white farmers and business-men, then promise more land to poor rural blacks. Dongo questioned why Sithole and Muzorewa were bothering to oppose him. 'The opposition do not have helicopters. They cannot reach the rural areas. I don't know why they are running, they are only giving credibility to Mugabe by making it look like we have a real democracy.'[55] Sithole withdrew on 12 March, claiming that he was being framed on charges of plotting to assassinate Mugabe. Muzorewa withdrew on 15 March, the day before the election, after the Supreme Court rejected his petition that electoral rules and law favoured the president and ZANU-PF. Mugabe had been campaigning, not to win – he was assured of that – but for a huge turnout. 'I know we will win but European countries want to see how many people will vote ... If, for instance, they see that half the people in say Bulawayo registered to vote, did not vote, they will say Mugabe's party is not popular.'[56] Now Muzorewa's eve-of-poll withdrawal threatened to ensure that half the registered voters everywhere would fail to vote.

The withdrawal was too late to prevent the election going forward on 16 March 1996. Muzorewa and Sithole's names remained on the ballot papers, printed weeks in advance. And, indeed, less than half of the 4.9 million registered voters bothered to make the effort. 1,557,558 did vote, and Mugabe received 90.2 per cent of their ballots.

Muzorewa, apparently, far from not having helicopters did not even have a telephone.[57] Sithole had campaigned with a secret itinerary.[58] This was explained as a means to prevent his own assassination, but it also meant that he and his small party could organise nothing in advance.

There were a total of 43,497 spoilt votes (about 2.8 per cent of those cast) and although Muzorewa and Sithole had withdrawn, their names were still used by those wishing to lodge a protest; but Sithole received fewer votes than the number of spoilt ballots. Muzorewa became the preferred protest vote and received most in the Matabelelands. In both Bulawayo and Matabeleland South, Sithole and spoilt ballots ran neck-and-neck, but Muzorewa did best of all – against both Sithole and spoilt ballots – in Bulawayo, despite being himself not Ndebele. Only in Bulawayo, Manicaland, Matabeleland North and Matabeleland South did Mugabe's share plunge to less than 90 per cent (83.6, 87.5, 87.1 and 88.7 per cent respectively). Muzorewa received 13.5 per cent in Bulawayo, and neither opposition candidate received double percentage figures anywhere else. Sithole crested 4 per cent only in Matabeleland North and South. Even in the most highly urbanised Harare, the combined opposition vote did not reach 10 per cent. It was not a rout – insofar as non-candidates cannot be routed – but in some way, and for some reason, not all of them negative, Mugabe had a measure of popular support. Here, he cherished the idea of winning the election, and only misjudged how far to go so as not to make it a non-contest.

LAND BRIEFLY AGAIN, URBAN PROTEST, AND NKOMO'S DEPARTURE

This is one of those junctures at which it might be well to remember that Mugabe has always been consistent on issues to do with land. What changed in the years after 1996 was the means of seeking to acquire it. Shortly after his very first electoral victory, at the independence elections in 1980, he gave an interview to the BBC:

> There must be fairness. Land must be shared. That is why we have a resettlement programme. We cannot deprive those who have large farms, arbitrarily, of those farms. We are going to acquire land. We must abide by legality, but also by the requirement of fair play.[59]

The introduction of arbitrariness, that is without due process, is a very recent phenomenon in the Zimbabwean land saga. After his 1996 presidential victory, Mugabe began the change of approach. There had been an electoral victor in Britain too, and that was Tony Blair. Mugabe's words were intended for his ears:

> We are going to take the land and we are not going to pay for the soil. This is our set policy. Our land was never bought (by the colonialists) and there is no way we could buy back the land. However, if Britain wants compensation they should give us money and we will pass it on to their children.[60]

In a way, these were startlingly blunt and clumsy words. They were a sort of demarche just ahead of the Commonwealth summit of 1997, to be held that year in Edinburgh. They had the finesse of the Nigerian nationalisation of BP on the eve of the Commonwealth summit in Lusaka in 1979. If Thatcher and Carrington had been unimpressed then, Blair was certainly unimpressed in 1997. Then, in the full pomp of his early first term, not yet putting feet wrong, he was anxious to rebuild Britain, and had no great funds to put right a colonial adventure that had begun more than a century earlier. He cold-shouldered Mugabe at Edinburgh, and the Commonwealth Secretary General, Emeka Anyaoku, had no influence on Blair – who thought as lightly of him as John Major had thought highly.

Perhaps the British Foreign and Commonwealth Office, under Robin Cook, and Blair made their first mistake over Zimbabwe at that point – for Mugabe was certain that John Major had reassured him that Britain would indeed assist with funds for compensation. Blair was, of course, hurrying on from the Major era, and thought that Britain was not committed to such previous understandings. It had been an understanding in principle; figures had been loosely suggested, but there was never any formal document of binding agreement. To that extent, Blair was within his rights. However, from the very first great push to resolve the Rhodesian issue in the mid-1970s, under Henry Kissinger, the matter of compensation – subscribed to in hefty sums by the international community – was always an accepted principle. It was implicit in the Lancaster House talks, but Carrington ensured that, although he recognised that a future government (of Zimbabwe) would want to widen the ownership of land, it found no formal enunciation in the final agreement. Mugabe was asked why he had given way, at Lancaster House, on the land issue. 'We had to. That is the "giving way" that I talked of, having to compromise on certain fundamental principles, but only because there was a chance, in the future, to amend the position.'[61] That chance lay not only in the powers of a new government. There was always that characteristic British 'nod and a wink' that Britain would help see the land issue right. But, as with all Albion's perfidity, those who accept the nod and wink do so at their peril.

After the Edinburgh Commonwealth summit, Mugabe's Government published a plan to take control of half the country's commercial farms – almost all white-owned. A list of 1732 properties was drawn up. Even now, the plan was for half, not all, and the state was still recognising a (meagre) principle of compensation: this compensation could now be whatever the state said it would be.[62]

Like all such tightenings of this noose – the 1992 Land Acquisition Act, discussed in Chapter 4, being a tying of the knot – the trapdoor never dropped. It was as if, always at each renewed moment of execution, it was the hangman who was praying for rescue.

*   *   *

Perhaps it was that, at this time, the hangman came under his own pressures. In January 1998, urban strikes and rioting broke out. The protesters had, by now, broadened their range of reference. They were dissatisfied certainly by economic decline, but there was also a linking of Mugabe's name to those of other authoritarian leaders in Africa – such as Arap Moi in Kenya, Mengistu and Mobutu – and the chanting in the streets was that it was time, all over the continent, for a new generation. After May 1998, with the first great protests in Indonesia against Suharto, and the prospect of his fall from power (which did indeed shortly occur), the Harare crowds shouted slogans linking Mugabe's fate to Suharto's.

In fact, at Non-Aligned Movement summits, Suharto had been a confidant and mentor for Mugabe – one accomplished dictator giving advice to his African student – so the street jibes were perhaps closer to the mark than the protesters realised. In that world away from food prices, hunger, inflation and unemployment; in the air-conditioned citadels of leadership, beleaguered leaders sit in conclave and take comfort from their own circles. Away from those citadels, they construct fortresses in their own capitals. For years it had been impossible to drive at night down the street in front of State House. Elite troops would seal it off, and even in the daytime pedestrians walked on the other side of that street, knowing that the President and his lodgings were a forbidden territory.

Within Harare, by now a truly passing imitation of a great city – office skyscrapers and penthouse apartment blocks rising by the day – the uneven distribution of wealth meant that those not destined to work or live in the gleaming glass would seek to live, and probably not find work, in an increasing squalor. In this world, vernacular radio was not the medium of information for debate. The independent and opposition newspapers had attained both a critical mass of circulation and sophistication in reporting, investigation and knowledge of the libel laws. The free press was a fine example of good journalism, and this, even more than the skyscrapers, indicated a city proper.

Not only that, but the street protests and riots were cognisant of something happening in the intellectual debates. The 1995 opposition demand for a constitutional debate had been kept alive, and in 1998 such an actual debate seemed possible. Intellectuals opposed to the Government wanted it; technocrats within ZANU-PF, seeking to 'modernise' their party, wanted it; and the old guard of the party, thinking it might entrench even further their own powers, wanted it. The President, wanting to avoid the fate of Suharto through sweeping new constitutional powers, agreed to it. The 1998 rioters, with their protests against shortages and decline, their international frame of reference, also knew that soon a great chance for change might come – not a change of government necessarily (although this was desirable, there was still no credible alternative), but a change in the constitutional conditionality of government. It seems romantic to say it, but the backdrop of information and the prospect of debate behind the 1998 riots were the final seal of developed urban culture in Zimbabwe. Only when the President, as we shall see, lost this debate did he embrace the land issue again. This time, he pulled the lever that opened the trapdoor.

*   *   *

In 1998, ZANU-PF was a party of distinct factions. There was, of course, the largely Ndebele/Nkomo ZAPU element; there was the faction (or factions) around senior party figures with their own voice – such as Zvobgo; there was the faction of Mugabe-loyalists; and there were the intellectuals and technocrats, their most visible spokesperson being Ibbo Mandaza – head of the key Zimbabwean publishing house SAPES, with its pan-African links and affiliation to Samir Amin's research and publishing group in Senegal, and now editor of his own newspaper – treading a line of 'constructive' criticism of the government, and veering away from condemnation. Called the *Mirror*, its production values rivalled those of the more fiercely independent, and truly opposition paper, the *Daily News*.

All these factions had their own histories and agendas. Within ZAPU, all awaited the death of Nkomo. Ill and without a nominated successor, he had held together the coalition with Mugabe. Zvobgo, audacious as ever, had recently issued a personal apology to the Ndebele people for the atrocities of the Fifth Brigade – thus signalling his readiness to cooperate with any successor to Nkomo – and was rumoured to be the source of radical contributions to the new constitutional debate, including a limitation on the numbers of terms held by any one president. However, he also was now sick, and had waited too long to be anything more than a shadow-warrior when the final battles for Mugabe's succession began. Mugabe himself was surrounded by his own Zezuru people – a Shona sub-group – and his faction also attracted opportunists, all those seeking the President's favour, the usual entourage of time-servers and genuine political loyalists. Mandaza, half-white and thus disadvantaged in any succession stakes, had himself suffered at Mugabe's hands, having been forced to make a self-sacrificial resignation from high civil-service office. He sought to revitalise the party intellectually and constitutionally – and to be himself a shadow-warrior, steering an intellectual colleague towards ultimate power.

Morgan Tsvangirai, leader of the Zimbabwe Congress of Trade Unions, had once criticised Mandaza: 'Zimbabwe has the misfortune of producing so-called progressive intellectuals who have the habit of lecturing workers and peasants through journals published from their mansions in low-density suburbs'.[63] In 1998, however, Tsvangirai was not moving from his trade union post. No one dreamt that he would very soon mount the greatest challenge Mugabe had faced – he had no political organisation or experience, he had no rural base – but many thought him behind the street riots and protests.

But now the cast for the events of the second half of this book had been gathered. It was time also to bid farewell to one of the founding actors. Joshua Nkomo was buried on 5 July 1999, in Harare's Heroes' Acre. To his people, whether or not he had been anointed by the shaman of the Matopos Hills, he was a king, the successor of Lobengula. Despite all his mistakes, his own corruptions and his litany of missed opportunities, many still felt he could have been a good president. Mugabe led the funeral orations. Perhaps he felt that he was being positive for the future – 'Do not be afraid that my government will neglect you [the Ndebeles] now that your great leader has gone. My government will treat Matabeleland just as it did when Mr Nkomo was alive.'[64] – but all in the Matabelelands remembered how indeed he had treated them. Even so, Nkomo's death did strike a sympathetic chord. This was a last instance of a nationally felt moment, even though it was one of mourning. From this moment on, the Matabelelands sided with the opposition that, also at this moment, began to spring forth.

WAR AGAIN

Mugabe had sought to humiliate Nkomo in the 1980s, just as he humiliated Sithole in the 1990s. All rivals, even if spiritual ones, had to be tamed. Now, as the millennium came to its end, Mugabe was once again under siege by the IMF – which had offered a standby credit of US$200 million over 12 months, provided that there were tightened monetary and fiscal policies. The hope was that credit would spark further lendings from the World Bank, the African Development Bank and rich governments, to the tune of some US$250 million a year over three years.[65]

But far from being minded to rein in public expenditures, Mugabe had suddenly two drains on his exchequer. The first had been a buying off of a sudden surge of war-veteran militancy – of which more below – led by Chenjerai Hunzvi. The second was that he had gone to war in Congo, and by the end of 1999 had 11,000 troops in that country. The new millennium began, for Anglo–Zimbabwean relations, with Tony Blair himself – not condemning the Congo expedition – insisting, against advice from his own Foreign Office, that the Zimbabwean airforce be sold spare parts for its British Hawk jets.[66] These were sold to Zimbabwe by Margaret Thatcher, and replaced the airforce blown up by the South Africans. Now they were bombing in Congo, and the war was costing Zimbabwe £1 million a day. The war had begun in 1998, in the aftermath of the Rwanda genocide, and pitted Congo's new warlord president, Laurent Kabila, aided by Zimbabwe, Namibia and Angola, against forces from or sponsored by the new Rwanda, Uganda and parts of Congo itself. It was the first African war of this magnitude, and with so many state players. The Zimbabwean player was suffering an inflation rate of 57 per cent, debt default and domestic fuel crises.

The opposition thought Mugabe had created the opportunity for it to move. On his chessboard, Mugabe moved the piece marked land once again – or, rather, it first moved for him to follow. In a time of crisis, once again, the 'liberation' Mugabe had confessed to in 1994, embracing then the IMF's measures, was abandoned and replaced by the staple issues of war and land.

The 1990s had begun with his last triumphs, in the Commonwealth and in Rome. Thereafter, it was decline from triumph and, for once, even the academic literature could offer only speculation and wonder. In Zimbabwe, the intellectuals and much of the population at large were choosing sides. A new cast had assembled and, at its centre, was an old President with very old certainties and a recourse to conflict both within and without his beautiful, benighted country.

NOTES ON CHAPTER 6

1   Ronald Weitzer, *Transforming Settler States: Communal Conflict and Internal Security in Northern Ireland and Zimbabwe*, Berkeley: University of California Press, 1990.
2   See Gavin Maasdorp and Alan Whiteside, *Towards a Post-Apartheid Future*, London: Macmillan, 1992.
3   Christopher Gregory, 'Zimbabwe's Second Decade: Little Room for Manoeuvre?', in Larry Benjamin and Christopher Gregory (eds), *Southern Africa at the Crossroads?*, Rivonia: Justified Press, 1992, p. 197.
4   Nancy Thede, 'Zimbabwe: From Structural Transformation to Structural Adjustment', in Nancy Thede and Pierre Beaudet (eds), *A Post-Apartheid Southern Africa?*, London: Macmillan, 1993.
5   Jeffrey Herbst, *State Politics in Zimbabwe*, Berkeley: University of California Press, 1990.
6   Gregory, op. cit., p. 226.
7   Thede, op. cit., pp. 98–9 gives a list of incidents, to which should be added the sheer costs of military preparedness.
8   US diplomatic source to the author, Harare, June 1993.
9   New Zealand diplomatic source to the author, Harare, June 1993.
10 *Sunday Gazette* (Harare), 6 June 1993.
11 *Sunday Gazette*, 23 May 1993.
12 US diplomatic source to the author, Harare, October 1995.
13 *Daily Gazette* (Harare), 28 February 1994.
14 *Financial Gazette* (Harare), 25 June 1992.
15 *Argus* (Cape Town), 11 July 1994.
16 *Daily Gazette* (Harare), 20 June 1994.
17 *Herald* (Harare), 15 June 1994.
18 *Herald*, 21 June 1994.
19 Ibid.
20 *Herald*, 22 June 1994.
21 *Herald*, 23 June 1994.
22 *Herald*, 25 June 1994.
23 Ibid.
24 *Herald*, 26 June 1994.
25 US diplomatic source to the author, Harare, June 1994.
26 *Guardian* (London), 25 October 1994.
27 *Guardian*, 27 March 1995.
28 *Horizon* (Harare), 6 April 1995.
29 *Sunday Gazette*, 16 April 1995.
30 For example *Financial Gazette*, 27 April 1995.
31 *Sunday Mail* (Harare), 30 April 1995.
32 *Horizon*, October 1996.
33 *Parade* (Harare), July 1999.
34 *Herald*, 28 September 1999.

35   *Standard* (Harare), 19–25 August 2001.
36   Associated Press, news release, 7 April 1995.
37   Associated Press, news release, 8 April 1995.
38   ZIANA, news release, 6 April 1995.
39   ZIANA, news release, 23 March 1995.
40   ZIANA, news release, 12 March 1995.
41   Welshman Ncube, 'A Review of Electoral Law and Institutions in Zimbabwe' *ZimRights Bulletin*, 1:2 December 1994.
42   US diplomatic source to the author, Harare, October 1995.
43   Ibid.
44   *Guardian*, 24 January 1998.
45   *Horizon*, September 1995.
46   ZIANA, news release, 17 August 1995.
47   ZIANA, news release, 25 September 1995.
48   ZIANA, news release, 8 September 1995.
49   ZIANA, news release, 17 September 1995.
50   *Herald*, 30 September 1995.
51   *Africa Institute Bulletin* (Pretoria), 34:5, 1994.
52   *Guardian* (London), 17 October 1995.
53   *West Africa* (London), 16–22 October 1995.
54   *Guardian*, 15 January 1996.
55   *Guardian*, 14 March 1996.
56   *Independent* (London), 16 March 1996.
57   SAPA, news release, 13 March 1996.
58   *Herald*, 5 March 1996.
59   Excerpted in Michael Charlton, *The Last Colony in Africa: Diplomacy and the Independence of Rhodesia*, Oxford: Blackwell, 1990, p. 152.
60   *Guardian*, 15 October 1997.
61   Excerpted in Charlton, op. cit., p. 80.
62   *Guardian*, 22 November 1997.
63   Cited in *Southern African Review of Books* (Capetown), 5:1, 1993, p. 19.
64   *Guardian*, 6 July 1999.
65   *Africa Confidential*, 40:16, August 1999.
66   *Guardian*, 20 January 2000.

SEVEN

Interlude: Houses of Hunger –
the Intellectual Debates
of Zimbabwe

What have Zimbabwean intellectuals believed? The backbone of small, urban opposition parties in 1990 and 1995? The technocratic wing of ZANU-PF? They came finally to loggerheads over the constitutional debates of 1998 and 1999. Before then, despite differences in how policy might be applied, they held a remarkably homogeneous view of how policy might be formed – homogeneous because still somewhat generalised, to an extent highly theorised, but not completely abstract. Already mentioned is their largely neo-Marxist orientation. From the 1990s – as with many Marxist and neo-Marxist groupings throughout the world – a certain borrowing from the Italian writer Gramsci entered their considerations. Now, revolution no longer overthrew a state, but a long and continuous revolution was to be fought within the constitutional provisions of the state and, particularly, the cultural processes of the nation and the institutions of what, everywhere, came to be loosely labelled 'civil society'.

In general terms, therefore, there is still a remarkably homogeneous intellectual paradigm within Zimbabwe. Within ZANU-PF outwardly, with its rhetoric of African roots and African processes, and its renewed rhetoric to do with socialism, there is room for a contemporary neo-Marxist to feel, contingently at least, at home. The only problems are that it is only rhetoric, and everything to do with African roots seems curiously Shona, therefore partial and partisan. For an opposition intellectual, the discourse on the institutions of civil society fits well within the urban base of opposition. The rural areas are given some genuflection in the recognition of cultural practices which validate, or fail to validate, political movement and leadership. The work, earlier cited, of Ranger, Lan and Kriger, to do with the importance of spiritual validation for the liberation guerrillas – and the pointed inclusion in Jocelyn Alexander's work on the Fifth Brigade and Ndebele dissidents of efforts also to validate spiritually those who returned to armed resistance in the bush – and Ranger's more recent work on the spiritual composition of histories in the Matopos Hills have all found a small Zimbabwean echo, even if no political praxis based on such culture and spirituality.

In short, the debate is not about theoretical principle – and never has been – but about constitutionally provisioned pluralism or its lack; about constitutional rights or their limits. The technocratic wing of ZANU-PF did not seek to foreclose the 2002 presidential elections but, as part of a beleaguered ZANU-PF, it now plays at Mugabe's hardball game with a shrillness and, sometimes, self-importance that is certainly innovative.

The problem of cultural issues – more often called 'social movements' in a secular literature still not fully comfortable with things spiritual – is that culture is, itself, politically manipulable, that is, it is not just that spiritual practice can validate the political, but that political practice can influence the spiritual. There are as many opportunist shamans and mediums in Zimbabwe as those in other trades, and Billy Mukamuri, writing a social-agrarian thesis rather than a political one, pointed this out.[1] So that, for reasons both of political opportunism among some spirit merchants and residual neo-Marxist secularism, there is no great taste in Zimbabwe for the new effort at an Africanist paradigm in the UK and France, to do with a prioritisation of informal African processes, and a privileging of 'witchdoctors' and their hitherto 'irrational' foundations.[2]

The Zimbabwean scholarship on 'social movements' is more likely to be published in joint volumes, with Western Africanists or African scholars from other parts of the continent, than in fully fledged volumes within Zimbabwe itself.[3] That, in itself, reveals a larger problem with Zimbabwean scholarship, however: it is revealed, in by far its greater part, in edited volumes. There is not a huge monographic list, meaning that positions are often elegantly and eloquently stated, but not rigorously sustained over several hundred pages. Such full-length work as have appeared have tended to be doctoral theses, published without too much amendment or book-specific rewriting. This is the case with political scholarship – not, for instance, with literary scholarship – but, shy of full engagement with spiritual practice as such, the outstanding

Zimbabwean contribution to political analysis did engage with a novella on spiritual bankruptcy and depletion. The Zimbabwean novel (and novella) are far more potent expressions of the political condition than Zimbabwean scholarship, and a short chapter will be devoted to them as a coda to this book. I shall return to Brian Raftopoulos's outstanding analysis, and its engagement with Dambudzo Marechera's novella *The House of Hunger*, exonerating Raftopoulos from the current international fashion for the tragic Marechera; he appreciated this short work sometime before an industry geared up around it and its late author. For now, it might be well to give a brief intellectual history and sociology of publishing in Africa, as it relates to Zimbabwe.

THE DAKAR–HARARE–DAR ES SALAAM TRIANGLE

Terence Ranger is often credited with having helped establish the Dar es Salaam school of African historiography, that is African studies premised upon an understanding of African culture and its values. What that has become now includes statements to do with an autochthonous politics – not to be autonomous in the world, but to be true to oneself in a world that, otherwise, imposes frightening conditions. This is a retreat, but not full-scale withdrawal, from Samir Amin's call for delinking from the West, and an endorsement of his critique of scholarship, thought and practice that is slavishly eurocentric.[4] Amin headed CODESRIA (Council for the Development of Social Science Research in Africa) headquartered in Dakar, Senegal; the other two most active centres are Dar es Salaam, led by Issa Shivji, and Harare, led by Ibbo Mandaza and his SAPES (Southern African Political Economy Series) Trust. CODESRIA and SAPES account for a huge portion of political research and publishing in sub-Saharan, north of the Limpopo, Africa.

In Zimbabwe, despite a preponderance in the political scholarship arena, SAPES was never fully monolithic. Unlike its northern neighbour, Zambia – where, in the Kaunda years, there was simply no book publishing of any merit at all without a foreign grant being involved – Zimbabwe has always had a full and vibrant range of publishing houses. Its most visible member in political scholarship was SAPES and, notwithstanding pluralism, there was a SAPES paradigm, closely linked to the CODESRIA paradigm.

The generalised sentiments of these are probably best expressed by
Issa Shivji, in his brief but famous booklet, *Fight My Beloved Continent*.[5]
Irremediably romantic, and unapologetically a clarion call, its best lines
are probably its literary coda (written by another) – from the Guatemalan
revolutionary poet, Castillo.

> On that day
> the simple men will come
> those who had no place
> in the books and poems
> of the apolitical intellectual
> but daily delivered
> their bread and milk ...
> and they will ask:
> What did you do when the poor
> suffered, when tenderness
> and life
> burned out in them?

It is not a call for engaged intellectuals that ranks alongside those of
Noam Chomsky, Ngugi wa Thiongo and Edward Said, but it is indeed a
call for engagement. The work betrays its author's founding Marxism,
with its bibliographical note celebrating John Reed's *Ten Days that Shook
the World* and Edgar Snow's *Red Star over China*. This is thus a founding
Marxism of action, even if (Edgar Snow may forgive me) rose-tinted
spectacles sometimes saw the red star. Shivji is looking for a new kind of
mass politics. 'The struggle will probably go through a phase where the
battleground of politics is the street before politics go to the battleground
of the countryside.'[6]

By this token, urban riots and parties in Zimbabwe are acceptable;
dissidence in the rural Matabelelands not. Somehow, out of this partial
beginning, a new type of democracy must emerge. Shivji doesn't know
what sort – the struggle will determine that – but it is clearly a sort
peculiar to struggle in Africa. In the first place, that means it is not
Western – although it could be capitalist.

> The New Democratic Revolution is primarily targeted at IMPERIALISM,
> i.e. MONOPOLY CAPITALISM not capitalism *per se*. This means against
> all imperialist property; domestic property which is closely linked or tied to
> imperialist property...(including) monopoly ownership of land such as
> feudal, settler...(it is not) directed against all private property, particularly
> peasant private property.[7]

So that, although this sort of call might almost be what Morgan Tsvangirai had in mind when he commented on 'so-called progressive intellectuals who have the habit of lecturing workers and peasants through journals published from their mansions', it is also a call that provides a rationale for land seizures and, not only that, for those land seizures directed from a first revolutionary stage in the cities.

If there are the generalised sentiments of the cojoint paradigm, the paradigm also expressed itself more subtly. Discussion at the 1992 General Assembly of CODESRIA was illuminating. Held every three years, this was the first to provide for reflection after the fall of the Berlin Wall and Communism in general. There were calls to refurbish resistance to the West by re-examining African culture, history and language. Not only that, but the democratisation of knowledge – as well as cultural practice – required a demarginalisation of the masses of the poor. New types of institutions were required.[8]

The 1989 SAPES conference (co-sponsored by the American Council of Learned Societies) had pre-echoed this theme. Although Shivji ended his contribution with a passionate call for the enforceability of rights, some very like the individual rights championed in the West, he asked for new forms of popular organ, suggesting popular assemblies that would cascade their influence upwards.[9] His programme here is, again, vague; but the principle was that a search for new democratic forms should take place, protected by the safeguarding of rights.

The new form should not be a one-party state.[10] How whatever form should grapple with the contradictions of international capital and those of internal politics was never articulated, from independence to the present time, except in Shivji's vague statements. The key was at least to articulate those contradictions.[11] And that has been the key contribution of SAPES. Occasionally, women and issues of gender were articulated,[12] but questions of homosexuality not. The first (non-executive) President of Zimbabwe, a constitutional figurehead behind the prime ministerial power of Robert Mugabe, was never given great space either before or after his humiliation, exposure and imprisonment as a homosexual. Canaan Banana, after he stepped down from the presidency in 1987 and Mugabe acquired full executive status, did make some brief appearances in the SAPES journal,[13] but he was never greatly defended when Mugabe ensured that the only other person ever to have been know as a Zimbabwean President (even if in a very different presidential capacity) was almost ritualistically transformed into a sodomising pariah. None of this had any political animus, although it did have a political effect. Banana's testimonial is his own intellectual writings to do with themes of liberation theology.[14]

To be fair to the Zimbabwean intellectuals, there was at that time a continental impulse towards establishing politics on new but indigenous foundations.[15] But the impulse was everywhere generalised, vague or romantic. Few works of detailed empirical analysis emerged in this epoch. Jonathan Moyo's study of the 1990 elections in Zimbabwe was an exception.[16] Brian Raftopoulos's work, based on the images of *The House of Hunger*, was also brief but, here at least, conceptual analysis reached a new height.

I LEANED BACK AGAINST THE
MASA TREE AND LAY STILL

Raftopoulos called his paper 'Beyond the *House of Hunger*: The Struggle for Democratic Development in Zimbabwe'.[17] Its rubric was a quote from Marechera's novella:

> I leaned back against the masa tree and lay still, trying not to think about the House of Hunger where the acids of gut-rot had beaten into the base metal of my brains. The House has now become my mind; and I do not like the way the roof is rattling.[18]

I shall discuss Marechera again in the book's coda. Suffice to say here that the novella is about psychological unease and decline and was, for years, unrecognised as the masterpiece that it is. Although expressed in personal rather than political terms, the page before Raftopoulos's quote is concerned with a repudiation of African heroes – which may be taken to include the heroes of the liberation which led to 1980 and the new state. It is among the very first pieces of Zimbabwean (certainly Rhodesian) fiction   and remains a rarity   that is not descriptive, concerned with conventional narrative, or purposely tells a story that is also a political or social lesson. It was just about gut-rot of the brains, and proposed no other programme than leaning back against the masa tree, lying still and trying not to think. Raftopoulos saw in this a superb political image, and picked it out brilliantly to use in his paper – identifying the declined Zimbabwean state as, itself, the House of Hunger. How to get beyond a state of gut-rot of thought and action was his concern.

The strong points of Raftopoulos's paper lie in his analysis and contemporary political history. When, however, the moment comes to publish a programme of action, Raftopoulos too falls into vagueness. Just as with the bulk of the SAPES literature, he saw the contradictions of external and internal pressures, and thought, working both for and against Zimbabwean development. He called these 'competing centres of force'. In doing so, he criticised Norma Kriger (whose work was cited earlier), and Christine Sylvester,[19] two prominent foreign Zimbabweanists, for failing 'to provide an hegemonic discourse that would sufficiently integrate the concerns of these 'competing centres of force'.'[20] And this is the crystal admission of Raftopoulos's paper: that the Zimbabwean intellectual world sought, somehow, a hegemonic discourse, a totalising presence, against the imperial world of monopoly capitalism; and that, admitting it stark and clear, notwithstanding debate within ZANU-PF, 'these are pessimistic times' for the party.[21] He could see, then, no alternative force.

The problem here is that – notwithstanding any calls for a popular movement that would itself define its own institutions and those of the state – the intellectual vision and its need for a centre, a force, a hegemonic point, was neo–Marxist up to a point but Leninist in its sense of necessary action. It was not just Shivji who was nostalgic for the days and certainties of Reed and Snow.

Even so, the importance of Raftopoulos's paper is that he not only brilliantly borrowed a metaphor to describe the political condition of Zimbabwe; he not only provided a fine analysis and conceptual argument; he said, in a way that the SAPES paradigmatic tribe did not, that ZANU-PF might no longer have an answer. This was a pulling away – not in political tracts or speeches, but in academic and intellectual discourse – from ZANU-PF, and marked a point of departure from those technocrats, like Ibbo Mandaza, who stayed within ZANU-PF, or remained its fellow-travellers.

In a way, Raftopoulos was right in what was to come. What was needed, and was to come from 1998, was not a hegemonic discourse, but a hegemonic moment. In those 1998 riots, something snapped and clarified itself – and, in that sudden clarity, ZANU-PF was, over two tests at the polls, defeated in the cities. It was not rioting simply about the price of bread – nothing so confined to literalness in the House of Hunger – but was also about a balance in society that ZANU-PF had lost sight of and, in any case, no longer cared about; not merely poetically, something to do with tenderness and life. Intellectuals may well have been laying still – though trying to think – against their masa trees, but a spontaneous agency broke through from 1998 that carried on to 2000. At this hegemonic moment, the man who had criticised the SAPES 'habit of lecturing' from mansions, Morgan Tsvangirai, stepped forward and, after almost two decades, a person of stature challenged Robert Mugabe.

NOTES ON CHAPTER 7

1   Billy Mukamuri, *Making Sense of Social Forestry*, Tampere: Acta Universitatis Tamperensis ser. A vol. 438, 1995.
2   Patrick Chabal and Jean-Pascal Daloz, *Africa Works: Disorder as Political Instrument*, London: James Currey, 1999.
3   For example Louis Masuko, 'The Zimbabwean Burial Societies', in Mahmood Mamdani and Ernest Wamba-dia-Wamba (eds), *African Studies in Social Movements and Democracy*, Dakar: CODESRIA, 1995.
4   Samir Amin, *Eurocentrism*, London: Zed, 1989.
5   Issa G. Shivji, *Fight My Beloved Continent: New Democracy in Africa*, Harare: SAPES, 1992.
6   Ibid., p. 45.
7   Ibid., p. 16.
8   CODESRIA Bulletin, 1 and 2, 1992.
9   Issa G. Shivji, 'State and Constitutionalism: A New Democratic Perspective', in Shivji (ed.), *State and Constitutionalism: An African Debate on Democracy*, Harare: SAPES, 1991, p. 43.
10 Ibbo Mandaza and Lloyd Sachikonye (eds), *The One Party State and Democracy*, Harare: SAPES, 1991.
11 Ibbo Mandaza (ed.), *Zimbabwe: The Political Economy of Transition 1980–1986*, Dakar: CODESRIA, 1987.
12 Elinor Batezat and Margaret Mwalo, *Women in Zimbabwe*, Harare: SAPES, 1989.
13 For example Canaan Banana, 'The Past Ten Years and the Future of Democracy', *Southern African Political and Economic Monthly*, 4:2, November 1990; 'Church and State in Southern Africa', *Southern African Political and Economic Monthly*, 4:11, August 1991.
14 Canaan Banana, *The Gospel According to the Ghetto*, Gweru: Mambo Press, 1980; *Theology of Promise*, Harare: College Press, 1982; *Towards a Socialist Ethos*, Harare: College Press, 1987.
15 For example Ahmed Mohiddin, 'Talking under a Tree', *Africa Events* (London), 7:3, 1991.
16 Jonathan N. Moyo, *Voting for Democracy: Electoral Politics in Zimbabwe*, Harare: University of Zimbabwe Publications, 1992.

17   Harare: Zimbabwe Institute of Development Studies Working Paper 17, 1991.
18   Dambudzo Marechera, *The House of Hunger*, Oxford: Heinemann, 1978, p. 13.
19   Christine Sylvester, 'Simultaneous Revolutions: The Zimbabwe Case', *Journal of Southern African Studies*, 16:3, 1990; 'Unities and Disunities in Zimbabwe's 1990 Election', *Journal of Modern African Studies*, 28:3, 1990.
20   Raftopoulos, op. cit., p. 7.
21   Ibid., p. 30.

PART THREE

THE OLD MAN'S RUTHLESS STAND

EIGHT

Mugabe's Path of Discomforts: One – Disease, War, the Constitution

THE NEW *DRAMATIS PERSONNAE*

Tendai Biti	Shadow Foreign Minister for the Movement for Democratic Change (MDC); legal counsel for Margaret Dongo and Ndabaningi Sithole
The *Daily News*	Well-produced independent newspaper with high production values and high-level journalism
Chenjerai Hunzvi	Polish-trained doctor, once married to a Polish woman; leader of the 'war veterans' and partial to the nickname Hitler; would die, almost certainly of AIDS
The *Zimbabwe Mirror*	Weekly newspaper edited by Ibbo Mandaza, critical but partial to ZANU-PF; mouthpiece of the technocratic wing of ZANU-PF; high production values and well-written backgrounders
Jonathan Moyo	Former professor of political science; sometime democrat and author on democracy; newly appointed minister in Mugabe's government and first-line apologist for Mugabe
Robert Mugabe	President, embattled, bitter, ruthless; not someone who should be demonised, but increasingly haunted by the *ngozi*, spirits or demons of the past
Morgan Tsvangirai	Former trade union leader, increasingly presidential, leader of the new opposition MDC

*   *   *

131

> Let us, you see, carry out this act once and for all. Those who will support,
> support, those who will want to sabotage, let them sabotage. We will go
> through that path of comforts and discomforts and we will evolve measures
> ourselves in the process of remedying that.[1]

Mugabe made that statement in 1992 as the Land Acquisition Act was racing through the Zimbabwean parliament. The 'once and for all' was delayed some eight years; then land acquisition – seizure – erupted in early 2000. By then, Mugabe had come under sustained pressure and attack over a number of epochal changes and, indeed, the period 1998–2002 was a new epoch for Zimbabwe. It is recounted and analysed here in three major parts: the first concentrating on the constitutional battle, but also covering the war in the Congo; the second to do with the fledging of the MDC as not only an opposition party but a significant parliamentary opposition party sweeping the Matabelelands and the cities in the 2000 elections; the third dealing with the land issue proper, the war veterans and Mugabe's diplomatic war with the international community.

Before beginning all this, however, it might be useful to glean from all the chapters before the sort of wheat or chaff that Mugabe might be seen to be. When the land invasions reached their initial height, British newspapers headlined and editorialised that he was mad. He was demonised in such a way that access to a more nuanced view became difficult. Kinder treatments suggested that, finally, he was living up to type, and that type had been moulded in the intrigues and ruthlessness of the liberation struggle – not on the field of war itself – but in the palace coups, manoeuvres, back-stabbings and assassinations that, whether he was involved with them or not, inexorably took him to the leadership of ZANU. Even opposition discourse in Harare could not quite fathom the President.[2] What, therefore, is the Mugabe who has, up to the period 1998–2002, emerged from this book?

1 Mugabe is himself not unintellectual. In kinder days, the West used to praise his intellect and academic achievements (more than five degrees). The African debate on culture would not be unknown to him, nor would he be unsympathetic to it. The debate often devolves to a certain Afro–centrism, and then an Afro–essentialism. This is not in itself racist, but in a time of globalism it carries hallmarks of a restrictive paradigm. Mugabe may well combine some of the essentialism of this debate with his earlier Maoist inclinations. It is not a Maoist cultural

revolution as such that he has initiated in Zimbabwe, but with land as the key motif, something wrongly advised, though a grandly gestured autochthonous action.

2 Mugabe, whether Maoist or not, does have Stalinist imprints in his record of treating not simply rivals and opponents but former rivals and opponents. He seems to have some need to suppress and reorder what reputation they have: Nkomo, Banana, Sithole. He did not need to undertake any of their humiliations, and certainly not by the grand gesture of a civil war in the Matabelelands. He moves to ruthlessness, both in moments of challenge and in memory of challenge.

3 Having said that, he is also not given to undertaking acts that may be inevitable but which he finds distasteful. His leaving Nkomo to open, for the first time, ministerial relations with a still-white South Africa in 1992 is a case in point.

4 He is also given to a presidential practice of one major item at a time. He had trouble, again in 1991 and 1992, operating tandem policies to do with the Commonwealth, Mozambique and drought. When he does undertake something, however, he can undertake it dramatically, swiftly and effectively. Drought crept up on him, but once he put his mind to the situation he rescued political victory from the jaws of disaster. He does so not so much by detailed technical command of the situation, but by grand policy strokes – which he imagines are not only correct, but correct enough to allow techniques and technical operations to evolve in a natural fit with the policy. He is prepared to take great risks, often with no or little fallback – his military intervention in Mozambique is a case in point.

5 Although Mugabe has zigged and zagged – a Maoist liberation leader, a 'liberated' economic liberal, and a rhetorical socialist once again (but tailored into an Afro-essentialism) – he would seem actually to believe what it is he is espousing in any particular epoch of his history. At the very least, he may be capable of greater moments of pragmatism than current wisdom suggests.

6 Having said that, in times of crisis, driven to a point when pragmatism is itself distasteful and smacks of defeat, he will wheel into play the issues of war and land. The latter is not only a bargaining ploy in international relations – as it was up to 2000 – but a long-term policy conviction.

7 With all his capacity for ruthlessness and severity, he still greatly values the endorsement of great states and leaders. He was anxious to

secure a higher than 50 per cent turnout in the 1996 presidential
elections as a signal to Britain of his popularity at home. When, however, that endorsement is repudiated or nor forthcoming, he will turn
vitriol against the withholder. He has developed, since the Edinburgh
Commonwealth summit in 1997, a genuine dislike – even hatred – of
Tony Blair. Mugabe's claim to his neighbours, as will be discussed
below, that it is Blair playing the land issue against Mugabe – not the
other way round – is not seen, by otherwise dismayed and concerned
presidents, as incredible.

8 As he can show with these neighbouring presidents, and as he showed
at the 1991 Commonwealth summit in Harare, and at key moments in
the 1992 talks over Mozambique, he can play a very fine diplomatic
game. Once committed to a grand policy, even if for spiteful or
vengeful reasons, he will not panic in the international articulation of
himself and it.

9 And he seems to have a need to hold elections, and then distort the
electoral process, as if even a stolen victory might be a validation.
Something in him seems to require a validation.

This is the complexity that is Mugabe, as the West seeks, and fails, to
understand his cruelties and crudities of the new millennium. He will
carry things out, once and for all – even if not always immediately; he
will evolve measures to deal with the situation that develops; and he will
invite the world to see what and who are, if nor right or wrong, victorious
and once again inescapable, or defeated.

With all this in mind, therefore, let us see how Mugabe was surrounded
by great issues, and how he approached them, from 1998 to 2002.

DISEASE

This first great issue he has done little about – although, to be fair, until
the economy improves sufficiently for education also to improve, and
until generic drugs at affordable prices spread into Zimbabwe, there is
little he can do. There has been little enough done in any of the Southern
African countries to combat HIV and AIDS. Indeed, in the rankings of
the 44 nations of Africa for which information is available, HIV/AIDS
prevalence (as a percentage of the adult, 15–49 years-old population),

Southern African countries occupy the first eight. Of these, a dubious distinction, in 1997 Zimbabwe was first – with an infection rate of 25·84 per cent. South Africa, where so much political protest has recently been raised to secure generic drug treatments, was eighth, with 12.91 per cent, about half Zimbabwe's rate.[3] 'In Zimbabwe by 2001 the likelihood of a 15-year-old woman dying before the end of her productive years will quadruple from around 11 percent in the early 1980s to over 40 percent. More than 2,000 Zimbabweans die of AIDS each year'.[4] The regional problem has been long recognised. In 1992, the Southern African Development Coordination Conference devoted a special issue of its journal to it, profiling the then-Zimbabwean Health Minister Timothy Stamps, a Welsh-trained physician who had come to Rhodesia in 1968 and joined ZANU in 1981. But it also indicated the political reluctance he faced in seeking to implement his policies on HIV and AIDS.[5]

This is not an election issue in Zimbabwe. Other matters have more than superseded the deaths due to AIDS-related illnesses – and a coy Zimbabwean public would rather refer to each death by the name of the final disease that preceded it, and not to the fact that disease had an easy time when entering a body shorn of its immunity. The President has done nothing presidential in this field – but thousands of citizens will die from HIV/AIDS, and their poverty will not help them postpone that death.

WAR

By contrast, Mugabe has been more than actively engaged in causing death yet again. The Congo war began in the wake of the Rwanda crisis. It might seem odd that upheaval in one of Africa's smallest countries should have a huge impact upon its largest. However, as Zaire, the now renamed Democratic Republic of Congo had a corrupt and barely functioning public administration. Even without Mobutu's legendary capacity for appropriating national wealth, the very size of the country would have made proper administration difficult. Local power interests could act as semi-autonomous – sometimes almost entirely autonomous – principalities within the nation. When the playboy rebel Laurent Kabila – rebel long enough to have had Che Guevara fight briefly for him, playboy intensively enough for Guevara to desert him – finally seized power in 1997, he had neither the personal capacity nor the apparatus to change the country. A new government in Rwanda, Tutsi-dominated after the Tutsis had overcome the genocide waged against them by Hutus, decided to take the battle to the Hutu rump who occupied freely the Congolese borderlands. Uganda sided with Rwanda, having its own geo-political concerns in the border provinces; and, for a time, the Eritreans, still idealistic and naive, and thinking that, like them, other African countries required a revolution, joined in. There were enough battle-hardened units in the assemblage, linked-in with Congolese factions who were against Kabila, to sweep well across almost all the eastern part of Congo. Zimbabwe's entry into the war was ostensibly occasioned by the Southern African states' concern for the resultant instability in Congo – Namibia and Angola also sent troops alongside the Zimbabweans – but the Southern African action was, to an extent, engineered by Zimbabwe, through its chairmanship of the regional organ for politics, defence and security. The summit that decided upon intervention in 1998 excluded South Africa, known to view involvement in Congo with great scepticism.[6]

It is hard to understand why Zimbabwe was so anxious to intervene militarily. Kabila was proving a most inept President. If anybody had 'just cause', it was probably the Tutsi Government of Rwanda. However, Congo was possessed of immense mineral wealth. Even Mobutu had far from exhausted it. Partly because of this there was a case for Congo's membership of Southern Africa's regional economic grouping – and there was the long-term African adherence to borders unchanged from their colonial origins, Eritrea being an accepted deviation, and Rwanda and Uganda's actions threatened to change Congo's borders by antique act of invasion. Of these, attention has most turned to Congo's wealth, not as an addition to the economic resource-base of an expanded region, but as something able to be appropriated – no longer by Mobutu, and not by the Zimbabwean state but by Zimbabwean military leaders, their political friends, and their expanded range of business colleagues. If the war began costing the Zimbabwean public exchequer £1 million a day, the private extraction of wealth remained steadfastly in private hands – even if those private hands were also meant to hold public office. The profiteering was immense. Almost as if to repair a diplomatic fence with Mugabe, Tony Blair insisted upon the sale of spare parts for the British-made Hawk fighter-bombers (that have no guidance systems for their bombs and rockets, so that bombing can never even pretend to be targeted away from civilians) that made up the backbone of the Zimbabwean airforce.

As generals and a sliding scale of their officers, together with their political friends and contacts – facilitators – back home became rich, those unconnected to the war suffered from the Zimbabwean inability to repay debts, to control inflation (57 per cent in 1999), or to purchase petrol and diesel. The head of the IMF, Michel Camdessus, described Zimbabwe's economic plight as 'very dangerous', and blamed the Congo war.[7] Zimbabwe entered recession, for the first time since independence in 1980. As protests grew, Mugabe's political repression began to grow; but this meant opposition grew still faster, and became, also for the first time, formidably organised.

By the second part of 1999, the opposition seemed strong enough for it to have a cautious political optimism amidst the financial gloom. In August 1999, a peace accord was signed among the Congolese factions. There is some reason to believe that, had it held, it would have been sufficiently face-saving for Mugabe to begin withdrawing his troops. Indeed, he probably at that point wanted to withdraw them. However, the accord did not hold, and the generals of the Zimbabwean army, for financial and military reasons, did not want to withdraw; as domestic opposition grew, Mugabe needed the support of the army, so it stayed in Congo. Its loyalty was bought, and the Zimbabwean polity was, in this exchange, given over to sacrifice. Huge additional expenditures on the armed forces, whether publicly or privately financed – through the Matabelelands war, Mozambican war and the Congo war – have created an alliance between Mugabe and his generals. The generals will not depose Mugabe, but may express an urge to prevent his deposition by anyone else. It would not be the present army, however, that would show its political hand first. That was something undertaken by those who claimed to have been an earlier army – the war veterans of the liberation struggle. They, however, did not show their hand in the first instance in support of Mugabe – but to oppose him. The contradictions of the eventual alliance with him can be understood in the melange of events that occurred from 1998 onwards – including the devising and electoral testing of a new constitution for Zimbabwe.

PRELUDE TO THE CONSTITUTIONAL DEBATE

There were three major outbreaks of protest and rioting in Harare in 1998: in January when teargas, sprayed from helicopters, was used to hold back riots against rises in food prices; in May and June, when students besieged parliament and likened Mugabe to Indonesia's Suharto, who had been forced to resign a few weeks earlier; and in November, over the price and scarcity of fuel. Soldiers opened fire on this occasion, with fatal consequences. Margaret Dongo said, 'These angry mobs cannot wait for the year 2000 elections to change the government. They know the government is milking the economy (over the Congo war) and they want to stop it now.'[8]

However, these riots had as their backdrop what was to come, in only a short time, to the forefront. Mugabe had begun playing, somewhat loosely, with the land card again; but enough for Western donors and financial institutions, in January 1998, to demand strict guarantees that the proposed nationalisation of 1480 farmers would neither hinder production nor cause the deficit to exceed the already-forecast 8.2 per cent of GDP for the financial year. A team of IMF negotiators, visiting Harare in January, left behind an ultimatum that farmers should be paid for their land and the improvements that they had made to it. Mugabe apparently agreed to pay for improvements and infrastructure, though not the land itself; but the IMF delegation thought it had sufficiently delayed the land programme for it, once again, to sink down Mugabe's order of priorities.[9] Meanwhile, from December 1997 to January 1998, the value of the Zimbabwean dollar had halved.

The second stage-set in the backdrop had been the Zimbabwean Congress of Trade Unions. It denied involvement in the January riots, was not in fact involved in the student protests of mid-year, but was certainly an actor – if not the instigator – of the November protests. On 11 November, a national strike was called, and was largely successful, as was another on 18 November. In the same month as Kabila, came to visit Mugabe in Harare, Morgan Tsvangirai was beginning to test his muscles.

The third part of the backdrop was the advent of the war veterans. In December 1997, in the face of a very well orchestrated campaign led by Chenjerai Hunzvi, Mugabe had agreed to pay veterans 'gratuities' of some £150 million – in recognition of their services in the liberation war. This, in itself – a sudden decision, or capitulation – knocked a huge hole in financial planning and precipitated a run on the stock market and threatened the value of the currency. At that stage, however, the veterans were not articulating the land issue. Mugabe had been doing that himself, and the two were not linked. But even after the IMF ultimatum of January 1998, the land issue did not, as the IMF had hoped, die away. It bubbled under the surface, and in November 1998, at the same time as the fuel crisis and the first national actions of the Congress of Trade Unions, a female white farmer was murdered, and her farmhouse torched, by what were then still called 'black squatters'. Mugabe himself was now restating his land policy, but with only 841 farms as his target, rather than 1480; with all this playing of numbers in a bluff/counter-bluff game with the IMF and others, others had begun to take the law into their own hands.

In November, as the embers of riots were still hot, Mugabe and Grace went to London to shop at Harrods. He stopped off, on the way – and against UN sanctions – in Libya, and asked Colonel Gaddafi for assistance with fuel (Libyan fuel did in fact come, and ameliorated a little that part of Zimbabwe's crisis; Gaddafi himself came, with a huge Bondish female entourage, and caused his own havoc with constant itinerary changes and the pitching of his tent in parts of the Zimbabwe countryside; Zimbabwean security could not hide relief at his departure). He stopped in Cairo, to buy arms for the Congo war; in Italy, to do the same; in Paris to discuss the war; and finally reached London, where Grace's bill at Harrods was less than the bill for arms. Mugabe had left behind warnings to Tsvangirai to stay out of politics.

But if Mugabe was buying arms for the war, not all troops sent to that war were happy. The senior officers certainly were; the 'grunts', or foot-soldiers, were not. In the early stages of fighting, several Zimbabwean soldiers were killed, but hundreds more came down with the virulent strains of Congolese malaria. Their officers did not yet understand the jungle terrain in which they were fighting, and November was the rainy season. Many began to desert. Popular disdain for the war became Tsvangirai's first rallying-call: 'Inflation is sky high, the economy is a mess. People question why we are in the war, when we have so many pressing problems here. We cannot afford this.'[10]

On 11 January 1999, the independent Harare Sunday newspaper the *Standard* published an article that 23 officers had been arrested for plotting a coup against Mugabe for his involvement in Congo and his mismanagement of the economy. The Government immediately denied the report and, on 13 January, military police arrested the *Standard*'s editor, Mark Chavunduka. They also arrested one of his reporters, Ray Choto. Later, the paper's publisher, Clive Wilson, was arrested. Where this case was different from run-of-the-mill press harassment was two-fold and ominous. First, it was military police who arrested the journalists. Second, two of them, Chavunduka and Choto, were tortured – suffocated, beaten with fists and planks, and given electrical shocks through their limbs and genitals.[11]

Mugabe remained stonily silent about the case at first, though his ministers commented contemptuously against the claims of torture. Tendai Biti, then co-chair of the Zimbabwe Lawyers for Human Rights, said 'the government does not care about the economy or about democracy or about basic rights. The only thing it cares about is power. And they will hold on to it at any cost.'[12] Riot police, with dogs and gas, broke up a demonstration of 300 lawyers on 26 January; shortly after, in a five-page letter, the judge of the Zimbabwe Supreme Court asked Mugabe to account for the military arrests and torture: 'What is of great consequence is the public perception that the military and the Central Intelligence Organisation can act with impunity in breach of the law'.[13]

But the military and the CIO did act in that way; and their very public precedent, including their use of violence against the defenceless, echoed in the minds of others gathering in the wings.

On 8 February, three more journalists were arrested. The *Mirror* had published an article, some time earlier, about the return of soldiers from Congo in body-bags. These arrests, for an old article, came just after a tirade by Mugabe against journalists and the judiciary. When the *Mirror*'s editor, Ibbo Mandaza, came to (this time) the police station to demand their release, he too was arrested and (lightly by comparison, but with sufficiently visible markings) beaten. At least the technocratic wing of ZANU-PF could claim it had its own independent views – but the point was that members of the army also had their own independent views, but the hierarchies of both the army and of ZANU-PF had their own agenda – and this was an agenda that was privileged above public law, and its constitutional foundation.

BATTLING FOR THE CONSTITUTION

Mugabe, however, cognisant of international criticism of his actions and confident still that he would win any election or referendum at home – if only because ZANU-PF was so comprehensively more organised than any opposition – moved to shore up his constitutional base. Constitutional reform had been an opposition demand at the 1985 elections, and Zvobgo's imperious condescension to this demand – implying there could be a constitutional debate at any time and ZANU-PF would win it – was still a part of the self-confidence of the ruling party. The opposition had sought, in any constitutional reform, to moderate the President's powers. Now Mugabe sought to use such reform to enhance them. Moreover, he sought to control the media more effectively, efficiently and quietly than sudden, public recourses to arrest and torture could provide. On 29 April 1999, therefore, he announced a constitutional reform commission to examine and recommend changes. He reserved the right to reject its findings, but ensured the composition of the new body was both huge and pro ZANU-PF. Of the 350 members, all 147 ZANU-PF MPs were included; the small opposition groups were represented, as were a number of professional people, clergy and academics.

It is here that academic battlelines were drawn in Zimbabwe, as some participated in the ZANU-PF effort to orchestrate the commission's work and others opposed it. Moreover, the small opposition parties aside, the majority of the civic groups in Zimbabwe had very recently formed their own National Constitutional Assembly (NCA), to push for reduced presidential powers and greater democracy. It was not represented on the commission, and its chairman was Morgan Tsvangirai.

There were two immediate preliminary skirmishes, therefore. Tsvangirai castigated the commission as having 'no legitimacy',[14] and the NCA was, in its turn, castigated for not wanting to play any role within it. 'The NCA should not have expected the government to sit back and watch while someone else took over the job of formulating' the constitution, that is the NCA.[15] The second skirmish was indeed between intellectuals. There was some trading of insults between academics who had sided either with the commission, or with the NCA. Moyo sided with the commission, and was disparaged by many of his colleagues.

As the commissioners neared the end of their deliberations, however – in September 1999 – an important battle of the new political era of opposition and turbulence took place within the NCA itself. This occurred as the commission opened itself to public comment. It held some 5000 meetings, conducted by eight provincial teams. It also prepared a national survey involving 140 researchers.[16] It was clear that the commission was not only going to present its constitutional recommendations, but do so with a show of extensive public consultation. The NCA, as an alternative, non-governmental constitutional body, would have been placed on the defensive. Moreover, it was a bulky alliance of groups, not well suited to opposition in a coherent way across a range of issues.

On the weekend of 11–12 September 1999, the MDC was formed, and Tsvangirai resigned as chairman of the NCA.[17] There were now some 30, mostly small, opposition parties. They were due to convene at a conference in Gweru, 25–27 September – so the announcement of the MDC took the wind out of the sails of many that had been manoeuvring for position. Nevertheless, the MDC did attend the conference and, according to the *Herald*'s editorial, treated the other parties with 'arrogance and surprising contempt',[18] Tsvangirai refusing even to stand up when introduced. Even so, this editorial, in what was now essentially a government mouthpiece, went on to express a surprising discourse of its own.

> Zimbabwe needs vibrant and strong opposition, hence the willingness of people to give new players, like the MDC, chances to prove their worth.
> As has happened before, the MDC will fall by the wayside if it continues to abuse itself of this big boy attitude. Life is an elaborate balancing act and the MDC will do itself a lot of good if it avoids rubbing everyone the wrong way.

Here the discourse was still one of pluralism – but it acknowledged that the MDC was a 'big boy' – and its note of caution to the MDC, to avoid 'rubbing everyone the wrong way', might well have been more properly directed to ZANU-PF itself. But now 'big boys' would contest the almost finalised draft constitution. Tsvangirai was immediately at pains to appear presidential. He insisted that he respected Mugabe. 'Even in my public addresses, I've never reduced myself to the position of dehumanising the position of the President. I feel that is inappropriate and should not be done'.[19] He announced a trip to Europe to discuss Zimbabwe's economic difficulties – thereby signalling both an MDC policy (and action) beyond the constitution, and an image of presidentialism. It was the idea of alternative government, rather than just opposition, that Tsvangirai sought to convey – and this, in itself, was new in Zimbabwean opposition politics. All opposition leaders had attacked Mugabe, but few had consistently undertaken to portray themselves as more truly presidential than he. Tsvangirai had a note to make on another issue as well: 'If people think that they have a soft target as far as the land question is concerned, then they have a serious problem'.[20]

Mugabe announced a referendum on the constitution for 12–13 February 2000. The MDC held its first party conference on 29–30 January, with a 6000 attendance as a show of strength. 'That draft constitution is not representative of what the people want. It represents what those in power want,' said Tsvangirai.[21] The draft constitution not only proposed increased powers for those in power, it was also clumsily written and alienating of groups it had no need to alienate. There were seven noteworthy provisions:

1 Increased presidential power. Among the new powers was an allowance for Mugabe to run for two more five-year terms.
2 Poorer women's rights. The majority of women would no longer be able to own property.
3 Poorer individual rights. Any right would be able to be overridden in the name of 'public morality and public security'.
4 Greater press censorship. A clause proposed a state-controlled media council to regulate the press.
5 Emergency powers. Providing draconian rights of arrest and banning, given to the President.
6 Sweeping Immunity. The president could not be prosecuted while in office, and could pardon anyone else.
7 Gay prohibitions. Apparently drafted by Mugabe himself, a clause prohibited gay marriage, and allowed individual rights to be overruled on the grounds of 'public morality'.

The MDC, therefore, fought against the constitution, both as a bad constitution, and as an entrenchment of a bad government. It turned the referendum on the constitution into a referendum on the government itself. Realising this, and belatedly recognising the opposition's strength, the Government's reaction became violent.

Of all the proposed constitutional provisions, the ones that seemed to evoke most dissatisfaction were those that increased the powers of the President. To an extent, the referendum was one on the President himself.

However, few commentators expected the constitution not to be approved. Andrew Meldrum, writing in the *Guardian*, reckoned 'it is almost certain that the constitutional referendum will pass. It is expected that less than 30 per cent of the electorate will vote.'[22] Moreover, as with the 1995 parliamentary elections, it was expected that the rural vote would swing automatically behind Mugabe – and the draft constitution pointedly provided for land nationalisation, of seizures from white farmers, as an incentive to the peasant voters.

However, the referendum coincided with the harvest, and a paraffin shortage – vital in areas not connected to electricity – and the ZANU-PF machine, either because of this or because of complacency, failed to marshal its rural vote. The cities turned out heavily, but it was only on the eve of the referendum itself that an upset seemed in the air.

There were 697,754 votes, representing 55 per cent of those who voted, against the draft constitution, with 578,210 in favour. It was, in Zimbabwean terms, a first and massive defeat for both Mugabe and ZANU-PF. Only 26 per cent of the electorate did finally turn out. Mugabe used this as a partial face-saver in his television address accepting the result. This acceptance itself stunned people. 'The world now knows that Zimbabwe is a country where opposing views and opinions can co-exist,' Mugabe said.[23] However, as suggested earlier, Mugabe had generally respected elections and tests at the polls – in the narrow sense that the poll itself and, by extension its result, had been respected. The campaigns leading to polls have been anything but respectful of the principle behind electoral tests. This is the nutshell – that outcome and its most narrowly defined process are more important by far than principle – of what might be said, this far into the game, to define Mugabe's strategic thinking. Even if it becomes a 'path of discomforts', he has been prepared to walk it. But he looked visibly shaken in his television address; and the celebrations of the opposition, particularly visible in the cities, could not have cheered his mood. Yet, as one nameless voter (in that charming British newspaper search for anecdotal comment and colour) was quoted as saying, 'I am amazed that they let the victory go through'.[24] ZANU-PF was left scratching its head over the rural vote. 'People from rural areas have really confounded analysts ... they have shown they should not be taken for granted.'[25] Mugabe convened an extraordinary session of the ZANU-PF politburo on 16 February, knowing that a similar vote in the forthcoming parliamentary elections, then scheduled for April, would unseat his party. The politburo meeting was followed by a meeting of the 220-member ZANU-PF central committee. Accusations were hurled at the rural party bosses who had failed to ensure voters turned out. But Mugabe also came under intense attack from his own central committee. It is important to say that from this moment on ZANU-PF was not simply a party with internal factions, but a party deeply divided. Winning elections was important to its retention of power, and if the President himself seemed likely to lose it those elections he would be deserted. Mugabe left the central committee crestfallen. On his seventy-sixth birthday he mused aloud about retirement: 'I do not want to wait to retire until I am back on all fours in my second childhood'.[26]

At this time, however, two things materialised to galvanise him anew. The land issue, long exploited by him as a rhetorical and electoral device, was suddenly – though briefly – taken out of his hands. And there appeared a new political figure of immense loyalty – or opportunism as his former colleagues saw it – and not a little daring. Moyo, by now spokes-man for the Government's constitutional effort, articulated what would be the opening gambit in Mugabe's fight to retain power. Speaking of the referendum polling days, he said,

> Preliminary figures show there were 100,000 white people voting. We have never had anything like that in this country. They were all over town. Everybody who observed will tell you there were long queues of whites. The difference between the 'yes' and 'no' votes would not have been what it was had it not been for this vote.[27]

Thus land and racism – naked – were thrown into the political atmosphere surrounding the period from the referendum in February to parliamentary elections in June (originally scheduled for April). Moyo was to become a Mandelson figure for Mugabe – restating the old rhetoric with new phraseologies. Land, racism, remarshalling the rural vote, and the advent of the ZANU-PF intellectuals all marked the next part of 2000.

NOTES ON CHAPTER 8

1   *Financial Gazette* (Harare), 12 March 1992.
2   Tendai Biti of the MDC recounted to the author, as did John Makumbe, a prominent academic commentator, the litany of Mugabe's liberation intrigues and betrayals in Mozambican exile between 1976 and 1979, Harare, August 2001.

3   UNAIDS, *Report on the Global HIV/AIDS Epidemic*, Geneva: UNAIDS, 1998, although this ranking table has changed since 1997.
4   Nana Poku, 'The Crisis of AIDS in Africa and the Politics of Response', in Nana Poku (ed.), *Security and Development in Southern Africa*, Westport: Praeger, 2001, p. 70.
5   *Southern African Economist*, 5:2, 1992, p. 16.
6   Maxi Schoeman, 'The Limits of Regionalization in Southern Africa', in Poku, op. cit., p. 151.
7   *Guardian* (London), 20 January 2000.
8   *Guardian*, 5 November 1998.
9   *Times* (London), 24 January 1998; *Guardian*, 20 January 1998.
10   *Guardian*, 14 November 1998.
11   Reports may be found in the *Guardian*, 22 January 1999, and the *Independent on Sunday*, 24 January 1999.
12   *Guardian*, 28 January 1999.
13   *Guardian*, 1 February 1999.
14   *Guardian*, 30 April 1999.
15   Claudious Chikozho, 'Will the Country's Laws be Rewritten?' MOTO (Gweru), 197, June 1999, p. 7.
16   *Sunday Mail* (Harare), 26 September 1999.
17   For quite good backgrounders, see the *Mirror* (Harare), 17–23 September 1999.
18   *Herald*, 28 September 1999.
19   *Mirror*, 24–30 September 1999.
20   Ibid.
21   *Guardian*, 31 January 2000.
22   *Guardian*, 12 February 2000.
23   *Times*, 16 February 2000.
24   *Independent*, 16 February 2000.
25   *Herald*, 16 February 2000.
26   *Guardian*, 24 February 2000.
27   *Times*, 16 February 2000.

NINE

Mugabe's Path of Discomforts: Two – Land and Persecution

The constitutional referendum had been held from 12 to 13 February 2000. Mugabe was still licking his wounds at the ZANU-PF central committee in the following week. In the last days of February and the beginning of March, thousands of – surprisingly urban-attired – 'squatters' occupied 70 white-owned farms. This seems not to have been wholly government-planned, although it was, by ZANU-PF factions at least, closely supported. Mugabe certainly moved to take advantage of the situation. Despite having only, days before, lost the referendum over a constitution with land nationalisation clauses, he introduced a constitutional amendment on 2 March authorising the government to take over white farms without compensation. The Home Affairs Minister, Dumiso Dabengwa – who had been imprisoned by Mugabe at the time of the repression of the Matabelelands, but who was now a staunch ZANU-PF supporter – ordered the 'squatters' to leave. They were not yet called 'war veterans'. Dabengwa said that there was no need for the squatters to take action, as the Government would now confiscate white land, without compensation, and redistribute it to the rural poor.[1]

Within only a few days more, Dabengwa had been overruled by Mugabe. The President, not only clambering aboard but scaling the public bandwagon, announced that the squatters could stay, pending the Government's allocation to them of land from the confiscated farms. Ten days into March, 500 farms had been occupied. Courts began ruling that the police had to enforce the law, no matter what the President said; but the police were, far more often than not, bystanders – even if, when taunted, aggrieved bystanders – and Mugabe began planning to target the courts.

The roots of the land problem had grown from settler seedlings. The appropriation of land, by Cecil Rhodes's British South Africa Company at the end of the nineteenth century, was not gentle. In 1896, a huge uprising of both Shona and Ndebele peoples killed some 400 settlers. This was the first liberation war, or *chimurenga*, of modern Zimbabwean history. The settlers' response was even more brutal than the uprising, and 'native' modes of self-organisation were destroyed. The formalisation of white hegemony over the land came in the 1923 constitution, which entrenched native reserves, and in 1930, with the Land Apportionment Act, whereby Rhodesia was largely divided into land privately owned by white settlers (by far the majority of land, and the best), and what became known in the Smith era as the 'tribal trustlands', a kind of peasant-farmer extended reservation.

The second *chimurenga*, the war of liberation that ended with independence in 1980, was a victory over the political structures imposed by generations of settler government and culture, but not over the land-ownership structures of the almost-century-long settler era. As outlined above, Mugabe had, from the beginning, regarded land as a great unfinished issue, but there were never the funds to purchase huge amounts of white land and, as the international community – Britain very much included – became disinclined to help, Mugabe's rhetoric became shriller. It was perhaps an arrant appropriation of the name, but the 'war veterans' who unveiled themselves as the squatters and invaders of farms in 2000 were echoing the unfinished nature of the *chimurenga*, and Mugabe, himself the devotee of that liberation and viewing himself as its spiritual heir – or at least as having political responsibilities to it – was disinclined to discourage them.

In Britain, commentators were inclined to condemn the farm invasions. There were, at the outset, some cautionary if not dissenting voices. George Monbiot noted that proper compensation for wholesale national-isation would have cost billions, but 'having hinted that we would pay for it, our government handed over only a fraction of the money required – £44m – to make it happen'. Monbiot said this was 'meanness', and that it had perpetuated a racial segregation on the soil of Zimbabwe.[2] Almost all of that £44 million was disbursed in the first decade of Zimbabwean independence. Even a continuation of that modest investment in the

second decade, particularly after the crippling drought of 1992, might
have kept the game of rhetoric from being taken over by pitch-invaders.
John Major hinted that he would indeed provide more funds, but Tony
Blair left Robert Mugabe with the strong feeling that Britain no longer
saw it as a responsibility or even judicious foreign policy. The argument
as to who said what to whom, inferred what, understood what, will never
be fully unravelled. What is certain from the record is that, although
rhetoric became shriller, and bluff ever more dangerous, no wholesale
appropriations of land occurred until 2000. Then, an unknown actor – at
least a seemingly placated actor – entered the game of bluff and rhetoric,
and took it over.

Chenjerai Hunzvi, who had nicknamed himself 'Hitler' (a self-acquired
nom de guerre, even though he had never fought in the liberation war),
was a Polish-trained physician, who had returned to Zimbabwe after
independence with a Polish wife. He was an obscure person until 1997.
Then, as the leader of the Zimbabwe Liberation War Veterans Association,
he confronted Robert Mugabe. How Hunzvi, without being himself a
veteran, became the veterans' leader is part of his mystery. Perhaps,
marginalised by a ZANU-PF that had grown fat, the unrewarded and
increasingly unrecognised veterans needed an educated and forceful
leader. Why Hunzvi wanted to undertake the role of their champion is
also unknown – perhaps as a route to power; but it was a risky route.
In any case, under his leadership, the veterans began demanding, with
increasing ferocity, some compensation   some pension – for their years
of service and sacrifice. In a way, they articulated the divide in Zimbabwean
society after independence between those who came to have and those
who remained the have-nots. Mugabe was ready to deal roughly with the
now-street-marching and protesting veterans: some beating and
teargassing – by now standard street measures against dissent – were
planned. Before the plans could be implemented, Mugabe and Hunzvi
held a meeting. Probably no one had spoken so roughly to Mugabe since
1980. Hunzvi threatened to unleash anarchy, and not only divide the
nation but divide it by depriving Mugabe of his spiritual heritage. The
veterans would be standing as those who had fought for Zimbabwe,
Mugabe would be called a traitor to them and their cause. The identity
of Mugabe's soul would be ripped from him. To Mugabe, the consummate
master of bluff and hardball, the threat of being met on terms that he
would normally set – and to have his sense of heritage, of personal

guardianship of the spirit of that heritage, so robustly challenged – was chastening. He gave in immediately, and the veterans received their pensions. At some Zim.$50,000 per veteran, the final bill came to £150 million. This was not, in isolation, a huge sum; but it was an unplanned expenditure and, amidst all the other strains upon the Zimbabwean exchequer, was the straw that broke the camel's back. Financial confidence dipped sharply. Money had to be printed and inflation soared.

There is conjecture as to how much Mugabe, in 2000, played Hunzvi, and how much Hunzvi was in fact leading the Government down a road that it had often threatened to walk but had never set out on. The logistical command of the squatters, impressive from the beginning, suggested major assistance from ZANU-PF. Moreover, only a small core of the farm invaders or squatters were actual war veterans – although the 'squatters' were being described as 'war veterans' by mid-March 2000 – so the recruitment of several hundred urban youths, not old enough to have fought or in some cases even to have been born at the time of the liberation war had to require party assistance. Government and party vehicles kept the invaders supplied, and many were meant to have been receiving daily allowances. However, if the Government or ZANU-PF had played this sort of initial role, it had been a suddenly-improvised role. Almost all of the early farm invasions were within commutable distance of Harare. There was not, then, any national plan. Second, not everyone in the Government and party knew of the local plan, Dabengwa's insistence that the occupiers should leave being a case in point. Third, if Mugabe had suddenly improvised a plan to play Hunzvi – to reignite the land issue sufficiently, and dramatically, to take attention away from Mugabe's own recent defeats – then there is some evidence that Mugabe intended the farm invasions to have a demonstration effect, a very visible demonstration effect, but not to have them become the foundation of applied Government policy. In April 2000, Mugabe was still saying that no white farmer would be chased from Zimbabwe, provided he or she wanted to stay in the country and share land with the landless peasants.[3] The more strident and open racism of his comments would come later – although Hunzvi was openly racist from the start. In early April, however, it seemed possible to suggest that Mugabe had been setting a stage for negotiations – with the white farmers, although with an unveiled fist, but also with the British, with whom an engineered diplomatic spat was in progress. The British were to lose control of that spat, just as Mugabe seemed to lose control of the land invasions (for a time) later that April. In early April, he seemed intent on making a point to Britain, not just about land but about the newly emerged MDC opposition. To crush the opposition electorally, Mugabe needed to redistribute land. A few seizures without compensation would encourage Blair's Government to think more urgently about negotiating some contribution to any possibility of compensation. Simultaneously, the British would be put on notice that any temptation it faced to support the opposition should be resisted. Mugabe could unleash violence: both the white farmers and the British had better cooperate. If this was his strategy, two things ruined it: the British misread Mugabe, perhaps entirely, and became themselves strident, almost themselves shrill; and Hunzvi, with or without Mugabe's help, having come this far, was going to crank up the pace and violence of his campaign to ensure that, even for a man like Mugabe, there could be no way back. The only way Mugabe could then re-control the land invasions would be by endorsing them all.

All this is to read events clinically, and to make some – perhaps imperfect   sense of contradictory signals and statements at the time. Moreover, the occupying war veterans were not always well controlled, and often when events spiralled into tragedy no one had planned that tragedy. Again, after April that too changed. Certainly, by April's beginning, Britain was sufficiently alarmed by the farm invasions to have drawn up contingency plans to airlift, if necessary, whites from Zimbabwe. Whether these plans had been drawn up in any detail, or were simply outline, is debatable. The prospect of evacuation had been raised by Foreign Office Minister Peter Hain – the former anti-apartheid cam-paigner – who now became a trenchant and official critic of Mugabe. His entry into a war of words with Mugabe was made without hesitation – perhaps with relish for his campaigning days.

BRITISH JAW-JAW AND THE ESCALATING LAND WAR

Alarmed by defeat in the February constitutional referendum, alarmed also by the apparent growth in strength of the opposition, and alarmed further by foreign reactions to the existence of an organised opposition – favourable – ZANU-PF entered a period of paranoia. Although the land issue and victory over the opposition were closely linked issues, they were not cojoint in equal terms. Electoral victory in the parliamentary elections, by now postponed from April to an indeterminate date in 2000 (August would have been the last constitutionally proper moment), was the greater priority. Pressure on Britain over land was a means to securing victory. It was a radical tactical manoeuvre. It accorded with Mugabe's longstanding principles over land, but was not an articulated strategy. Even with the Mugabe-esque penchant for evolving measures as a grand plan sweeps along, this was not yet grand.

In March, tipped off that the British diplomatic bag bound for Harare contained more than papers, the Zimbabwean Government arranged its interception – with news crews present – at Harare airport. This was a flagrant breach of protocol and diplomatic conventions. Apparently, the Government had expected to find weapons destined to arm the opposition – a crude speculation – but found instead electronic eavesdropping equipment. No doubt MI6, not inconsistent with its practice – and that of a few others – elsewhere, was upgrading its 'political reporting' capabilities. The Zimbabwean Government has long known, and tolerated, such activities. There are jokes in the Zimbabwean Foreign Ministry as to which embassy houses the worst spies. In the political atmosphere of Harare in March 2000, however, anything could be turned to its worst interpretation; and if there was disappointment over the non–discovery of arms, surveillance equipment was the next best thing – especially in a war of propaganda.

Whether it liked it or not, Britain was about to be 'suckered' into Zimbabwean electoral politics. About this time, both US and New Zealand sports shooting teams were detained at the airport – with actual arms – and the Zimbabwean fear was again of guns reaching the opposition. The US and New Zealand response was to address the 'misunderstanding' as quietly as possible.[4] Perhaps the British felt that they did not have that option and, indeed, international diplomatic protocols had been breached in the opening of the diplomatic bag. In any case, the exchange of strong words rapidly became surly, then insulting, then shrilly insulting. Mugabe labelled the British Government one run by gays; Peter Hain called Zimbabwean repression of demonstrations 'thuggery, licensed from on high … attacks encouraged, if not actually organised, by President Mugabe'.[5] It became an extraordinary exchange. Indeed, in my quarter century of covering international relations I can recall no equivalent series of attacks by a British junior minister on a head of state. The British response to Amin's Ugandan expulsions of Asian British citizens was, by contrast, stiffly measured. This is not to raise the issue of whether Hain's comments were merited, but Mugabe then simply adopted them into his election campaigning speeches. Hain was, henceforth, painted as acting as if he were the 'last governor of Rhodesia', and Mugabe proclaimed that Britain 'has declared war on us'.[6] The idea became – this much was transparent – one of painting the opposition MDC, as fully as possible, as stooges of the British.

The Foreign Secretary, Robin Cook, also attacked Mugabe, in emphatic though slightly less robust terms. There was to be a EU–Africa summit in early April. He knew that he had better begin to close the gap. By some arcane mischance (or mischief) British and Zimbabwean delegations were seated close by at the summit. Cook very deliberately snubbed Mugabe when the two encountered each other by accident in the hotel lobby. Nevertheless, Cook and Mugabe met in their own private session on the evening of 3 April. Mugabe stressed the land issue.

Meanwhile, Mugabe had begun to rush through his constitutional amendment, the sixteenth since independence, providing that if Britain did not pay compensation for nationalised land it could be nationalised without any compensation at all. The Justice Minister, speaking on the amendment in parliament, charged that 'the current British government has reneged on the issue of paying compensation on land acquired for resettlement'. This was a reference to the Blair attitude at the Commonwealth summit in Edinburgh and what had followed since. To be fair, the British had begun to offer to provide compensation funds, but only on condition that land acquired was indeed redistributed to those actually poor, and in a transparent manner. The Zimbabwean Government saw this as a conditionality which would mean Britain dictating the process of land acquisition, a cheek since it was British settlers in the first instance who had 'acquired' land in a somewhat less than transparent manner from the actually poor. Zimbabwe was beginning to portray the issue, with some success regionally, as a British unfairness. Hain's manner of speech had indeed not helped to counter this perception. Returning from his meeting with Cook, Mugabe said, 'I insisted that the meeting with Cook would not include Peter Hain as I do not want to have sight of him. He has already predicted we are going to rig the elections. I told Cook we have never rigged elections.'[7] And in the very narrow way described above, he had not. He had hardly, however, provided for fair campaigning, and Hain had been attacking a particularly brutal breaking up of a large demonstration in Harare on the first of April. Nevertheless, the twin tracks of Mugabe's election strategy had now been established. He would attack Britain and the MDC as an agent of the British – still behaving in their imperial pomp – and he would attack the land issue at full throttle, assuming a complete command of it, and when the time was right marginalise Hunzvi, then dispense with him. First, however, he would give Hunzvi his head and let him escalate the invasions; Hunzvi would be a sort of cover for Mugabe; Hunzvi, however, thought he could escalate the issue sufficiently to take it beyond Mugabe's control – so that Mugabe would legitimise Hunzvi, not Hunzvi cover Mugabe – and both men were looking to win an election for ZANU-PF, and for Hunzvi victory over Mugabe would mean a cabinet seat, preferably with official responsibility for land redistribution. In a sense, Mugabe was fighting two campaigns: a parliamentary election, in which he was using the land issue, and, having chosen to use the land issue, a campaign for the leadership of the resurrected *chimurenga*, for the spiritual mantle from the days of liberation. If Hunzvi controlled the war veterans, he was a far more potent opponent than Tekere in 1990 or Muzorewa in 1996. Although this was a parliamentary election, there was a kind of 'presidential' jostling as well. Both men were setting out to play a very dangerous game, and neither cared greatly about the casualties caused along the way.

Moreover, although Mugabe had begun by seeing land in terms, among other things, of an election issue, Hunzvi seemed quite dedicated to the concept of land as a natural indigenous Zimbabwean right. His rhetoric, shriller than any before and certainly more nakedly racist, took no prisoners, brooked no compromise, afforded no negotiation. He stared Mugabe in the face, and he refused the judgements and the sanctions of the courts. He was, in that casual but very accurate parlance, 'going for broke'; and he was going at speed.

THE COURTS TRY TO MAKE A STAND

The largely white Commercial Farmers Union had tried to obtain court orders against land occupation from the outset. Up until the end of 1999, with the military arrest of journalists, the independent authority of the courts had been generally respected in Zimbabwe. Even after those arrests, the trenchant court response – as noted above – suggested an ongoing check to executive powers, and a balance that prevented a wholesale descent into arbitrary rule. On 17 March 2000, the High Court, under Judge Garwe, issued an order declaring the land invasions illegal, and instructing the police to evict the occupiers within 24 hours. At the hearing, Hunzvi swore that he had not been involved in farm seizures: 'I must categorically state that I am not and was not responsible for the occupation of farms'.[8] This was patently false. In any case, the police, realising the political significance of the issue, balked from obeying the court order. Through the Attorney-General, they applied for a variation of the order, arguing that it was ill-advised for an under-resourced force to intervene in something so obviously political and with racial over-tones. They also argued that it would be iniquitous to use law to protect a system of land ownership so obviously inequitable. On 13 April, in response, Judge Chinhengo ruled that the invasions were both illegal and riotous, and that the police had a clear duty to enforce the court order. The invasions nevertheless continued, and the police took no action to prevent them. On 19 April, the High Court held Hunzvi in contempt. Hunzvi pleaded that he strove always to obey the law and that he would certainly work with the white farmers to 'ensure the peaceful vacation of the war veterans from the farms'.[9] The farmers, by this time desperate and prepared to cling to even remote hope, even argued before the court that Hunzvi should be given time to work with them. On 5 May, the High Court granted them this request.

By May, elections were close. Hunzvi promised one thing to the courts and did other things on the farms. He would have a few more months as the *führer* of rural Zimbabwe, but the courts were also entering their last months as truly independent bodies. After the elections, Mugabe would ensure that he had sufficient legal instrumentality to make a stand before the highest court in the land; and then he ensured that the bench of the Supreme Court was replaced by judges of his own choice. At this stage, before the elections, now firmly scheduled for June, the courts had demon-strated their fidelity to law.[10] Mugabe faced a growing opposition at the hustings, a limit to his arbitrary powers (at least in the declaratory form of court orders and judgements), and an ambitious agent (or co-worker) in the land-seizure programme. By now, it was indeed a programme.

THE LAND SEIZURE PROGRAMME AND THE ELECTIONS

In April, the first of a handful of white farmers had been shot; but several members of the MDC had also been killed. The British press, by and large, highlighted the white deaths, and again this suited Mugabe. Not only did it, in itself, suggest a racially segregated British interest in the country, it also veiled the great violence done to opposition members. Already, if you were a campaigner for the MDC, you were very brave. Hunzvi cranked up the rhetoric, and aimed it expressly at both the white farmers and Britain. 'The white farmers have two options: to hand over the land and leave or to stay and see what land we leave them. The whites are foreigners, they are British! They should go back to Britain.'[11] ZANU-PF placards rubbed in the official discourse: 'Zimbabwe will never be a colony again'. The farmers were being portrayed as the last of an occupying force – they were literally occupying the land of Zimbabwe – and the state to whom they owed true allegiance, Britain, was trying to defend them. So long as the British centred their views on the issue of land and white farmers, these views were turned into pro-ZANU-PF election propaganda.

Meanwhile, Hunzvi hinted at an expansion of his own role: 'We are here to ensure that ZANU-PF's reign shall never be interrupted by sell-outs.'[12] The term 'sell-out' was a dreaded accusation during the war of liberation. Guerilla 'justice' could be somewhat untransparent, brutal, and people could be selected for gratuitous but exemplary execution. Hunzvi's more than transparent coding was that, both in the time remaining before the elections and after them as well, a pogrom might be in order. Perhaps he was nominating himself as master of the pogrom. Certainly he was a most visible campaigner for ZANU-PF, and scourge of the opposition. In April, 14 MDC members were killed. Tsvangirai responded defiantly: 'We are not throwing in the towel. Our people are being killed but we will continue.'[13]

However, as May broke Mugabe considered that all the initiatives were running his way. The 'war veterans' commanded huge strategic chunks of the countryside, and were attempting to ride some sort of electoral shotgun over rural voters. The opposition was still active, but having to work hard to absorb its losses and, above all, maintain the morale and fortitude of its canvassers. The police were standing aside and the courts were making judgements that the Government had no intention of upholding. Moreover, the Government was rushing through both temporary and permanent measures to justify in law all that was occurring on the farms. It was in early May – with Commonwealth and other international pressures starting to chime in with those of the British, but far more centred upon the electoral process – that Mugabe thought the time was right to call the elections. They were slated for 24 and 25 June, and ZANU-PF considered that the seven weeks of formal campaigning would allow them to consolidate the gains made by intimidation and ruthlessness. Meanwhile, more farms were invaded, more farmers died, and this process ran both in tandem with and parallel to the election campaign. It was in tandem since the seizure of land was an election promise of redistribution to come; it was parallel since its external purpose was to distract attention from too close a scrutiny of electoral tactics of violence. Violence, in short, was calculated to cover violence. It was ingenious, and the British Government and press took a very long time to wake up to the dual-track nature of Mugabe's work. In diplomacy too, Mugabe worked another dual-track trick: to the British and their complaints about farm seizures, he responded defiantly – 'Britain will not decide our destiny'[14] – and to Commonwealth concerns over elections he responded by finally calling elections. He was sure he was going to win; and the opposition, initially buoyed by the unexpected referendum results, were downcast. Tsvangirai began musing aloud about boycotting the elections. 'Faced with this situation of lawlessness and murder against our members, the MDC must consider new strategies, including a possible boycott of the parliamentary elections'.[15]

Britain finally froze its arms sales to Zimbabwe. The Zimbabwean response was, again, insidiously calculated. In talks with the Commercial Farmers Union, Mugabe offered to suspend violence on the farms in favour of peaceful handover of land for redistribution. The campaign against the white farmers had finally sapped their resolve. However, ZANU-PF wanted even more from them. Conscious that farm seizures had alienated many black workers, whose livelihoods had now been ripped away from them, ZANU-PF now wanted their erstwhile employers, the white farmers themselves, to campaign for ZANU-PF and win back the votes of the rural workers. If Mugabe had been conciliatory in his talks with them, other ZANU-PF figures spelt out the overall strategy more bluntly. One provincial governor said, 'we are not happy with the attitude of some white commercial farmers who are supporting the opposition. We do not want another war. If you want peace you should support me and the ruling party. If you want trouble, then vote for another party.'[16] In fact, the violence on the farms did not end, but Mugabe had done or attempted three things with one stroke: first, he had wrung a concession from the white farmers in the struggle; second, by suggesting that they should now campaign for ZANU-PF, he had rubbed salt into their wounds; third, if they had indeed cooperated with him, the sting would have been drawn from the British protest. There was no madness or simple-minded ruthlessness at work here. At the very least, even if shorn of principle (but he would have said land redistribution was indeed his principle), he was proving, as before, a master tactician. On the chessboard, the British pieces were in disarray. Mugabe moved forward again, ensuring the British remained on the back foot, and announced the stripping of citizenship from white Zimbabweans who had, surreptitiously, maintained their British passports as well (dual citizenship had in fact been banned in Zimbabwe since 1985). The aim was, yet again, to keep British interest firmly focussed on white Zimbabweans, while the majority black population was conditioned away from the opposition. (In addition, non-citizens would be ineligible to vote.) By mid-May, the 'war veterans' were as busy committing acts of violence upon the opposition as they were occupying farms. Yet more opposition workers were beaten to death.

With a month to go before the elections, the glossy British gossip magazines finally caught up with the Zimbabwean tragedy. *Hello* ran a five-page colour spread in its 23 May issue on the fortitude and Christian forgiveness of a white farmer's widow. In the Zimbabwean election campaign, MDC campaigners were opening rallies with the song, 'Mother and father, if I die today don't cry for me. It is I who gave myself to die for Zimbabwe.'[17]

By the end of the first week in June, with elections only two weeks away, 29 opposition workers had been killed; 1400 farms were occupied; 841 farms were officially designated for appropriation and redistribution; Mugabe was saying that the final number would be much higher; and Mugabe had begun verbally attacking High and Supreme Court judges of British descent.

Looking back, the calculation of violence – as much as the violence itself – is what chills. People who died were considered as so many ciphers in a cold-blooded campaign conducted on several levels. Looking back also, the British responses and efforts at intervention were amazingly maladroit and, even if truly intentioned, were such that Mugabe quite seamlessly incorporated all British criticism to demonstrate a key point of his electoral message. Looking back, the courage of the opposition was particularly impressive. Outgunned, it never lost its composure and conviction that Zimbabwe deserved better. It organised itself through a baffling array of constantly changing mobile telephones (something quite new to Zimbabwe), so much so that it never quite kept up with itself in terms of which number was, at any moment, attached to which organiser. What kept their roadshow very much on the road was a steely determination. As June matured, there was even the glimmer of optimism that, perhaps, just perhaps, it might win. It was a belief that the Zimbabwean people deserved better and, above all, that the Zimbabwean people were better than Mugabe and ZANU-PF considered them

THE ELECTION RESULTS

In the campaign leading to the 2000 parliamentary elections, Mugabe accomplished two things. First, more than ever before – with the exception still of the Matabelelands in the 1980s – he committed violence against his own people. It would seem that winning an election is of great moment to him, and the stronger the challenge the more ruthlessness and violence he is prepared to deploy in the run-up to elections themselves. Second, he put behind him the judgement of observers from 1991 and 1992, that he was a President who excelled at doing only one thing at a time. In 2000, he operated at several levels simultaneously: confronting a powerful opposition, while playing a game of leash and unleash with Hunzvi and his 'war veterans'; unleashing a farm seizure programme that was also a diplomatic cover; playing Britain thereby, and distracting that country's attention while persecuting the opposition; conducting the electoral campaign proper, while preparing the ground for a later pogrom, not of all opposition as Hunzvi had hoped, but of the judges who, even more than the opposition, expressed themselves as an institutionalised check on his exercise of power. And he had done this while conducting a most exacting diplomacy with Zimbabwe's Southern African neighbours, playing down their fears of instability, convincing them he really was the only game in town, and constructing a myth of white colonial interference that touched raw nerves across the Limpopo River in the very recently freed South Africa. If a man might come of age in his seventies, then Mugabe did; but, if ever a man simultaneously came of age and sold his soul, Mugabe gave every impression that he was prepared to do that – to embrace anything that would permit him to enter an election with the expectation of winning. For this Faust, the hollow Helen was validation by a preconditioned count of numbers.

As it was, the count ran him close. The provinces where the 'war veterans' had been most numerously deployed remained with Mugabe. This was almost all of central rural Zimbabwe. Sithole's ZANU-Ndonga retained one seat in the east. Otherwise, all 19 seats in Harare fell to the MDC. ZANU-PF won nothing at all in the capital. All eight seats in Bulawayo fell also to the MDC – who also won 13 of the remaining 15 seats in both Matabeleland North and South. Essentially, the huge bulk of the Matabelelands, Nkomo having died, remembered the atrocities of the Fifth Brigade and voted against Mugabe. Even Dumiso Dabengwa – imprisoned by Mugabe during the 1980s and the general of Nkomo's liberation forces but who had restored his links with Mugabe and become a minister – lost his seat with a massive swing against him. Tsvangirai, fighting a birth-place seat in the heart of ZANU-PF territory, did not enter parliament.

However, Chenjerai 'Hitler' Hunzvi did. Several ZANU-PF seniors lost their seats, but in the end Mugabe had just scraped it. ZANU-PF took 62 seats to 58 for the opposition (57 MDC, one ZANU-Ndonga). All of the west, Manicaland, the spiritual heartland of liberation, was lost to ZANU-PF – so that the narrow victory, made more comfortable by the additional 30 seats nominated by the President, was, in terms of heritage, a little hollow. With only a four-seat electoral majority, court challenges predicated on localised rigging, might have seemed a prospect – and indeed the MDC launched several such challenges – but the total 34-seat majority, thanks to the 30 nominated seats, meant that the overall result would not be overturned.

The actual days of the election itself were, again, and also by contrast to the pre-election violence, reasonably quiet, and polling was reasonably fair. Certainly the international community moved quickly to accept the result – if only to have elections retained within the Zimbabwean political structure. Both major parties in Britain accepted the result, while emphasising the strength of the opposition and its newly validated claims to some participation in running the country. Thabo Mbeki, the South African President, lauded the result as an evidence of democratic process taking root; and the UN's Kofi Annan said that the result should be respected, despite reports by observers that pre-election violence could have affected the outcome.[18] In all, the international community had let Mugabe off lightly. It accepted what he had narrowly and pain-stakingly maintained: in Zimbabwe, elections were fair. It was just that, in Zimbabwe, electoral campaigning can be very far indeed from being fair, and in 2000 the Government had become not only unfair but savagely unfair. This was an election very different from all before, and the Mugabe who emerged had crafted himself into a Mugabe of even more complex hue than before, and if before it had been possible to speak both well and ill of Mugabe, after the 2000 election it was possible to speak only overwhelmingly ill of him. Complexly bad – not mad – but very complexly bad.

Mugabe did not make Hunzvi a minister. Having used him, Mugabe chose not to reward the man who had once spoken to him as an equal and, for a time, had seemed an equal. Hunzvi was infuriated, and turned his attention once again to terror on the farms, thinking to retain and expand his powerbase among the 'war veterans', in case Mugabe sought to do with him as he had done to Nkomo, Banana and Sithole before – and also to maintain his springboard in case he could bring about an eventual leap to power. Whatever Hunzvi's motivations and ambitions, this violent footnote of a man set about wreaking yet more violence for just short of a year. He collapsed on 21 May 2001, and died on 4 June of AIDS – the disease against which Mugabe had done so little. It is said that Hunzvi did not have a good end. There were many, probably even within the President's office, who were not sorry about that.

If Hunzvi did not enter the cabinet, Professor Jonathan Moyo, of the ZANU-PF technocratic wing, did. He did not set about a reformist or enlightened agenda, but became in very short order Mugabe's most articulate spokesman. Once again, as with Hunzvi, Mugabe worked with a lightning-rod preceding him. Moyo became execrated by his former colleagues and the opposition press, but the new lightning-rod and hammer of Mugabe took to his new duties – chiefly it seemed of crushing the opposition – with a relish and talent rare among academics.

THE UNFOLDING OF MORALITY PLAYS

Although some academic commentators had seen Moyo as 'rightist' and elitist ten years earlier,[19] the general view of him after his elevation in 2000 was as a turncoat. The opposition newspaper, the *Daily News*, by now the largest-circulation paper in the country – and with far higher production values than those of the government mouthpiece *Herald* – took delight in republishing a 1977 article by Moyo on political openness, in order to contrast the Moyo then with the 2000 version.[20] The particular physiognomy of Moyo gave the political cartoonists a field-day. Recognisable by his large head, he was the 'egghead' professor of the stereotypes. So he was drawn with this head growing ever larger, swollen with ministerial pride and, it was said, even presidential ambition.[21] (Mind you, it was Moyo – his characteristic wit not quite lost – who quipped, when the US presidential race was torn by accusations of voting defects in Florida, a state governed by the brother of the eventual winner, that Zimbabwe would be very happy to send election observers to the US to ensure the freeness and fairness of the election there.)

Moyo was a lightning-rod for Mugabe. He was also, if a loose analogy might be drawn, a Peter Mandelson figure, a spin-doctor by virtue of his facility with words. He was, finally, as Minister of State for Information and Publicity – lodged directly in the President's office – not without some influence in the days to come over the freedom of expression. Certainly, with a broadcasting brief as well, vernacular radio was closed off to the opposition. Moyo became a tenacious and vigorous defender of Mugabe. He entered into the shrillness that characterised Zimbabwean debate and set about raising its pitch – though not very much its tone. In a way, the label of turncoat was one that applied to Mugabe as well. In the very early days after liberation it was the intellectuals who placed a special faith in what Mugabe and ZANU-PF could deliver. They were not conspicuously vocal at the time of the Fifth Brigade atrocities in Matabeleland but, by the end of the 1980s were certainly disenchanted with the overall drift of ZANU-PF – away from internal party democracy, and away from any semblance of state socialist economic policy. It was not so much that they thought that the state had a choice in adopting structural adjustment and a form of neo-liberal economics, but that the very recent sovereignty of the country seemed now mortgaged to the IMF and World Bank without any countervailing discourse of eventual escape and the replenishment of, at least, an African social democracy. Even so, of the two issues – economics and ZANU-PF internal democracy – it was the latter that propelled the intellectuals into the ZUM camp of Edgar Tekere for the 1990 elections. Having switched sides then, many never forgave Mugabe the local intimidations and riggings that had baptised them into actual, as opposed to ivory-tower, politics. That Moyo should now become the mouthpiece of Mugabe – especially when national democracy was having to struggle constantly – simply compounded the sense that Mugabe himself was a font and epitome of betrayal. The unease of the intellectuals at the end of Zimbabwe's first decade of independence had been most elegantly – and with careful restraint – articulated by Brian Raftopoulos, in a work described earlier.[22] Raftopoulos became, by the end of Zimbabwe's second decade, chairman of the Zimbabwe Crisis Committee, comprising some 250 civil-society organisations. That there should exist so many NGOs concerned about the political health of Zimbabwe suggests, as much if not even more than the sudden rise of the MDC, a proactive health in the Zimbabwean polity. For it is not simply a response to arbitrariness and authoritarian, self-serving autarky; it is also a quest for a different future to overcome the legacy of betrayal. In short, there is a proposition made by this polity, not simply a protest. That proposition, however, seeks a moral government and a moral governance.

When looked at from this perspective, the commentaries of opposition figures make fine sense. It was not that Mugabe rigged the 1990, 1995 and 1996 elections, and won them because of rigging. He would have won them with or without what were, by comparison to the elections of the 2000s, paltry stage settings. Beneath the insistence that play was not fair[23] is the keen knowledge that neither play nor the lead player are moral. In the 2000s, there is a sense that normative and moral concerns have supervened the neo-Marxist analyses of the intellectual left in Zimbabwe, and their censure has been directed against not only Mugabe but a member of the intellectual right – Jonathan Moyo – who, as the satirists unremittingly trace it, rose up the hotel cocktail conference circuit, through the constitutional commission, to become attached to Mugabe's political anatomy. The exact mode and juncture cannot be expressed here.

It was within this sense of a moral frustration at large – and watching a similar frustration far away spill over – that Tsvangirai made his speech likening Mugabe to Milosevic, and likening the possible fate of his Government to that befalling Milosevic's on the streets of Belgrade and on the steps of the Yugoslav parliament. The notion of overthrow, and overthrow on moral grounds, touched a nerve in Mugabe. He entered a period when he sought not only to crush the MDC, but to crush Tsvangirai. Simultaneously – for he continued to operate on several levels – he continued with the farm invasions, determined now to complete a belated revolution, with or without Hunzvi, and if not create the new Zimbabwean create the new Zimbabwe – standing alone against both the external pressures of residual colonialism and colonialism's residual fifth column within. In this version of a spacious political moral goal, Mugabe confronted those who said he was immoral with a very precise amorality.

THE BATTLE TO DEFINE THE BATTLELINES

After the June 2000 elections, the next six to eight months were occupied with a prolonged sparring duel between ZANU-PF and the MDC. Each sought to test the other's strength and resolve, feeling for weak points, seeking to consolidate their own bases, and engaging in diplomatic manoeuvres in which each side sought to attract international support. A great deal of Scandinavian money helped to finance the MDC's effort to establish a proper political structure and infrastructure – for it remained a somewhat loose coalition of the disaffected and the idealistic. Little bound them except opposition. If Tsvangirai began to project himself as a credible alternative president, few others in the MDC appeared to be potential members of a cabinet. Tendai Biti began to cut ice as a prospective foreign minister, Welshman Ncube and David Coltart were both possible ministers of justice (all three were lawyers), but ministerial material was thin on the ground. Biti had less than half a dozen party members whom he could trust – as having enough knowledge and skill – to send on diplomatic missions. The result was that he and Tsvangirai had to conduct most of the MDC's foreign relations and make the overseas visits while directing political strategy and organisation back home. Even here, the gaps within the MDC could be seen. Biti was not a supporter of cross-cutting links with dissenting members of ZANU-PF, but Tsvangirai was; Biti was against any political deal that would allow Mugabe any future amnesty in return for a peaceful presidential election in 2002, but Tsvangirai was in favour. In any case, faced with too little technocratic strength and expertise within, some MDC seniors projected the possibility of an MDC cabinet that included ZANU-PF members. Old and occasionally principled opponents of Mugabe within ZANU-PF, such as Zvobgo, could be useful quasi fifth-columnists for the MDC in opposition, and heavyweight cabinet ministers when office was attained. At the very least, idealism and *realpolitik* made uneasy bedfellows within the MDC.

Yet people such as Zvobgo held certain keys. A longtime ZANU-PF baron, with a history of selective public opposition to Mugabe – particularly over press freedom – he had an immense personal following in his home region. If he and a few other dissenting barons, it was felt, sent out the word not to vote for Mugabe in the presidential elections, then their people would not vote for him. It was one thing to ensure a ZANU-PF parliament; it was another thing to ensure the future of this particular ZANU-PF President. To a huge extent, these were all wishful calculations as 2000 progressed – some would have said fanciful – but everywhere in Harare, from township bars to Western embassies, the cut and shape of future governmental cloth was constantly measured in the dream tailoring of a moment when some sort of change seemed nearer than ever. For Zvobgo and his ilk it was a case of ditching a President to save ZANU-PF. The party would still command parliament; it could have ministers in an MDC cabinet; and it could wait out the inevitable fractious unravelling of the all-too-loose MDC, while nurturing its own future president. There could, thereby, be a second coming of ZANU-PF – just as in Eastern Europe somewhat reformed Communist parties had begun reacquiring power. The reverse side of this coin was, of course, that the dissenting party barons were a minority. Many more had nothing to offer the future except as the coat-tail-holders of Robert Mugabe. Ibbo Mandaza's *Mirror* ran a front-page headline, 'Party chiefs preventing Mugabe from quitting',[24] thereby ensuring readership of a somewhat speculative non-story, but also indicating the sense of fluidity and possible bargaining now in the air. For every idealist within the MDC there was a counterpart ready to 'talk business', but it was fantasy business in October 2000. Even so, the mood was such that Tsvangirai, on his foreign travels, urged Southern African governments to press Mugabe to hold early presidential elections. He had begun to be met by ministers in surrounding countries, so was being sized up as to his presidential capacities. And yet he could remain surprisingly naive about international relations. Passing through London on a trip to Scandinavia, he did not know whether or not to meet with the new Commonwealth Secretary General, Don McKinnon,[25] despite the Commonwealth's (admittedly slow and almost ritualistic) capacity to insert election observers even in troubled countries and suspend from membership rogues that had turned against democracy – and thereby send a signal seen by the wider international community. However, Tsvangirai was impressed enough by international events to watch the overthrow of Milosevic on television. He was struck by the images of a peaceful and popular uprising, and the ease with which the Belgrade crowd had simply marched into parliament. He might have been less impressed by the clandestine deals done with the Serbian military immediately afterwards, but as October 2000 dawned Tsvangirai compared Mugabe to Milosevic, and predicted that the fate of one would become the fate of the other, and that if Mugabe was reluctant to leave office the people of Zimbabwe would push him aside.

It was the mistake the Government had been awaiting. Charges of incitement to violence were prepared. Later, these became charges of treason. The Government had two primary motives in pressing charges: the first was, particularly with the treason charge, to besmirch Tsvangirai; the second was the mistaken belief that a criminally convicted person was constitutionally debarred from the presidency. (In fact this is not so, but it was a widely held misconception at the time.)

It would take time for the trial to take place, and the MDC response throughout October, and more sporadically until December, was a series of strikes, boycotts and township protests. The call to protest fell on ready ears, for shortages of fuel and the rising prices of food had caused great resentment in the Harare townships and in cities across the land. These were a show of force on the part of the MDC. The Government's response was also a show of force, with teargas and police beatings once again wheeled into action. In January 2001, suddenly upping the ante dramatically, saboteurs – almost certainly prompted by elements in the Government – blew up the presses of the *Daily News*. Some £1.2 million worth of equipment was destroyed in the 28 January attack (but the paper, using borrowed presses, did not miss a single issue); and in February Mugabe began his attack on the white judges.

The attack on the judges had not come out of a blue sky. To an extent, the judges had bravely attracted the storm clouds. In mid-2000, the

Government had completed its 'fast-track' land acquisition provisions, and these provided some superficial measure of law by which to cover the seizures. Despite law, however, the process remained inherently arbitrary and without process – in that fast-track settlers needed to have no lease, permit or other documentation of land having been assigned them. Moreover, it seemed that the mode of identifying which farms were to be seized was random, as was the means of selecting the new settlers. Under action brought by the Commercial Farmers Union, the Supreme Court ruled, in the closing months of 2000, that the Government, having provided law, had failed to comply with its own law in acquiring land. The judgement was prefaced by an extraordinary political rubric, agreeing that land reform was necessary (when that was not the point of law being contested), and only then judging that it required a proper legal format. If this was a figleaf defence against Government anger towards the court, it gave little protection. The Government was outraged, calls went out for the Chief Justice to resign, the Minister of Justice questioned the desirability of white judges, 'war veterans' stormed the Supreme Court on 24 November 2000, and on 14 December Mugabe himself told a ZANU-PF congress that 'the courts can do what they want. They are not courts for our people and we should not even be defending ourselves in these courts.'[26]

The Government thus began its campaign to force the white judges to resign. First it sought the resignation of the Supreme Court Chief Justice, Anthony Gubbay; then it began piling pressure upon another Supreme Court justice, Nick McNally. However, Gubbay, although at first seeming cooperative, issued a defiant refusal at the end of February 2001. By then, McNally had also refused to resign. Despite their brave but quixotic stands, the judges finally felt no choice but to go. Even then, Mugabe could not rely upon the judges. It was a white High Court judge, James DeVittie, who overturned two constituency results from the previous year's parliamentary elections in April 2001; and in May a black High Court judge, Moses Chinhengo, dismissed the action brought against Tsvangirai for speaking of a people's overthrow of Mugabe, in the manner of the Yugoslav people's overthrow of Milosevic.

In June, Hunzvi died, but the farm seizure programme continued; if anything, it escalated. On 29 June, Mugabe listed a further 2000 farms for seizure, bringing the total to 5200. Only 300 white commercial farms remained ungazetted.[27] At the beginning of July, the Zimbabwe Congress of Trade Unions called a successful national strike over two days. But Mugabe, through it all, held firm. He persevered with the farm programme, unrest was met with increased police beatings and teargas, the 'war veterans' also participated in the repression, Jonathan Moyo began preparing new repressive legislation, and it seemed as if Mugabe was challenging his opponents to step up their pressure – indeed to launch the people's insurrection in the manner of Belgrade – and to accept the consequences. In July, 11 people were killed, 61 disappeared and 288 were tortured in the escalating political violence.[28] Unwilling to risk the prospect of a bloodbath, it was the MDC in this trial of nerve which blinked first. By July 2001, having thrown all its urban strength against Mugabe, an exhausted opposition seemed to have run out of ideas. It did not give up, but, in the standoff, the president seemed still to be holding all his cards and, indeed, more cards than before. He no longer had Hunzvi to contend with, and all he commanded he now commanded alone.

In concluding this section, it is well to recall the progress – over ten years – of the land issue. Britain's intervention at a number of earlier stages of what became a bloody programme may well have reduced both blood and the number of farms seized. This is well to say in retrospect, but in any case here is a review:

First ten years of independence:
   3.3 million hectares of land purchased by the government
1992: Land Acquisition Act
   5.5 million hectares were proposed for purchase, of the 11.5 million hectares owned by white farmers – less than half
1995: still a white Agriculture Minister, Denis Norman
1997: first direct warning from Robert Mugabe to Tony Blair of land acquisition without compensation; numbers of farms used for the first time, rather than hectares; list of 1732 farms for acquisition drawn up
2000, February: first farm invasions occupy 70 farms
2000, April: constitution amendment rushed through parliament to legitimise seizure without compensation
2000, June: 1400 farms occupied; however, only 841 officially designated for acquisition
2001, June: 5200 farms designated for acquisition; only 300 or so white farms not yet designated.

DIPLOMACY AND THE OLD MASTER AT WORK

When the farm invasions began in early 2000, Britain's diplomatic efforts were firmly emphasising the violence and arbitrariness of the seizures. The fledgling opposition was much more concerned with navigating its way through elections and being treated fairly. To be sure, Peter Hain weighed in against the violence directed towards the MDC, but treated both farm violence and electoral violence as two manifestations of the same thing – whereas, as discussed above, the two were not fused from the beginning, and later one was used to cover the other. The farm invasions dominated the diplomatic agenda, to the relative cost of the democracy agenda. Zimbabwe's neighbour South Africa fought hard at first not to be involved in any public way, although there were certainly behind-the-scenes remonstrations and expressions of concern. The regional diplomatic effort soon became one of seeking to persuade Mugabe towards a reasonableness in terms of permitting political expression. Tsvangirai was still an unknown quantity to them, and many Southern African presidents were wary in case the former Zimbabwean trade-union boss should finally prove as limited as his former Zambian counter-part, the lacklustre President Chiluba. Tsvangirai embarked upon regional tours to impress upon all who received him his credentials as an alternative president; and he was received politely, by the second half of 2000 by ministers – not yet by presidents.

Mugabe, however, was an old master of diplomacy. Conscious of the nuances of horse-trading – and having somewhat more to trade than Tsvangirai – he worked the regional presidents tirelessly. His theme was basically that Britain's failure to fund land acquisition, despite its practice of doing so in the 1980s and despite assurances from John Major in the early 1990s, was the real culprit in an issue not so much of nationalisation drawn out of context but of nationalism pure and proper. For the young neighbours, the oldest not much more than 30 years into independent statehood, it was a resonant theme. Britain should, indeed complete a decent legacy and facilitate Zimbabwe's nationalisation – and do so without conditionality. The conditionality attached by Blair and Cook to any suggestion of funds for land compensation was always far too public, 'front-loaded' and ethically ostentatious for regional consumption. Privately, the Southern African presidents urged Mugabe to ensure democratic processes, and privately Mugabe assured them that he would. In public, therefore, the Southern African presidents, in August 2000, called upon Britain to fund land acquisition. Mbeki and Malawi's Bakili Muluzi were deputed to apply pressure to Tony Blair.[29] Later, these same leaders would apply pressure upon Mugabe for failing to honour his pledges to them to ensure proper democratic practice; but the early diplomatic rounds went very much to Mugabe. It took Mbeki until October 2000 to condemn the farm invasions in a strong but very carefully worded lecture to the foreign press corps in South Africa. But this audience had been specially chosen also to ensure a basic caveat was recorded for Western, particularly British, leaders: if Zimbabwe collapsed, Mbeki said, 'we would have to absorb that shock'.[30] In short, even then the MDC was not yet seen as a fully credible alternative government. It was still getting used to parliamentary behaviour. Its ministerial talent was very thinly spread. Tsvangirai looked promising but was, as yet, undeveloped. Mugabe was the only show in town and, while criticising him, the presidents had to ensure that he did not become so weakened that Zimbabwe could not be governed. It was a thin moral line – if morality entered it at all – but it was a political judgement most of all.

Meanwhile the MDC was indeed finding foreign policy hard. Tsvangirai was so pressed to accomplish all the duties he should normally have passed to expert deputies that his time for reflection was limited. Blessed with a sharp mind that could glean the kernel of complex information quickly, he oversaw the MDC by a series of on-the-road decisions. Tactical brilliance, however, is not in itself sufficient substitute for diplomatic strategy, and he took time to understand the full nature of patient international alliance-building – particularly if an international organisation should be, by both bad habit and long tradition, particularly requiring of patience. In one, condensed conversation, Tsvangirai managed to impugn both the UN and the Commonwealth leaderships. On Kofi Annan.

> The UN Secretary-General has had a close association with Mugabe, yes, and I think he has been far too accommodating of the extremes of Mugabe. This is very unfortunate; and I myself have not met Kofi Annan. I regret that people like the Secretary-General forget that Mugabe has been transformed. He is not what history says once he was.

And on the new Commonwealth Secretary General, Don McKinnon:

I'll be in London on the 5th and 6th of November (2000), and I might or might not – I'm not sure – whether I'll see the Commonwealth Secretary-General, Don McKinnon. You know, such men want the best of both worlds. They're unaware of realities on the ground, and think a few passing, choice words will suffice.

Finally, on the 1991 Harare Declaration to do with human rights, a Commonwealth cornerstone and something to which Mugabe – even some two years after his Commonwealth triumph – gave enthusiastic endorsement: 'The Harare Declaration, ah, ha, you know this is the saddest thing about Africa, all these flowery declarations and all without commitment... the declarations are not worth the paper they're written on'. [31] And, in a literal sense, much of what Tsvangirai said was (and is) true. The problems with saying it, however, were two-fold. The first was that, at that point, Tsvangirai had not yet even met Annan or McKinnon, so these were not exactly cordial prelude notes for meeting them. The second was to do with the instrumentality of international relations, when declarations can be made to return to haunt their signatories. The Harare Declaration could have been made into a key whip with which to flog Mugabe – but the British concentrated on land, Tsvangirai concentrated on a quest for international condemnation of Mugabe without giving his interlocutors any strategy, instrumentality or entry point – save that Tsvangirai and the MDC also condemned Mugabe. What alarmed many leaders in those early days was a sense of latent brilliance that could be as parochial as any moment of Mugabe.

By 2001, however, the diplomatic chase had changed very greatly. Jack Straw had succeeded Robin Cook as British Foreign Secretary. Tsvangirai had been well blooded into diplomatic method, and Mugabe had become tiresome (though not fully unconvincing) in his constantly reiterated theme that it was a struggle between a Zimbabwe, pure and free, and a Britain with revanchist overlord tendencies. Moreover, despite taking a terrible beating at the hands of ZANU-PF violence, the MDC emerged still intact and still determined, and very sober and hardheaded. It was now Tsvangirai, not just regional presidents, calling upon Britain to play a softer public game. The key to the future would be in the presidential elections in early 2002 – when Mugabe himself would be on the line. The emphasis now should be ensuring that those elections were held, internationally observed to ensure sufficient freeness and fairness for Tsvangirai to contest them on equal terms, and not to give Mugabe the excuses he might seek to abort those elections, or to ban observers. Throughout the end of 2001 and the early stages of 2002, the discussions were entirely about diplomatic strategy.

Even so, the MDC was still short-staffed on the diplomatic front. It did not send a delegation to the 2001 OAU summit, but it did to the meeting of regional Southern African leaders – 'and it showed. Positively. They isolated [Namibia's] Nujoma, possibly Mugabe's last true ally. No, no mistaking it, the MDC has matured. They're learning to do it.'[32] The learning to do it was still not fully accomplished. In the end, the September 11 attack on New York meant that it was postponed, but in August 2001 the MDC was uncertain whether and how to send a delegation to the October Commonwealth summit in Brisbane, Australia. It was 'probably the case' that Tendai Biti, the shadow foreign minister, would go, 'but Morgan may have to be at an important EU meeting at the same time. If Morgan goes to Brisbane, he'll have to leave early.'[33] And yet it was the Commonwealth that had the greatest leverage to insert election observers – the practice having been started, by ZANU-PF's own admission, by the Commonwealth in Zimbabwe in 1980 – to recount the Harare Declaration to Mugabe's face, and even suspend Zimbabwe from membership, a mild gesture in the sense that it lacked sanction, but a gesture full of symbolism and designation. It would make Zimbabwe a pariah, and the proud Mugabe, used to presidential accolades, equally a pariah. Europe in 2001, would not move without the Commonwealth also moving. The greater meeting would be the Brisbane summit, but in late 2001 the MDC was still constructing itself into, not a fully fledged opposition – it was that – but into a visibly fledged government-in-waiting. It was getting there, but it was not the march into Belgrade for which Tsvangirai had once hoped. But in his patience and endurance, and in his increasing maturity, he was now being taken by presidents and commentators in international relations alike as a prospective government leader. The Tsvangirai of 2002 was not perfect, but had far fewer rough edges – in a way, by making him work so hard Mugabe may have done Tsvangirai a favour – and the MDC had been blooded, very literally so, as well as by way of political metaphor.

COUNTING DOWN TO THE PRESIDENTIAL ELECTIONS

The endgame of the Mugabe presidential term could only be as he had crafted its prelude. It was too late to change tack; indeed, he introduced a few old favourites into his repertoire of political manoeuvres; and he sought to buy time from Britain, the Commonwealth and Europe, by seeming to show reasonableness on the land issue. This he did by joining and then stretching out a negotiating period, by agreeing to what was finally negotiated, a deadline for implementation being among the items negotiated, and then allowing the deadline to lapse without actual implementation; then begging for patience by suggesting that best efforts were indeed being made; then, effectively, making the international community start all over again. This was the tactic used over the so-called agreement crafted by the Nigerians in Abuja, and which was hailed as a breakthrough on the land issue. In fact, all the agreement did was to suggest that the end of violence on the farms would result in some £36 million being forthcoming from Britain to help compensate white farmers. The British had not raised the figure from what they had, for some time, suggested might be forthcoming under various conditions. By itself, £36 million would not compensate very much, and certainly not the land already seized. However, it was billed as a great triumph for Straw, while it was probably more a triumph for his Nigerian counterpart, Sule Lamido. The 'very strong commitment' to the agreement, as Commonwealth Secretary General Don McKinnon put it, from the Zimbabwean side was from Foreign Minister Stan Mudenge.[34] Nevertheless, the 'breakthrough', coming in September 2001, not only suggested (a sudden) agreement after a full 18 months of farm invasions, but an agreement made before powerful Commonwealth representatives – apart from Nigeria: Australia, Canada, Jamaica and Kenya, black nations outnumbering white.

However, for the Zimbabweans a September agreement was tactically important. One month before the then-scheduled Commonwealth summit in Brisbane, it sent a signal designed to defuse calls for suspension of membership; it was also a short enough time to protest goodwill but logistical difficulties in achieving the end to violence. And, as with Nkomo many years before being left with the decision to open contacts with South Africa, Mugabe was conspicuously not heard endorsing the Abuja agreement in public. The Zimbabwean 'climbdown' hailed in the British press had not involved Mugabe at all – except as its tactical instigator. The man who was 'committed' to the agreement was Stan Mudenge. Mugabe did not bring himself to swallow, personally, any bitter pill, but left himself aloof and free enough, having bought time, to do as he wished. An orchestrated diplomatic campaign to have him keep his word, involving strong words from African presidents throughout September, left him shaken but unmoved. Mbeki stormed out of a meeting with Zimbabwean leaders on 11 September. The farm programme, with its violence, continued.

By October, Mugabe was giving speeches about a return to socialism, and espousing a revolutionary rhetoric from decades before. He fended off both EU and Commonwealth calls for an end to violence; Europe began talking of sanctions as Mugabe began talking of socialism. In November, Mugabe began playing the election-observers card in earnest – threatening to prevent independent local observers from monitoring the presidential elections – and sending signals that EU observers might also be banned. Month by month, Mugabe cranked up the gears towards repression domestically and defiance internationally. New laws to curtail expression and dissent were signalled in November – although these were not to have an automatic ride through parliament – and the same month saw Mugabe begin a campaign against foreign journalists in Zimbabwe. In the wake of September 11, and President Bush's war against terrorism, Mugabe appropriated the discourse to say that he too was warring against terrorists from Britain. In December, a Supreme Court by now packed with Mugabe appointments declared the land seizures legal. Army commanders uttered noises to suggest a full military backing for Mugabe, and in January 2002 Mugabe began to have the new laws of repression piloted through parliament. These are discussed below. He also stepped up recruitment for a youth brigade, and this also is discussed below. Europe, the Commonwealth and regional presidents were, month by month, stunned by a new barrage of initiatives from Mugabe. Each upping of the ante made a return to an earlier, less extreme position seem a diplomatic goal – but that earlier position was now just one stage of a succession of escalations that had, some stages before, left the realm of the reasonable.

THE YOUTH BRIGADES

The rescusitation of the idea of youth brigades – mobilised youth to be given both employment skills and political indoctrination – was owed to Mugabe's Employment Minister, Border Gezi – after Hunzvi, a key protagonist and organiser of the farm invasions. Recruited from rural villages by the military, the inducement was not only a degree of training but possible military careers for the best of the recruits. Like the Malawian Young Pioneers of two to three decades earlier, however, they were also trained and used as political saboteurs and agents of petty terror (only in Malawi they were also used as agents of mass murder). A training camp was named after Border Gezi, a faithful Mugabe lieutenant, and the virtue of the youth brigades was not even having to pretend any more that they were war veterans. Not only that, training could make them even more effective than the often ramshackle 'veterans'. The youths were trained and deployed in groups of 50, and the training was designed to inculcate a bond within each group. They became agents of violence and intimidation, a militia for ZANU-PF, and the militia was meant to have a multiplier effect – each group training further groups. They were, moreover, taught to handle small arms.

Yet, however instrumental on behalf of Mugabe and ZANU-PF, they indicated two things: the first was that Mugabe was still adding, as constantly as before, new ingredients into the violent electoral mix – always something new to keep his opponents and critics off guard; the second was that this was hardly new at all, but Mugabe turning a circle, returning, as with his renewed calls to socialism, to an earlier epoch. It would be fitting to apply the answer from Oedipus to the sphinx here: a creature who begins in youth crawling, who walks at midday upright and proud, but who declines in twilight in a crouch and a crawl just like the original child. But this was not a decline into helpless old age. This was a vigorous, if old, man; and even if he was turning a circle, it was to renew – not relive nostalgically – his roots; and these roots were to create a new country, freed from Britain and white settlers, populated by new Zimbabweans. It was not Mao's cultural revolution, but it was violently and ruthlessly romantic enough: to think that the entire world could be defied, a lone President holding out, enemies without and within, and thinking that he alone carried Zimbabwe within his veins.

And, although Teurai Ropa had now metamorphosed into Joyce Mujuru and was, once again, a senior ZANU-PF personality, she was no longer involved, but the youth brigades of late 2001 and 2002 were trained, if need be, also to spill blood.

THE NEW LEGISLATION

In January 2002, Mugabe called presidential elections for 9 to 10 March. Simultaneously, he introduced three new bills to parliament. By now, court judgements had overturned sufficient results from the June 2000 parliamentary elections for ZANU-PF and the opposition to hold equal numbers of elected seats. The ZANU-PF majority was entirely composed of Mugabe's 30 appointed MPs. These were easily enough to ensure passage of the bills – provided all the ZANU-PF MPs remained loyal and were not inconveniently absent on the days of voting. For many in the party considered the new bills steps too far, and the ZANU-PF whips were to be busy in the weeks ahead. The bills were to do with access to information, whereby foreign journalists were banned and local journalists had to be registered; public order and security, whereby the police were given huge powers, and it became illegal to speak in hostile or abusive terms of the President; and electoral amendments, whereby registration to vote became harder, local, independent election observers were banned, and foreign observers were limited. Mugabe also amended the labour-relations act, banning strikes without government approval.

The bills – with the exception of the access to information, or press bill – were passed on 10 January. The MDC's Tendai Biti spoke of them savagely and bitterly: 'We are going to challenge this package of fascist rules in the courts. They are trying to clothe fascism with this whole set of bills.'[35] Meanwhile, Mugabe stepped up the redistribution of farms seized. In the first week of January, 1000 families received their new farms. However, inflation was running at 100 per cent and there were shortages of every staple food and commodity. The regional presidents cautioned Mugabe: Malawi's Muluzi pointed out that a clean election involved not only the days of polling – thus nailing Mugabe's hitherto narrow band of respect for elections – and Mozambique's Chissano chastised the Zimbabwean military for its talk of support for Mugabe. Mbeki, however, was showing signs of frustration, not just with Mugabe but with

Britain's diplomatic pressure upon South Africa to take a tougher line against Zimbabwe. He was reported as feeling unfairly landed with a problem largely of Britain's making.[36] Nevertheless, he was hardly happy with Mugabe either.

Alone, the press bill – probably the most controversial – had not passed into law. Harare resounded to rumours that ZANU-PF MPs were refusing to appear in parliament for the vote. In the third week of January, if the bill had been put to the vote on any day, ZANU-PF would have been defeated. In the final week of January, the bill was reintroduced to parliament, with a handful of minor changes. Its effect would still, however, be the same. The parliamentary boycott of the previous week had been led by Zvobgo, long a champion of a free press, and critic of Mugabe over this issue more than a decade earlier. Moreover, he was one of the ZANU-PF barons with whom members of the MDC thought they could work. So far, Zvobgo had remained loyal to ZANU-PF, but not slavishly so. As early as September 2000, he had launched a stinging attack on Mugabe's farm acquisition programme, with the by now famous and condescending words, 'We have tainted what was a glorious revolution, reducing it to some agrarian racist enterprise'. Now, true to his record, he again delayed the bill, launching a list of accusations against the Justice Minister and provoking sufficient mayhem to force parliament to adjourn.

He could not delay the march of repression, however. Having been passed by parliament, the President signed into law the public order bill on 23 January. The new law made it almost impossible for the opposition to hold rallies and demonstrations without police approval – and this was going to be difficult to obtain. The press bill finally received parliamentary assent on the last day of January. Zvobgo gave up the parliamentary battle with caustic words, calling the bill 'the most calculated and determined assault on our liberties guaranteed by the constitution'. And he singled out the bill's author, Moyo, as having given himself 'frightening powers'.[37] Meanwhile, as both Europe and the Commonwealth began to discuss 'smart' sanctions, targeted upon Mugabe and his most senior lieutenants, the name of Moyo was included in their list. On 4 February, the first journalist was arrested under the new laws, for having led an unauthorised demonstration in favour of press freedom. In that demonstration, reporters carried placards with the words 'Zvobgo was right'. Somehow, the parliamentary tactician of the occasion had not been a member of the MDC, but a baron of ZANU-PF.

If possible coalition lines for the future were being pencilled in, the election battlelines were drawn in indelible ink. At his very first campaign rally, Mugabe attacked Tsvangirai as a 'puppet of Britain'.[38] Blair's government was not only colonial, but unnaturally stuffed with gay and lesbian ministers who were forced to marry each other. Clearly, the same themes of colonialism, and the MDC being colonial stooges, were to be constants – but with shrill abuse thrown in. Tsvangirai, for his part, opened his campaign by, effectively, challenging the military leaders – with their fat bankrolls in Congo, their payoff from Mugabe, and their warnings that only a Mugabe presidency would gain their support. He said, point-blank, that he would sack them.[39] In the past, this would have been an ill-considered and extemporaneous act of bravado. After all, Mozambique's Chissano had already chastised the Zimbabwean generals. The new Tsvangirai, however, was making several points: one was indeed to the regional presidents and the international community, demanding that they keep their attention on the Zimbabwean generals; the second was a domestic declaration. In the referendum, the military rank-and-file had voted overwhelmingly against Mugabe's constitution. The rank-and-file, who had to do the fighting, had not been enriched by the Congo war. It was a call to them, not only to vote for Tsvangirai but to protect him as well. In a way, the battlelines were literal; not without fifth columns however: much Harare opinion talked of contacts between the MDC and very senior officers.

Mugabe had prepared for this election since the MDC ran ZANU-PF close in the parliamentary contest of June 2000. The farm issue had been calculated so that if Britain had cooperated Mugabe could have proclaimed himself the great victor over colonialism, and if Britain had not cooperated he could proclaim that his opponents were the stooges of colonialism. In this calculation, it was a win–win foundation for a President who wanted to win the presidential elections. The only problem was that it had been no more than an 'agrarian racist enterprise', a small-ness in the face of the world. Its umbrella protectors were repressive laws, thugs in youth brigades and masquerading as war veterans, and a military leadership engorged with their ransack of a country belonging to others. Ironically, Tony Blair himself had supported the early stages of Zimbabwe's Congo adventure, insisting on the sale of arms to the Zimbabwean airforce. All this was quickly to become merely an enterprise of looting, home and abroad, and this was a shadow – even if a shadow turning circles – of what Mugabe had once been. Even that once being carried his own internal shadows, as the next chapter suggests.

NOTES ON CHAPTER 9

1   *Guardian* (London), 3 March 2000.
2   *Guardian*, 20 April 2000.
3   *Herald* (Harare), 8 April 2000.
4   New Zealand High Commissioner to the author, Harare, October 2000.
5   *Observer* (London), 2 April 2000.
6   Ibid.; *Guardian*, 31 March 2000.
7   *Guardian*, 6 April 2000.
8   *Standard* (Harare), 19–25 March 2000.
9   *Herald*, 20 April 2000.
10 I should at this stage declare a debt to papers presented at the conference 'Crisis in Zimbabwe: A Time to Act', Harare, 3 August 2001, especially that authored by Sternford Moyo. Newspaper reportage, both in Britain and Zimbabwe, does not always master legal detail and nuance in the way that longer papers can. I thank John Makumbe for providing me with his own copies of these papers.
11 *Guardian*, 20 April 2000.
12 *Independent on Sunday* (London), 30 April 2000.
13 *Observer*, 30 April 2000.
14 *Guardian*, 4 May 2000.
15 *Guardian*, 11 May 2000.
16 *Guardian*, 13 May 2000.
17 *Independent on Sunday*, 21 May 2000.
18 *Guardian*, 28 June 2000.
19 Andries Matenda Rukobo, 'Misplaced Emphasis in the Democracy Debate', in Ibbo Mandaza and Lloyd Sachikonye (eds), *The One Party State and Democracy: The Zimbabwe Debate*, Harare: SAPES, 1991, pp. 130–31.
20 Jonathan Moyo, 'Politicians look at issues with open mouths and shut minds', *Daily News*, 24 October 2000; first published in *Parade* (Harare), January 1977.
21 See the cartoon in the *Daily News*, 23 October 2000.
22 Brian Raftopoulos, *Beyond the House of Hunger: The Struggle for Democratic Development in Zimbabwe*, Harare: Zimbabwe Institute of Development Studies, Working Paper 17, 1991.
23 Foe example John Makumbe and Daniel Compagnon, *Behind the Smokescreen: The Politics of Zimbabwe's 1995 General Elections*, Harare: University of Zimbabwe Publications, 2000.
24 *Mirror* (Harare), 20–26 October 2000.
25 Morgan Tsvangirai to the author, Harare, October 2000.
26 Cited in Sternford Moyo, op. cit.

27   *Times* (London), 30 June 2000; these figures vary from those in the *Guardian*, 4 July 2000, which suggested that an additional 1400 farms had been gazetted, but still agreeing on a total of 5000, while indicating a residual 500 farms not yet listed.

28   *Guardian*, 20 August 2001.

29   *Guardian*, 9 August 2000.

30   *Times*, 26 October 2000.

31   Morgan Tsvangirai to the author, Harare, October 2000.

32   British diplomatic source to the author, Harare, August 2001.

33   Tendai Biti to the author, August 2001.

34   *Guardian*, 7 September 2001.

35   *Guardian*, 11 January 2002.

36   *Guardian*, 15 January 2002.

37   *Guardian*, 1 February 2002.

38   *Guardian*, 2 February 2002.

39   *Guardian*, 4 February 2002.

TEN

Mugabe's Path of Discomforts: Three – Ghosts and Spectres

People were always having parties. There was excitement in the air. Independence. People getting new jobs. Moving into new houses. Getting married. Showing off. And everybody was young. Optimistic twenties. Now we are in our forties. We have children. We are tired of our jobs. Stuck with mortgages. Tired of our wives. Tired of our families. Plagued by ESAP and AIDS and bad government and fatigued political vision and traditions gone awry.

Shimmer Chinodya
Can We Talk and Other Stories[1]

There has been a long and vibrant cultural tradition in Zimbabwe. By that I mean that authors, musicians and sculptors have, in particular, produced works of beauty and meaning. Harare has had thriving publishing houses – although they have had harder times of late – a recording industry, and Shona stone sculpture was a revelation to the international art world after independence. Slightly clichéd now, the sculptures nevertheless depict a spirit trying to emerge from stone. And recorded song was always an avenue of protest. Sung in vernacular languages, the Rhodesian authorities often did not know that the chart-topping discs of Oliver Mtukudzi and, particularly, Thomas Mapfumo, were songs of defiance. Mapfumo became known as the King of Chimurenga, king of the liberation war, and the Guru of Chimurenga.

There are internationally renowned authors in Zimbabwe: Shimmer Chinodya, whose work is quoted above, Chenjerai Hove, Charles Mungoshi, the female writers Tsitsi Dangarembga and Yvonne Vera; this book has several times quoted from Alexander Kanengoni, whom I hold to be an underestimated and strikingly powerful writer; and, of course, there is the late Dambudzo Marechera, around whom a sometimes facile scholarly industry has grown, but whose work struck a chord in the academic writings of concerned Zimbabweans, and whose novella, The *House of Hunger*,[2] gave them a metaphor to describe what Zimbabwe had become. I want, however, to begin this brief chapter by touching upon a difficult and little-appreciated aspect of Marechera's life.

Marechera died young in 1987. He was only 32, and died of AIDS. He at least did not have to endure too much ESAP, but he died in poverty, a deeply disturbed young man who, despite his brilliance, managed to get sent down from Oxford. David Caute wrote a brief and moving memoir of him,[3] and this helped to establish his vogue. The person who has done more than anyone, both to help Marechera in his illness and to insist that the world read him, is the German scholar Flora Veit-Wild.[4] It is in her writings that we glean a biographical knowledge not readily amenable to Western sensibilities. The newly arisen Marechera industry celebrates him not only for his rejection of tired African heroes and his seeming political refusal of the state, but for his post-modernity: a fractured author of fractured writing, stammering in his speech and abandoning grammar in his writing; psychologically at odds with himself and politically alienated from Zimbabwe. What the industry does not deeply investigate is the spiritual cause of fracture within the delicate being of Marechera. Possessed of a spirit, Marechera's mother relieved herself of it by having it ritually transferred to Marechera. The young author never forgave her. He could not cleanse himself of the transferred spirit. It hung within him, and suspended his mental balance in its own esoteric scales.

To take this at face value in a book on Robert Mugabe's political history might seem to inject the gratuitously esoteric. However, as Terence Ranger, Jocelyn Alexander and other authors cited earlier have been at pains to point out, spiritual endorsement of the liberation struggle was vital to the guerillas, both as a link to the rural people who helped protect their whereabouts and as a validation of themselves who were at risk of being killed. Recent Africanist scholarship has come to insist upon the foundational importance of spiritual linkages with the everyday workings of Africa, and to say that Africa cannot be otherwise understood.[5]

There is a further dimension to spiritual validation of those about to die, and that is to do with spiritual cleansing of those who have killed. To resist cleansing is to refuse to end war. To resist cleansing is to carry war within you, and to be warring forever with those whom you have killed. The deeply sympathetic work of the anthropologist Pamela Reynolds deals with the importance of ritual cleansing and healing.[6] The importance and form of this cleansing constitutes the climax of Alexander Kanengoni's novel *Echoing Silences*,[7] which I have quoted from earlier. The main character of the novel, Munashe, has been a guerilla during the liberation war, and had been forced to commit atrocities. For the rest of his life, even after the end of the war, Munashe can find no peace. A spirit haunts him and makes life unbearable for him. Kanengoni tells none of this simplistically. His horrors of war are stark and moving, as are Munashe's memories of war and atrocity. The ceremony of cleansing – which leaves Munashe dead, the only way left to release so powerful a spirit we might call guilt – is superb writing. But Munashe, after his death, enters a heaven where the heroes and heroines of the liberation remain anguished about what has happened to their legacy. They condemn the political leadership of Zimbabwe, and accuse it of having betrayed its original impulses, of having become impure.

It is the idea of the impurity of Mugabe that haunts much of contemporary Zimbabwean history. He has never apologised for the atrocities in the Matabelelands, and thus has not begun to cleanse himself of the deaths caused in the 1980s. He has not allowed the true veterans of the liberation war to undergo any state-blessed cleansing for the blood shed during the *chimurenga*. And before the *chimurenga* was successful there were the assassinations of ZANU leaders Herbert Chitepo and Josiah Tongogara. There are streets named after these two in Harare today; but many still suspect Mugabe of involvement in these killings – certainly of Tongogara, the popular military leader who would share the risks of his soldiers. Of his death Mugabe has not been cleansed.

In fact, by refusing to allow the *chimurenga* to die, by resurrecting its name and blessing the 'war veterans' of 2000 to 2002, by continuing the war in this way, Mugabe has indicated that there can never be cleansing because there cannot be an end to fighting, and that for him to fight is more important than to be cleansed.

All this of course sounds, and may actually be, fanciful. However, Harare gossip has its psychological as well as political nuances. In April 2001, the Employment Minister, Border Gezi – the latter-day planner of farm invasions and youth brigades – was killed in a car accident. In May

2001, Defence Minister, Moven Mahachi – who in 1975 helped Mugabe escape to Mozambique, supported Mugabe's Congo war, and in more recent times ordered the military arrest and torture of journalists – also died in a car crash. The deaths, by the same means, so close together, of two key architects of Mugabe's new millennium repression of Zimbabwe stunned both ZANU-PF and the President. Senior ZANU-PF figures were heard talking aloud about the withdrawal of spiritual blessing from their cause. For some time, the mood in Government circles was apocalyptic. It was said that since the parliamentary elections in 2000, with the upsurge of the MDC, Mugabe had been having premonitions, and that Grace's disenchantment with her husband dated from this time. It was said that Mugabe had been seeing a psychiatrist, a certain Dr Vlad Rankovic (a Serbian, adding colour certainly to Tsvangirai's comparison of Mugabe with Milosevic), had been prescribed anti-depressants, had not sought help from the Catholic church, but had become increasingly Shona in his superstitions. Of these, the primary source of grief was the haunting of Mugabe by the ghost of Tongogara. Mugabe sought to placate the ghost by laying a place for him at dinner every night. Tongogara, the theory went, having died in a car crash, had re-entered Mugabe's life via the car crashes of his two ministerial lieutenants. The angry ghost who died in bitterness, and who died at Mugabe's uncleansed hands, would have, Shona belief suggests, easy access to the mind of his murderer. The ghost, or *ngozi*, who is aggrieved can only be placated by a redressing of his grievance. Something must be paid. That which is paid must be symbolic and symmetrical with the cause of offence. No cleansing is possible until the price is paid.

In a way, the books of Zimbabwean authors have been pointing to this confluence of psychological guilt and political destabilisation. If not impure, the country has grown middle-aged and disillusioned, tired of the same old struggle – perhaps tired of the same old men haunting the welfare of the state. In 2000, the most popular song in Zimbabwe was by Oliver Mtukudzi. It was top of the charts. It could be heard sung all over town, and it was sung at MDC rallies. It was from the album *Bvuma*, and the title of its hit song was translated as 'tolerance'. And, at first hearing, the Shona lyrics of the first track, the hit song, suggest tolerance – that the old come naturally to tolerance. The song has double meanings, however, and here the old *chimurenga* trick of rousing the population without the authorities being able to point a finger is replayed. The lyrics seem to suggest, gently, that the old should tolerate the young, since age means that there are many things that can no longer be done. I am told, however, that the verb forms used are the imperative, and that the true translation of the key refrain of the song should be 'stand down' or 'retire'.

The song also artfully makes the point that even those who are old and 'mature' are but children to be played with in the eyes of God. It is, the psychological gossip in Harare says, Mugabe's presidential State House – the one whose street cannot be entered at night – that is truly the God-forsaken *House of Hunger* now.

NOTES ON CHAPTER 10

1   Harare: Baobab, 1998, p. 103.
2   Oxford: Heinemann, 1978.
3   David Caute, 'Marechera in Black and White', in Preben Kaarsholm (ed.), *Culture and Development in Southern Africa*, London: James Currey, 1991
4   Flora Veit-Wild, *Dambudzo Marechera: A Source Book on his Life and Work*, London: Hans Zell, 1992; Veit-Wild and Anthony Chennells (eds), *Emerging Perspectives on Dambudzo Marechera*, Trenton: Africa World Press, 1999.
5   Patrick Chabal and Jean Pascal Daloz, *Africa Works: Disorder as Political Instrument*, Oxford: James Currey, 1999.
6   Pamela Reynolds, *Traditional Healers and Childhood in Zimbabwe*, Athens, OH: Ohio University Press, 1996.
7   Harare: Baobab, 1997.

ELEVEN

Elections 2002

The Book Cafe, upstairs in the Fife Avenue shopping centre, is not far from downtown Harare, and just around the corner from the beautiful gardens of the Bronte Hotel. Yet not many tourists go there – just off the beaten track and, for that reason, a place of refuge and intellectual recreation for the beleaguered liberal community of black and white Harare. There is sometimes music and poetry; there is a good bookshop with titles from the local presses – Weaver, Baobab – drinkable coffee, atrocious pasta (no one can make a good pasta in Harare), and rudimentary mixes of alcohol. Set on a large, partially enclosed terrace, it is the perfect location for cafe society, African-style. Harare is not all dusty townships and luxury high-rises – often the city pads of what were farmers – and the Book Cafe, for all its potential for self-satire and irony, is some sort of middle-ground. It is not just the liberal community that hangs out there. Central Intelligence officers do too – but some of them actually seem to enjoy the atmosphere, and eavesdropping is casual.

The majority of the denizens of the Book Cafe still have their siege humour intact – and reinforced – and now the jokes in February 2002, the presidential elections looming in March, are of how ridiculous the President looked on state television as, celebrating his seventy-eighth birthday he affected a romp across a stadium field, showing off his vigour to an election rally, waving balloons and wearing the sort of self-praise shirt, with portrait and slogans, that went out of fashion with Hastings

Banda and Kenneth Kaunda. That is an irony that seems to have escaped Mugabe: that the last authoritarian presidents who wore such shirts, advertising themselves and their self-profession of virtues, were overthrown in elections.

But he is astoundingly vigorous for 78. His campaign schedule is hectic – so that this election is an altogether weird combination of intimidation and 'normal' election rallies. Well, normal for the President anyway. The opposition rallies are triumphs of courage. If not beaten or teargassed on the way, those who reach the rally wait until they are safely inside the stadium before taking out, and putting on, the MDC T-shirt. It carries a giant open hand. It says 'halt' to Mugabe. Inside the stadium, the MDC supporters wave red cards – football's indication of a sending-off. Mugabe is being, they hope, sent off. All the emblems of the campaign are ones of vigour, and Mugabe is trying to sell himself, at 78, as the repository of vigour and wisdom that will take the nation forward. He runs across fields. He eats birthday cakes while famine begins to enter the land without working farms.

And, as he does these things, his lieutenants plot murder and mayhem; and if ever there were conversations on surrealism at the Book Cafe they are taking place now. Only many of the customers there have themselves bravely gone to the MDC rallies, have campaigned at least a little. They can say that they have done something; but it is in the townships and rural areas that the real beatings and serious intimidation take place. Here, the election will be won or lost – and this is a world away from the Book Cafe, but perhaps the two worlds might be successfully united by the desire for change. The days ahead would tell.

PURITIES AND IMPURITIES

Ever since Peter Hain and Robin Cook's time, both Tony Blair and the British media have been unrelenting in their castigation of Mugabe. There was much with which to castigate him, but not all who supported him have been intimidated or bribed to do so. In that sense, there was a real election campaign amidst the surrealism, and there were many in Zimbabwe who believed that, whatever his methods, Mugabe had been empowering of them. The spectre of colonialism is still great in Africa. Huge numbers of those voting remember vividly the days when a white man was, by definition – legal and political definition – greater than any black. The more Blair castigated Mugabe, the more Mugabe built such attacks into his campaign platform.

There were tiny exceptions in the British media's acceptance of their cue from Blair. Seumas Milne lamented that the media 'has now abandoned even a veneer of even-handedness, as reporters and presenters have become cheerleaders for the opposition MDC'.[1] Perhaps this was the British fondness for the underdog, and Tsvangirai was relentless in portraying himself, internationally, as such. It was probably more, however, a certain parochiality in both British leadership and journalism. Allied to Blair's sense of certainty, and the hectoring that comes from it, the castigations and condemnations flew fast and stuck fast. At the March 2002 Commonwealth summit in Brisbane – of which more below – African Commonwealth leaders despaired of Blair. It was not that they supported Mugabe. Many despised him. Obasanjo of Nigeria and Mbeki of South Africa had had promises broken by him. But Mbeki, in particular, thought the Zimbabwean problem was something gravely exacerbated by British, Blair-led maladroitness. He was too diplomatic to say so in public. Blair had no such reservations about criticising his African colleagues. The *Guardian* editorialised that Blair had made 'an embarrassing mess' in Brisbane, and lamented the sidelining of Foreign Secretary Jack Straw – effectively accusing Blair of grandstanding and extemporising foreign policy.[2]

But Tsvangirai was not pure either. In the dirty world of Zimbabwean politics, he too had cut and chased, made deals and contemplated the undemocratic and unlawful. The infamous video that purported to catch him plotting Mugabe's assassination is discussed below; but, quite apart from ZANU-PF's attempts to besmirch him, and quite apart from his own tactical mistakes along the way, Tsvangirai had put out his feelers to key members of the armed forces, dissident barons in ZANU-PF, and even to the 'war veterans' who had spearheaded Mugabe's land seizures – of which the British premier and media had made so much. In fact, Tsvangirai was probably successful enough in his overtures to the veterans that, even though they never ceased to squat on the farms, they were no longer completely reliable from Mugabe's point of view. The advent and spectacular growth of the youth brigades or militia – nicknamed 'green bombers' because of their uniforms and their resemblance to a ubiquitous species of fly that feeds on faeces – is partly a tribute to the MDC's courtship of the veterans. Tsvangirai promised that he would require the veterans to leave the farms – and even they would have known that if they didn't leave agricultural production could not be restored – but this was a pact with the very people called devils by the British.

Mugabe at least didn't wear fly-green fatigues on the hustings. But he sported a white baseball cap bearing the legend, 'Land for Economic Empowerment'. He wore a red armband with the slogan, 'Total Independence and Liberty'; and his garish shirt was adorned with portraits of himself – slightly younger, slightly more dignified. The leaflets strewn in his wake carried his portrait again, and the legend, 'He has done all these things for you', meaning that he had suffered the slings and outrageous arrows of British and European attack for the sake of a truly free Zimbabwe. He referred constantly to Tsvangirai as Tsvangison – as a black man who was truly white, and truly an agent of a Britain seeking re-entry to Zimbabwe as its colonial master.

Tsvangirai, by contrast, constantly wore a suit, seeking to exude presidentialism, and talked of a post-election Zimbabwe of reconstruction and respect for the institutions of good government and governance. The MDC policies were judicious and plain-spoken: among them, that the land occupations had not only to end but be reversed so that white farmers could resume food production for an increasingly hungry nation; and that with this reversion to an older order a new order could be more systematically and fairly implemented. These were bold policies in a land of stark symbolisms. Moreover, it was clear that Tsvangirai would have to depend heavily on foreign help to accomplish all he said – and the ZANU-PF heartland was not slow to point this out.

As for that ZANU-PF heartland, it was not merely lulled into rhetoric about a third and final *chimurenga* (this was the youth brigades' motto), it believed in Mugabe's Mao-like writing of an historical moment at which, not just in Zimbabwe but internationally, political upheavals were possible, and that, however rudely and ruthlessly, new destinies were being forged. Mugabe's autarky was not alone in the world, and in this changing world self-empowerment was the dominant theme. Tsvangirai depended on the old world order. Mugabe was somehow going beyond this. In the swirl of the campaign, a Zimbabwean election was also somehow an international one – and the attention of the world was evidence of this. Resisting the demands of the old world, the imposition of their observers, was not just an election stratagem, it was a form of election promise, a policy. In this view of events, ZANU-PF campaigners were the ones who saw themselves as pure – while the British were painting only the MDC as pure. The pure, however, were capable of committing many impurities.

AUSTRALIA: VIDEO PRELUDE TO A SUMMIT

The ZANU-PF strategy was not confined to a campaign within Zimbabwe. It took very much into account that the Commonwealth summit, postponed in the wake of September 11, would take place in Australia just a week before the elections. Mugabe counted, of course, on the summit's proximity to the elections making it, effectively unable to steer him away from his course. Before the summit's original date, as described earlier, he had allowed promises to be made in Abuja, Nigeria, in front of Commonwealth grandees, in order to defuse criticism then. Before March in Brisbane, however, he added further ingredients to his recipe for keeping his critics constantly on their heels. If they were constantly having to defend themselves or, more beneficially, from Mugabe's standpoint, having to defend Tsvangirai, they would have less time to attack him.

As a prelude to the 1996 presidential campaign, Mugabe had accused his rival, Sithole, of plotting to assassinate him. If, before Brisbane, he tried a similar tactic with respect to Tsvangirai it was by much more sophisticated means (even if technically flawed ones). There might be resort to old tactics – but with new instrumentalities. Accordingly, on 13 February 2002, Australian television broadcast a video that seemed to portray Tsvangirai plotting to 'eliminate' Mugabe. The joins in an obviously assembled video were highly visible. Nevertheless, it was clear that, in one context if not another, Tsvangirai had got himself involved in a discussion about the desirability of Mugabe's death. This, it might be said, is a common fantasy in Zimbabwe. Even ZANU-PF barons have mused on the easier nature of life without the old man. MDC circles have wishfully projected this same scenario in their own private conversations. It has almost certainly been the subject of at least casual conversation between second-rank MDC figures and junior army officers. It would be quick, clean – a coalition transitional government leading to free elections, populated by relieved figures on both sides, could be engineered, and a post-election coalition cabinet appointed, saving everybody a lot of trouble. It would be itself undemocratic, but in the greater service of the nation.

Only after 25 February, when Tsvangirai was charged with treason (but later released) on account of this video, did the British leap to his defence. Jack Straw called the arrest 'yet another attempt by the Mugabe regime to obstruct the conduct of the election'.[3] Tony Blair called the affair 'deeply suspect'.[4] Yet neither Straw nor Blair had actually seen the full video, and the Australian journalist in whose programme the video appeared, the award-winning Mark Davis, staunchly defended his broadcast. 'We have not manipulated a single word or a single sentence'.[5]

Indeed, Davis had probably not. The MDC had hired a Canadian lobbying firm to represent its north American interests. One of its principals, Ari Ben-Manashe, subsequently turned out to be working for Mugabe. It was he who had made the video and provided it to Davis. So this had the hallmarks of a 'sting'. There are, however, two deeply troublesome aspects to the affair that the British Prime Minister and Foreign Secretary swept aside. The first is, obviously, to do with the adroitness of a potential president in talking, at length, about his rival's 'elimination'. The second is that Ben Manashe's lobbying firm, Dickens and Madson, has been heavily involved in Africa's war-diamond trade – the very trade from which Mugabe's generals have profited in Congo. Was Tsvangirai using Dickens and Madson to craft a deal with these very generals? If so, what residual diamond corruptions might have been cut into any proposed deals? This, in itself, never mind fantasies of assassination, cannot echo the finer rudiments of democracy. As it turned out, the revelations of the video seemed to be no more than just another sideshow in the heated Zimbabwean election campaign. Its object, however, was to elicit just the sort of response with which Blair and Straw obliged Mugabe. Even a putative assassin, Mugabe could say, will be instantly defended by his masters. And if Tsvangirai was learning fast how to appear and act in a presidential manner, then the rough diamond he had been (the tape had been made in mid-2001) could return to haunt him. Mugabe could now also say, without too much direct reference at all to the actual contents of the video, that his opponent lacked 'experience'. To the ZANU-PF repertoire of campaign slogans came one to do with Mugabe's great experience and wisdom.

AUSTRALIA: THE SUMMIT

At the Commonwealth summit in Lusaka in 1979 the vexed question of how to deal with Rhodesia, and its possibility as Zimbabwe, threatened to divide the assembled leaders and damage the Commonwealth. Careful staging of the agenda, accomplished by Commonwealth Secretary General Shridath Ramphal and summit chairman Kenneth Kaunda kept the issue from even surfacing until the third day. Even then, the real discussions and decisions took place out of session, as the British were first marginalised, then courted, then converted – in such a way that they believed it had all been their own idea. In Brisbane in 2002 no such skills were forthcoming from Commonwealth leaders, and no such flexibility was forthcoming from Blair. More obdurate and didactic than Thatcher, less accommodating of his own Foreign Secretary than Thatcher was of Carrington, he cut a figure – although he didn't know it – of earnest, depth-free arrogance.

Despite the British media reports of a split over Zimbabwe – which dominated the agenda from day one – it is incorrect to typecast it as one along racial lines. The Caribbean, Asian and Pacific states voted on either side of the split. The African leaders, however, unanimously rejected the idea of suspending Zimbabwe's Commonwealth membership – until after the elections, in a single week's time from the summit, in the event that the elections were found, by the Commonwealth's own observers, to have been unfair. As described above, it was these very leaders to whom Mugabe had lied. It was South Africa to which Zimbabwean political refugees were escaping. It was the failure of Zimbabwe's food production, occasioned by drought but to a large extent by the farm invasions, that was throwing regional food planning into disarray. It was the very farm invasions in Zimbabwe, briefly mimicked in parts of South Africa, that raised Mbeki's fears of economic chaos in his own rural areas. In short, no country had suffered more from Mugabe's policies than South Africa, and no leaders had been lied to more earnestly and directly than the ones Blair now sought both to lecture privately and, in a barely restrained way, impugn publicly. Carrington, on behalf of Thatcher, and Major would have made a show of listening to those most affected.

The African leaders had both reasonable and unreasonable motivations. Unreasonable since, not far below the surface of fine words, they too were custodians of imperfect democracies – some more imperfect than others – and their latest colleague, the very recently-elected Levy Mwanawasa of Zambia, probably owed his place to a tainted election. Now the last thing they sought was a British premier laying down guidelines and precedents as to which of them might, in future, sit beside him. To that extent, once again, Blair's deconstruction of Mugabe acted against him. More than one African president was heard to mutter the words 'Northern Ireland', whenever the imperfections of their democracies were implied. Not all, but many of them were trying hard – and lectures on democratic theory were not what they wanted to hear.

More reasonably, they were very aware that the Zimbabwean elections were only a week away. EU observers had already left in dudgeon. Commonwealth observers needed, they felt, to be kept in place – both to help ensure some fairness in the voting process, and to report back to them. That there should be no suspension until all of the evidence was available was their own approach. Contributing to that was their feeling that, as in the past, the actual days of polling might, in themselves, pass peacefully and fairly. The Zimbabwean Foreign Minister, Stan Mudenge, represented Mugabe at Brisbane. He was well known to exactly those Commonwealth leaders, to whom, through Mudenge, Mugabe had lied at Abuja in September 2001. They felt a little sorry for him. In their private discussions, Mudenge seems to have assured them that if Tsvangirai won there was a real chance that the results of the election would be respected.

The MDC representative in Brisbane was upset about the decision to delay a possible suspension, and upset that the possibility of sanctions would also thereby be delayed. However, the MDC had itself dithered for weeks as to whether or not it wanted EU and Commonwealth observers in place, or sanctions and suspension immediately. It could not have both, since sanctions would mean the departure of observers from the sanctioned body. The Commonwealth decision in Brisbane meant that Commonwealth observers would remain in place.

The Commonwealth set up a small team to review the report of these observers: Nigeria's Obasanjo, Australia's John Howard and South Africa's Mbeki. Apart from Blair, these were the Commonwealth's most senior heads of government, and their assemblage in this guise was a curious rerun of 1986, when Obasanjo and Australia's Malcolm Fraser had headed the Commonwealth group of eminent persons that had visited apartheid South Africa and recommended Commonwealth sanctions. Now, all three were looking in the same direction – but sanctions again were a possibility; so too was the possibility of the Commonwealth, as in 1986, being unable to reach complete agreement.

The MDC had prepared, finally, for the Commonwealth summit. It had earlier sent out a delegation to speak at the University of Queensland and at other venues organised by civic organisations. Tsvangirai, like Mugabe, could not attend the postponed summit since the election campaign demanded all their time. But the MDC did not make a great impact at Brisbane, most of its senior talent being engaged in an election campaign that was having its surreal, but also its very bloody moments.

THE DEPARTURE OF EU OBSERVERS

Shortly before the Commonwealth summit, EU observers were pulled out of Zimbabwe. This was the result of a protracted dispute between Europe and Zimbabwe as to which states might be represented in the team of observers. Zimbabwe had posted a list of countries whom it regarded, from past comments, as hostile to the Mugabe Government: Britain, Germany, Sweden, the Netherlands, Finland and Denmark. These, Zimbabwe said, should not send observers. The EU said that it could – and would – select whomever it wished, and the Zimbabwean response was that Zimbabwe, as a sovereign state, could host whomever it wanted, and not host those it did not want. Pierre Schori of Sweden was appointed to head the EU observer team. He entered Zimbabwe on a tourist visa and was expelled for violating the terms of his visa. The struggle, however, was over much more than types of visa. When, as a result of Schori's expulsion, the EU launched sanctions – with the US following suit – Moyo made the pointed comment that, 'we are now dealing with organised economic terrorism whose aim is to unseat a legitimately elected government which has decided to defend its national independence'.[6] To an extent he was, of course, right. No European state would brook such an imposition. And these very same states had indeed accepted the results of previous Zimbabwean elections. The Zambian press response, in its most liberal newspaper, compared the West's treatment of Zimbabwe to its treatment, and befriending, of the military dictator of Pakistan – suddenly useful to the West in Afghanistan – and called the EU sanctions an 'imperial arrogance'.[7] And the *Herald* in Zimbabwe editorialised with the carefully calculated words of an affected democratic maturity – that nevertheless struck chords among undecided voters – that the withdrawal of EU observers 'represents an important epoch in the evolution of the African continent into a region that can now stand on its own and define its own political processes without the endorsement of former colonisers'.[8]

The MDC had vacillated for weeks over whether to plump for this sort of EU action. At first it had sought the retention of observers. But British weight in the EU discussions had forced the MDC to tilt its support behind sanctions and the withdrawal of observers. It was all grist to the mill of those who called Tsvangirai 'Tsvangison'.

ELECTION BIASING

Not content to demonstrate his experience as superior to Tsvangirai's, and not content to harp upon the theme of Tsvangirai as Blair's poodle – Blair having made enough of a dog's breakfast of supposedly helping Tsvangirai – Mugabe sought also to bias the election in his favour by manipulating the legal instrumentalities at his disposal. Commenting on the run-up to the 1995 parliamentary elections, Welshman Ncube – now a senior MDC figure, charged alongside Tsvangirai with treason – had made a number of pointed accusations about Mugabe's far-ranging powers. These are described in Chapter 6, above. I also made the comment in that chapter that, broad as his powers were, Mugabe did not actually exploit them at that election. Now, in preparation for the 2002 presidential elections, he did exploit them.

The powers of which Ncube complained were that the President could appoint key electoral officials, including the chair of the Electoral Supervisory Commission; Mugabe now appointed recently retired Colonel Gula-Ndebele. Colonel Gula-Ndebele, in turn, appointed Brigadier Nyikayaramba as Chief Election Officer. Both were viewed as Mugabe supporters, and other military and Central Intelligence officers found their way onto various levels of the electoral machinery.

In addition, the Government now proceeded to cut the number of polling stations in the MDC urban strongholds, and increased the number in the rural ZANU-PF fastness. The scarcity of stations in the cities, coupled with a protracted bureaucratic checking of names against the register, would cause great frustration and controversy on the polling days. The painstaking checks against register were to ensure that elaborate exclusions were not circumvented. The electoral rolls had been culled of white Zimbabweans who had not renounced their British rights; large numbers of young, first-time voters were unable to register on the rolls, and although later overturned under legal challenge Zimbabweans overseas were to be deprived of voting rights. (As it was, despite the court ruling, arrangements were never put in place for overseas Zimbabweans to vote.)

Under ordinary conditions, not even all these measures would have overturned the swing towards Tsvangirai that the opposition and the urban opinion polls predicted. Accordingly, for Mugabe and ZANU-PF, the key to election victory had to be through nationwide efforts to intimidate voters, and as a last resort to rig the count. Whatever may or may not be said about the strengths and weaknesses of Mugabe and Tsvangirai, no matter how much the British media's demonisation of Mugabe is balanced by more judicious and balanced assessments, the fact remains that Mugabe, in his desire to be elected, put into play a massive and sustained programme of brutalities and persecutions, of beatings and murders, of coercions and threats. There are no means on earth that could describe the conditions for electoral campaigning as free and fair. Mugabe did himself a greater disservice than any number of British premiers could earnestly contrive.

INTIMIDATION

Thousands of Zimbabweans were intimidated during the campaign, and the ripple effect – the spreading of fear of intimidation – was designed to affect tens of thousands more. Intimidation usually took the form of beatings. Although there were several deaths, the policy – by and large – seems to have been one of violence just short of maiming and death. In many rural areas, citizens suspected of harbouring MDC sympathies were abducted by the youth brigades, taken to their camps and assaulted. Flesh wounds were inflicted as a visible warning to others. In one case, a youth had the MDC initials carved into his back with a dagger. There were reports of some huts being torched, and comparisons were made to the atrocities of the Fifth Brigade in the 1980s,[9] but these are overblown, and underestimate what was perpetrated by the Fifth Brigade. What went on throughout the 2002 campaign was nationwide, and was designed to set examples and give warnings. ZANU-PF youths even stoned a convoy of EU observers – by mistake, perhaps – before they were withdrawn; shots would sometimes be fired at MDC convoys. Even Tsvangirai's car was shot at and teargassed in the last week of February. Some MDC members of parliament were quite savagely beaten. Urban violence involved a great deal of teargas, in addition to beatings, stonings and occasional gunfire. Attending MDC rallies became a highly risky business, and it must be said that, no matter whether MDC leaders always maintained their dignity or not, their supporters consistently displayed a heroism and belief in democracy that must shame many in the West.

Although the youth brigades played a highly visible role in the intimidation of the rural areas, they were not used in the way that their forbears and partial inspiration, the Malawi Young Pioneers, were. The Malawian antecedents were much more organised, efficient and ruthless. Thousands died as a result of their pogroms. Their Zimbabwean descendants had been hastily recruited and trained, and although often deployed alongside and supported by army units, they were a motley bunch who were, in their very eagerness to earn a wage in this manner, an indictment of ZANU-PF's provision for the countryside. Penniless and poorly educated, these youths were cynically used and given the bully's power: to have this power was an antidote to their years of deprivation at the bottom of Zimbabwe's social heap.

In the cities, ZANU-PF youth activists – usually not part of the brigades – engaged in particularly urban forms of intimidation. Slashing with broken bottles was more commonplace here; and gangs of these youths – aided not by the army but given free rein by the police – would roam the township streets as a constant threat and constant reminder. The police themselves were deployed to facilitate ZANU-PF operations and to hamper and harass those of the MDC. They would break up MDC rallies, threaten supporters with arrest, indiscriminately fire teargas rounds, and club people with their batons and rifle butts. The continual prevalence of all these forms of intimidation meant that even apolitical citizens, travelling innocently in any city or part of the countryside, would be liable to navigate large numbers of roadblocks and made to profess their loyalty to ZANU-PF and to Mugabe. As food shortages began to bite into Zimbabwe, the army, the police, the youth brigades, and urban ZANU-PF militants ate well.

TALES FROM THE RALLIES

The refusal to be cowed by intimidation will be an enduring hallmark of these elections. Opposition supporters braved huge obstacles just to attend rallies. Many smaller gatherings were broken up. Rallies had trouble gaining permission to proceed under the new legislation rushed through parliament. Even the ones featuring Tsvangirai himself had sometimes to be cancelled for fear of violence. However, the MDC did succeed in holding a large number of rallies, and some were very well attended indeed. On Sunday 3 February, despite a Saturday night of ZANU-PF youths marching the streets and warning against attendance, 12,000 people crammed into the stadium at Sakubva township, near the eastern city of Mutare. Police roadblocks caused half-mile tailbacks, but people patiently waited – some saying that, after all, they had already waited for years. When Tsvangirai appeared, the crowd roared 'Chinja!', 'change', and the atmosphere was more exuberant than any football match, red cards being waved and all. Tsvangirai addressed the crowd from the bumpy football pitch, without a lectern, speaking directly and talking of change and, in particular, of policy changes. He spoke of restitution, not retribution, of constitutional propriety and the rule of law, of respect for the judiciary, then urged the crowd to be sure to vote: 'We must all go and vote, because at the end of the day, let not the future generations accuse us of being negligent and allowing a dictator to destroy the country in our faces'.[10]

Mugabe rallies featured the President, attired colourfully, and speaking not of policies but of an historical process undergoing completion. Those attending benefited from being trucked in, in some cases unwillingly. Many, however, did want to hear his message which, apart from its anti-colonialism, promised seed, fertiliser, land. Mugabe did not address the question of immediate food shortages, and he spoke from beneath a canopy and behind a bulletproof lectern that dwarfed him, his white baseball cap hovering between the two. The songs and manner of slogan-chanting – a voice-leader giving the cue, the crowd offerings an appropriate chorus – were from his former era; and his imagery was also from a former era. His clothing was from a bygone time of African one-party state leaders; his anti-colonial vocabulary was from the days of liberation. And all this begged the question of what he had accomplished since those days of liberation.

As Mugabe supporters left their rally, their homegoing precautions were very different from those at MDC rallies. At the latter, people removed their MDC T-shirts, some put on plastic helmets – but from the expressions on many faces, it was difficult to tell that it was this party that had been put under siege. Meanwhile, at the ZANU-PF camp all seemed, behind the meticulous orchestration, grim and forced. The old party and the old warrior, with their old policies and older rhetoric – albeit restated for a new global order, which Zimbabwe alone would defy – were having to crank themselves up, one aged limb after another, to climb the mountain that democratic challenge had planted before them. By the end of the campaign, Mugabe would not be running across stadium fields. He simply appeared exhausted and, in his garish dress, a crumpled doll of himself.

THE MDC CONFRONTS THE VEXED
QUESTION OF LAND POLICY

The contrast in campaign promises could not have been more marked than over the land issue. Mugabe had built an entire policy rationale and personal *raison d'etre* on restoring white land to the majority black people. Now he accused Tsvangirai of planning to give that land back to the whites; and Tsvangirai was. However, he addressed the issue by pointing out the food shortages: 'There is a need for land resettlement in this country but we also have to deal with a very serious food deficit'. In short, he pointedly linked the growing hunger to Mugabe's policy of land seizures. These had radically affected agricultural production, and been compounded by drought. 'We believe,' he said, 'we can find a lasting solution, a more equitable solution, by creating space for the landless and at the same time also recognising that commercial agriculture is important for the long-term economic stability of the country'.[11] These things begged the question of how the squatters and war veterans were to be removed from the land they had occupied, or how non-squatters and veterans – who had been assigned seized land under the legal processes Mugabe had instituted – might be persuaded to move; or to where they might be moved, what land they might instead be given. Tsvangirai promised that they would not be landless, but this would be a difficult policy to fulfil. However, as a policy statement, it was bold; and, in the contradictions and misfortunes of Africa it was drought and the spectre of hunger that made this boldness seem sensible to a voting public Mugabe had courted precisely by land seizures.

The encroachment of hunger was felt first in the rural areas furthest from Harare. Matabeleland South was, as in all previous periods of food shortage, the first to feel the stomach pinch. In these rural areas, however, the very persistence of the youth brigades began to have an effect very different from the one intended. 'It's ending the cultural order if a young person of 14 can raise his hand to slap an older woman in the face.'[12] ZANU–PF and Mugabe had counted on reducing the opposition vote in the cities, and coercing a maximum rural vote for themselves. Now, if they had overplayed their hand in the rural areas – particularly those parts where hunger intruded – then that rural vote might not be as assured as in the party scenarios. As the polling days, 9–10 March 2002, approached, the Harare rumour mills were awash with the 'news' that Mugabe had transferred some US$3 billion abroad.[13] At best, this would have been Mugabe hedging his bets, not necessarily planning to flee. More prosaically, it was probably just another rumour – although, like all Harare rumours, supposedly from impeccable sources, and possibly containing a grain of truth. But as the first day of polling dawned, with people in the cities having begun to queue from the night before, there was everywhere the feeling that, whether in Mugabe's terms or not, an historic moment had arrived.

TALES FROM THE POLLS

By Saturday morning, 9 March, the urban queues were often several thousand long.[14] The reduction in the number of polling stations in the cities was designed to test the patience of the pro–MDC electorate. In addition, extended bureaucratic register searches preceded every casting of a ballot. One station was reported to average a throughput of one voter every seven minutes. At another station, Saturday saw 200 voters cast their ballots from a queue of several thousand. The register search was designed to ensure that all those who had been effectively de-registered could not circumvent the system, but it was also designed to slow the process down. In short, by pleading electoral thoroughness, the Government was seeking to win an election in which traditional rigging could be disclaimed. This much, at least, was transparent. The South African observers estimated that, with the slow rate of progress, it would take five days for Harare to vote.[15]

The very small number of international observers could not deploy themselves in any thorough sense, particularly in the rural areas. The withdrawal of the EU observers may have been making a point to Mugabe that, on the ground, benefited him. With an estimated 2000 polling stations, redistributed to favour the rural areas, it would have been impossible even for a unified, several-hundred-strong observer mission to monitor proceedings. Several small, uncoordinated observer missions, often landing in Zimbabwe a mere week or two before the elections, were a paltry international effort, and spoke of Mugabe's success in reducing their number and their effect. Having said that, they did have some effect; and this was abetted by the redesignation of local international agency staff as observers – these at least knew their way around. Both youth brigades and ZANU-PF urban thugs would rein in their intimidation whenever observers appeared. However, from having personally helped plan and conduct the very first such mission in Zimbabwe, in 1980, I can say that in no sense could the assorted observers have developed sufficient infrastructure and logistical systems to monitor the entire country. What went on in the cities was very visible. What went on in the rural areas was far less so.

Insofar as efforts were made in the cities to reduce the MDC vote, this did have an effect – in that many people, holding down jobs or with dependent relatives, simply could not wait for hours – sometimes most of both Saturday and Sunday – in order to vote. Many people simply became dispirited and left the queues. However, the morale within the queues could be amazingly buoyant. People reserved places for those alongside them who needed to find a toilet or have a quick bite to eat. Black and white mingled together, waiting it out in the same queue, under the same conditions – and cordial camaraderies developed, almost as a rebuttal of Mugabe's racially charged campaign. In the queues, people kept up one another's spirits by saying, 'people have died for this', and they were not going to sacrifice their moment of democracy now.

There were instances of ZANU-PF plans not always going well. Many white voters, whom ZANU-PF had worked to deregister, found sympathetic election officials who, after an extensive search of the register, 'found' their names. With the majority of officials government-appointed, these were rare exceptions, but it demonstrated that, in all walks of Zimbabwean life, the previously monolithic ZANU-PF no longer held total sway. This was evident also in the few rural reports of voting. It was not always the case that this electorate was solidly behind Mugabe. And, here, many voters – upon whom the President would have relied – simply stayed away.

So it was that, by Sunday, the atmosphere, nationally, was explosive with expectation, not 'Will the government win?' but 'Will the government still lose despite all?' Tsvangirai turned up to vote on Sunday, at the Avondale polling station in a middle-class area of Harare. It was his fiftieth birthday. Cameras were everywhere, and he was given a birthday cake shaped like State House. He looked every inch the president-to-be. He had made often major mistakes along the way, had several rough edges still, but had matured in this campaign and was – remaining warts and all – a very different figure from the trade-union leader who had helped form the MDC such a short time before.

But by Sunday night, the queues still as long and slow as ever, people began to despair. They had done everything they could in their thousands and thousands, and now the election was to be stolen from them by simple slow-motion. The Government was going to say it had merely insisted upon proper procedure, point to the relative absence of violence on the actual days of polling, and declare the President freely re-elected. The MDC went to the High Court and argued for a third day of voting – and, despite all Mugabe's earlier efforts to tame the judiciary and pack it, the High Court agreed that there should be a third day.

Monday 11 March, dawned with queues and much confusion. Some polling stations opened briefly, were closed again by the Government, and then a number – five hours after normal voting would have begun – reopened, but only in Harare. Neither side knew what the result, if fairly counted, might be. Every single voter in Harare now might be crucial. The Government media, and Minister of Information Jonathan Moyo, began predicting a Mugabe victory and scorning the opposition's predicament.

TOWARDS THE RESULTS

Moyo spoke of a huge turnout in the rural areas – of which there was no independent conformation – and of a low turnout in the cities. He pointedly referred to queues not being an indicator of turnout, but only votes cast,[16] somewhat disingenuously failing to note that the length of queues was causing the lack of votes. But the Government's accounts of voting turnout was unconvincing to many observers. Whereas 69 per cent of registered voters were meant to have cast their ballots in the Mugabe stronghold of Mashonaland Central – the province to the north of Harare – only 47 per cent were meant to have voted in both Matabeleland North and South, an area the size of England, and traditionally hostile to Mugabe, the place where the greatest ever intimidation of Zimbabwean citizens took place in the 1980s, and where one might have expected to see a large turnout for the opposition. One Commonwealth official remarked that this was all part of a 'coordinated strategy by Mugabe to steal the election.'[17] Large numbers of MDC party agents and election monitors were either arrested or prevented from travelling in the convoys accompanying the ballot boxes being transported to the counting centres. Fears of box stuffing, switching of boxes, or addition of fresh boxes were raised. Welshman Ncube was arrested as he tried to visit neighbouring Botswana – on the grounds that a person charged with treason could not leave the country – raising the spectre of a Mugabe persecution of his rivals in the event that he won what was now evidently a highly unsatisfactory election, unable to meet international criteria of freeness and fairness. The mood at MDC headquarters, which had been buoyed by hope being piled upon hope, began to deflate as these hopes were clawed away. Police began firing teargas to disperse the remaining queues in Harare, and Tsvangirai released an extraordinary press statement. It was quietly dignified and tremendously sad. It retained hope, but was already recognising a certain inevitability. It is probably the most presidential and statesmanlike document of the entire election campaign, and is worth quoting in full:

> My Fellow Zimbabweans: I thank you for your courage as you continue to vote in your millions. We see your determination. We hear your support. We share your impatience. The power is in your hands. What the people of Zimbabwe now deserve is a celebration.
>
> But there are those who say that dark clouds threaten the horizon of our country.

Together we have travelled a very difficult road to achieve democratic change. Your resilience to reclaim your rights, as expressed by the over-whelming turnout, has shaken the corridors of power. Rarely in the history of mankind have a people faced such brutality while retaining such gracious exuberance.

But the forces of darkness may yet try to block your path to victory.

As I address you, it is sad that this regime still seems intent on defying your will. Whatever may happen, I as your loyal servant am with you all the way. They may want to arrest me and at worst kill me, but they will never destroy the spirit of the people to reclaim their power. We have said that this election is about the choice between hope and despair. We may have moments of fear but we must never let despair overwhelm us.

The tide of change is irreversible but we must be prepared to pay a high price for our freedom. President Mugabe and his colleagues are afraid of the people and we have heard they may do anything to kill the messenger. If they do, you must stay strong and carry on the work we began together. Among you walk heroes – heroes who waited hours and hours to vote, heroes who refused to be turned away. These are the heroes of the new Zimbabwe whose voices must be heard around the world.

Now is the time we have been waiting for and we are ready. But let us first wait peacefully for your votes to be cast and counted. Restrain yourselves so you do not allow their sinister plans to succeed. As you wait for the results, do not succumb to their provocative traps. I know they are trying very hard to provoke you. Yes, we share your fear that the result will be rigged, but let us complete the process we began together in our campaign for a better life for all Zimbabweans.

In closing, let us pray President Mugabe, his party, and the security forces shall uphold the Constitution while peacefully honouring and respecting the will of Zimbabwean people.

May the Lord bless you in your continued efforts for freedom.[18]

THE RESULTS

The results were announced on the morning of Wednesday 13 March. Those Zimbabweans with work had already arrived at their jobs or their fields. The army was deployed throughout the cities and placed on high alert. Across the border, the South African army was also on alert and a camp for refugees had been prepared. The announcement was that Robert Mugabe had taken 1,685,212 votes to Morgan Tsvangirai's 1,258,401.

Mugabe's support was a little more than in the 1996 presidential elections where, against two minority candidates who withdrew before polling began, he secured just short of 1.5 million votes. Many more people did vote in the 2002 elections – one and a half million more – but Mugabe's support stayed firm, and pulled back some of the MDC support in the 2000 parliamentary elections.

Even if all the queues in Harare had voted, this would have run Mugabe much closer, but would probably not have overturned his margin. The clues behind his victory lay in the countryside, where lawlessness had reigned for two years – since the advent of the war veterans – and violence had become more systematised with the advent of the youth brigades. Despite the loss of rural livelihood and the increase in hunger, intimidation has held considerable sway here. Whether the actual counting was rigged or not is another question. Historically, this has not been the case on an orchestrated basis in Zimbabwe. There have been local instances in parliamentary elections, but rigging of a presidential count would demand careful planning and military precision – switching of exactly the right number of boxes with exactly the right number of ballots recorded at the polling station. In a nationwide system of ballot-rigging, the possibility of whistle-blowing or plain incompetence must be high. Here, the role of the military must bear scrutiny. Only the army might do this well. If there had been ballot-rigging, then the most suspect areas would be some in Matabeleland South and a great deal of the spiritual heartland of the liberation war, in Manicaland. The scarcity of international observers, and their lack of sustained and comprehensive penetration of the countryside, must be pointed out yet again. Harassment, arrests and detentions of local observers and monitors would have created opportunities for box substitution. Having said that, such substitution has not historically occurred in Zimbabwe, and there were no serious suggestions immediately after the elections that it had occurred on any wide and orchestrated basis in 2002, although claims of rigging did increase in the months afterwards. Mugabe has always, on the narrow grounds of what happens only on polling days, claimed that elections are not rigged. As it was, in the 2002 elections what happened on the polling days was far from satisfactory and, even by his own narrow standards, there cannot be a sustained claim for freeness and fairness. It probably all comes down to two things: first, the long, meticulously laid-out plans for intimidation, ruthlessly carried out – always taken to the brink of what the opposition and the international community might call a hopeless situation, always to the point where hope could be constructed and an election go ahead. The dashing of hope has become the Mugabe hallmark during his years. Second, a significant proportion of the electorate believed his message: that the white world was seeking to order Zimbabwe's affairs, and that the local manifestation of this – white ownership of most of the land – was what Mugabe had been combating. Once he began combating this, he was forced also to combat the white world internationally. Britain, in particular, obliged him in his promotion of this message.

The immediate opinion of African observer teams and presidents was more mixed than the British media generally allowed. The South African team called the election 'legitimate', but did add the rider, 'we have steered clear from the words free and fair. We cannot openly declare it free and fair'. A team of regional MPs, assembled by the Southern African regional economic body, was more pointed, saying that 'basic standards' for democratic elections had not been met, because of state-sponsored violence against the opposition. But the Tanzanian President probably expressed the general African reservation about the election: not that it was unfree and unfair, but that external dictates had been, by definition, unfair to an independent country and militated against its freedom. 'It would be a great tragedy for anyone to try and determine the outcome of an African election in Europe.'

The comment of the Nigerian team was the most revealing, however – not in the sense of what was said by the Tanzanian President, but in the sense of how it arrived at its verdict: 'We recorded no incidence that was sufficient to threaten the integrity and outcome of the election, in areas monitored by the team'.[19] This team, like most African observer teams, concentrated largely on the elections themselves, and the immediately preceding official campaign period. While the regional MPs, as noted above, spoke of the longer campaign of intimidation, most African observer teams spoke only of what little they saw in a short period of time. They, like Mugabe, took a narrow and legalistic view of what an election entails; and, even with this narrow view, their deployment was so limited that they, finally, took a narrow view of a narrow view.

For, if one were to apply categories that privileged only very broad descriptions, one would have to say that the long-term election campaign was unfree – many were killed and many thousands prevented from expressing themselves politically; and one would have to say that the days of polling were unfair – in that many were unable, even with extreme patience, to register their votes. Concentrating, however, only on the days of polling and a short period beforehand, observer teams were able to say two things: that, Harare aside, most Zimbabweans seemed to have had a reasonable opportunity to vote; that the opposition, by very virtue of having contested this election, had itself given the election legitimacy.

This would seem the gist, for instance, of the South African case.

SOME ANALYSIS

A breakdown of voting figures, however, suggests a certain pattern:

1 In Matabeleland North, where the scourge of atrocity is well-remembered, the turnout was only 53 per cent. Here the split was 61 per cent for Tsvangirai and 35 per cent for Mugabe.
2 In Matabeleland South, with a similar memory of atrocity, turnout was only 54 per cent, and here Mugabe ran Tsvangirai more closely. Tsvangirai gained 50 per cent, Mugabe 44 per cent.
3 In Bulawayo, the capital of the Matabelelands, turnout was a very low 45 per cent. Tsvangirai gained 79 per cent and Mugabe 17 per cent.
4 In Manicaland where in Zimbabwean election history the battle has always been to capture the spiritual heritage of liberation that the region represents, turnout was 55 per cent, with Tsvangirai gaining 48 per cent and Mugabe very close behind with 47 per cent.
5 Finally, in Harare itself, turnout – as measured by votes cast, not by numbers in the long queues – turnout was 47 per cent. Tsvangirai received 75 per cent, Mugabe 24 per cent.

Tsvangirai did not beat Mugabe in any of the remaining five major areas. In these areas, turnout was 69 per cent (Mashonaland Central), 61 per cent (Mashonaland East), 56 per cent (Mashonaland West), 68 per cent (Midlands) and 61 per cent (Masvingo). In all these areas, Mugabe won large majorities, from 63 per cent to 84 per cent.

A total of 3,130,913 voted, out of 5,647,812 registered.

The first contrast is between respective turnouts. In areas where Tsvangirai did well, turnout averaged only about 50 per cent. In areas where Mugabe did well, turnout averaged more than 60 per cent. If turnout had been uniform at 60 per cent throughout the country, and the same voting percentages were applied, Tsvangirai would just have won.

Either the MDC was unable to get out its vote, or it was prevented from doing so. By contrast, ZANU-PF ensured, by both free and coercive means, that its vote turned out.

The second contrast is between expectations based on polls and electoral history, and the 2002 outcome. Both Matabeleland South and Manicaland were expected to return higher majorities for Tsvangirai. It was in these areas, however, that particularly high incidences of intimidation were reported. In Matabeleland, memory of atrocity might indeed precipitate fears of its return. The threat of a new *gukurahundi*, a new whirlwind, could not be welcomed.

The third contrast is, of course, between expectations in Harare and the reduced outcome caused by voting delays.

None of this arithmetic, by itself, demonstrates that the election was stolen. It does indicate, however, far greater cause for concern than some observer teams allowed. And behind these figures, of course, what is meant by the word 'intimidation' is not what most observers would wish to experience. This election, in the most literal sense, did violence to Zimbabwe.

THE FUTURE

The most pointed comment in this direction came from the Commonwealth observer group. Released two days later than the reports of most other groups, and the result of both greater consideration and a greater degree of observation, its verdict was damning. It was read by the group's head, Abdulsalami Abubakar, himself once a military ruler of Nigeria and now in the camp of democrats. It listed major electoral deficits: first the level of violence and intimidation; second the failure of the police to protect the opposition and, as a result, the biased application of law; third the legislative framework, which was described as 'basically flawed', especially its restrictions on assembly and free speech; fourth restrictions placed upon civil society groups; fifth restrictions placed upon local poll monitors; sixth the lack of transparency in the electoral registration process, meaning that 'thousands of Zimbabwean citizens were disenfranchised'; seventh the reduction in urban polling stations; eighth the delay in reopening polling stations after the High Court had ordered a third day of polling; ninth the too-wide discretionary powers of the electoral registrar general. 'It is our view that the ruling party used its encumbency to exploit state resources for the benefit of its electoral campaign.'

As a result of its observation, the group came to 'the conclusion that the conditions in Zimbabwe did not adequately allow for a free expression of will by the electors.'[20] The restraint of the last sentence could not disguise the severity of the group's judgement, and the catalogue of its reasons for coming to such a judgement. But this meant that, whereas Nigerian and South African observers had – albeit with some misgivings – basically validated the elections, the Commonwealth group had not. It was this group which was meant, as a result of the discussions at Brisbane, to guide Mbeki, Obasanjo and Howard in determining the response of the entire Commonwealth towards Zimbabwe's future membership. The diplomatic traffic became intense. Mbeki's deputy came to Harare to try, fruitlessly, to persuade Mugabe to form a coalition government, with Tsvangirai as Vice-President. Mugabe refused. Mbeki flew up from South Africa, and Obasanjo down from Nigeria, to meet in person with Mugabe on 18 March. By this time, Mugabe had been hastily sworn in for his new presidential term and was not giving ground easily. Nor, however, were the Presidents of South Africa and Nigeria prepared to give him too easy a ride, having pointedly not attended his inauguration. Mbeki and Obasanjo flew on to London, to begin their Commonwealth discussions on 19 March.

In the light of the narrow caution shown by various African observer teams, and the reluctance of Africa to be seen to be dancing to a tune dictated by the West, there was great scepticism that the Commonwealth would expel Zimbabwe from its membership. In addition, Western leaders were resigned to a pragmatism on the part of South Africa, since it had to continue to deal with Mugabe – and try to temper the disaster there arising from the spillover problems of Zimbabwean policies. However, to the surprise certainly of the British Government, the three Commonwealth heads of government did indeed suspend Zimbabwe's membership. It was, with immediate effect, to last 12 months, and then to be reviewed in the event that Mugabe had made progress towards what the three called a 'reconciliation' that recognised the need for a fair treatment of the opposition. Mbeki, in particular, had vacillated in the days after the election results as to whether he would recognise the verdict of South African or of Commonwealth observers. Many in his own cabinet advised him to recognise the former. The West spoke, in barely veiled terms, of a possible retreat from a new policy of increased aid to Africa; but finally the verdict of the Commonwealth observers had been simply too stark to be avoided.

The West had been more immediately angry at the election result, but the swift endorsement of it – by so much of Africa – meant it saw how little it could do. The Commonwealth decision at least meant that Mugabe could not simply insist upon a black–white division in the world. The West had other measures also in mind. Its 'smart' sanctions, targeted at Mugabe and his senior people, would at least mean that Grace, who had appeared alongside her husband as they cast their votes, would not for a while be shopping with him at Harrods. Certainly the West would also move to prevent ordinary Zimbabweans from starving. A humanitarian provision was always going to be forthcoming, and ZANU-PF always knew that.

> You see, the ministers say that the West will, despite everything, feed the hungry. Food aid will come. As for us, even if we tear the country down, we can and will just build it again. We did it before – build from nothing – and we can do it again. And the West will know that it is in its interests to help us do this.[21]

Both the West and the multiracial Commonwealth would, however, urge fairer political play in the future. This may be scant comfort to those whose will was ignored in the Zimbabwean elections.

Nothing in Zimbabwe's case can, however, be prophetic. Everything changes and those who have played prediction games have almost always been disappointed. As the election and all its traumas fell behind the international disquiet that followed it, there was talk in more than Commonwealth quarters of helping to heal Zimbabwe's wounds, of sending signals to other African leaders that such elections should not become the norm – but much of this was rhetoric. A pragmatism will, in the nature of international politics, eventually arise; and Mugabe will, himself, become more pragmatic in his dealings with the outside world. Whether he will first unleash a pogrom against the opposition must be, however, a real fear.

More pressing for him, at 78 – and mindful of the already uncomfortable parallels developing between himself and the finally senile and incontinent dictator of Malawi, Hastings Banda, a man who held on too long, even in African eyes – Mugabe must set his mind to the reunification of ZANU-PF. He must choose, and stick with, a successor. And he must bring back into the fold men like Zvobgo, who opposed his repressive legislation in parliament and who refused to endorse Mugabe's candidature for the presidency. The very existence of more liberal-minded people in ZANU-PF, even if now only at that party's margins, means that there is not a monolith. There are enough factions and margins for bargains to be made, and Mugabe can make them. For the one thing the West has learned from 2002 is that Mugabe is a much more complex and extraordinary mover than it had expected or estimated. What he did was to accomplish a great political act. It was not a great moral act – except in the terms of his own autarky – but it was a great political act all the same. As he comes up to his eightieth year no one will underestimate him again.

And the MDC? On 14 March, it placed full-page advertisements in the *Daily News*, and one read:

The struggle for democratic change continues.
We have lost a battle
But not the war.
Do not despair
Do not lose hope.
The will of the people shall prevail.
Together we will complete the change.

Another advertisement gave excerpts from Tsvangirai's sadly dignified press statement of 11 March, reproduced above – the 'amongst you walk heroes' statement. A third thanked all the voters, especially those in the rural areas – many of whom had done their best, despite intimidation, to vote as they wished.

As soon as the results were announced on 13 March, the Italian Bakery was suddenly deserted. The bustling morning coffee crowds went home, fearful of what would happen next. Many went home to cry, to sit despondent, simply to worry. MDC supporters gathered together to commiserate and support one another. On a veranda in Harare, one wrote a poem, and she will forgive me, I hope, my reproducing some lines from it:

Together we told our stories:
of driving to rural polling stations
of ducking police road blocks
of being arrested
of the chaos and cigar smoke in the command centre

a brilliant tapestry of tales of courage and humour and love
newly woven
There is no going back with this fabric in place.
Held together with such laughter.

Yesterday I awoke to grief
and went to bed
knowing I was connected to the universe.

For the first time, with these elections and the parliamentary ones that preceded it Zimbabwe has a mass opposition. As a political accomplishment, given Zimbabwe's political history – election by election, as I have recounted them in this book – it is something even greater than what Mugabe did. If that opposition does not indeed despair, and is not crushed, a very great deal more will be heard from it. African presidents can, at least, seek to protect Tsvangirai, and this was an underlying text in the Commonwealth suspension of Zimbabwe for 12 months.

MUGABE

It might seem an academic note upon which to build a comparison, but, just as I have tried to be even-handed about Mugabe in this book – not simply demonising him – so too I have tried to be even-handed about Tsvangirai – not simply praising him. I would not like, however, Mugabe to have entirely the last words here, so a note about words seems to be in order.

Some years ago, when Tsvangirai was still a trade-union leader, but already expressing his dissatisfaction with Government policies, a Zimbabwean scholar analysed his speeches for their linguistic construction, and through this their political suggestiveness. This is all to do with what is now called 'discursive practice', but it provides useful insights. Alison Love found that in Tsvangirai's uses of speech – counterpoints with ZANU-PF ministerial statements, questions, negatives, alternatives, allowing for possibilities but establishing priorities and avenues for further thought and discussion – he was using speech that was an invitation to dialogue and inclusiveness.[22] In short, they were not simply oppositional – nor were they demagogic or hectoring. It is important to point out that, throughout the entire history of the MDC, and throughout the election campaign, Tsvangirai continued to speak like this.

By contrast, Mugabe's speeches became increasingly oppositional, accusatory and demagogic, as if he were the opposition leader and not the President, as if he were a man at war. And, in a very real sense, Mugabe was at war with the world. To say that starkly would be to end this book with the sort of caricature it has sought to avoid. Let us, therefore, revisit some observations made near the beginning of chapter 8. These were interim appraisals of the man, up to 1998, and much has changed both in Zimbabwe and Mugabe since then.

In my observations, I made four primary points. I said that in times of political crisis he will wheel into play issues to do with war and land. He has certainly done this in the years leading up to 2002, with war in Congo and the use of the land issue as a political instrument.

Land, however, is not merely a political instrument. I have said that there is both an intellectual Afro-centrism to Mugabe and a cruder autarky. He has made of his actions a great virtue, or believes that this virtue has impelled his actions. This is the virtue of self-determination, despite all rational calculations to do with short-term pain and despite all international pressure. By turns reasoned and unreasonable, he has both kept the international community second-guessing him and persuaded – in virtuoso diplomacy – many of his colleague presidents in Africa that his could be understood as a genuine policy of liberation.

I said that by 1998 his record was one of dealing with one issue at a time. This has certainly changed since then. Mugabe, from the beginning of the new millennium, kept several balls in the air simultaneously: land seizures; playing himself off against the 'war veterans'; piling pressure upon the new MDC opposition; winning parliamentary elections; engaging in a heated diplomatic battle with Britain and, more recently, Europe; engaging in a calculated African diplomacy; and fashioning for himself a presidential victory.

And that leads to the fourth major point: he has a need to hold elections – even if it means engineering the validation he seems to extract from them, as if nothing and no one has ever validated him enough. In the face of criticism and condemnation, he seems to need a bedrock that he can – even if implausibly – call his own.

A POLITICAL LIFE

The rains failed over the normally wet season in 2001–2. Shona belief is that the heavens withhold rain if angry with wickedness below. Certainly there is political anger in Zimbabwe on both sides as Mugabe's fifth term struggles to get underway. The problems he faces are massive and, to an incredible degree, of his own making. He has ever been one to take huge risks and make grand gestures. These have been full of conspiracy, as he manoeuvred his way to the top of the liberation leadership; these have been of reconciliation, as he took up leadership in an independent Zimbabwe for the first time; these have been full of savagery, as he launched atrocity in the Matabelelands; these have been full of liberal pragmatism, as he, at the turn of the 1990s, embraced market economics and rhetorical democracy; these have been full of decisive foreign intervention, as in his deployment of troops in Mozambique and his subsequent Roman diplomacy that helped bring war to an end; and they have been full of intolerance and ruthlessness, as he has rooted out white farmers, attacked opposition and shored himself up within a fortress of deceits.

The moments of his greatest international acceptance were, Rome apart, within Commonwealth circles. The 1979 summit in Lusaka had paved the way for negotiations, and those negotiations – greatly abetted by the Commonwealth, had paved the way for independence, and his leadership of the new country. The 1981 summit, held in Harare itself, celebrated him as a man of human rights and democracy – albeit both prematurely and with significant blind spots. Nevertheless, these were themselves validations as well as celebrations, and it is unlikely that he will ever be so celebrated again, or so internationally validated.

There is no simple explanation of Mugabe. Western politicians who have sought one, or assumed one, have always been left floundering in the wake of his complexities and complex stratagems. It has been said that he is given to repeating stratagems from the past – that he is a prisoner of his own violent past, and should always have been predictable (and untrustworthy) on that basis – but, if this is indeed even partially true, he repeats himself in ever more complex and unpredictable ways. No, there is no one key to Mugabe. This book has tried to indicate how he has led his political life. In a way, he overcame his personal demons – doubt and despair, perhaps guilt – after the closeness of the 2000 parliamentary elections. Perhaps he could only fully overcome them by securing, by any means, the validation that votes marked in his name can bring. Beyond that, I do not wish to engage in further speculation. Others may paint psychological portraits of the man, but I do not feel that, outside novels and gossip, there is sufficient clinical evidence on which to base this. That he is, in 2002, after a complex political life, complexly bad is what I want finally to say.

As his motorcade swings out of the State House presidential mansion, it has to turn into Josiah Tongogara Avenue. Huge jacaranda trees litter the broad avenue with purple flowers. Newspaper-sellers knock on car windows at every traffic light, but they won't approach the President's motorcade. In any case, with outriders sounding their sirens, the long motorcade is oblivious to traffic lights. He will drive past the old sports club on his right that was once a social bastion for a white elite; on his left are high-rise luxury apartment blocks. Josiah Tongogara is a long avenue, changing its name a few times as it heads westward. The motorcade probably won't turn south to pass the hard urban slum of Mbare. Psychological portrait or no, even Mugabe must sometimes reflect, behind the smoked glass of his Mercedes, watching or avoiding the mixed results of his 22 years in office, that he has missed his chance to enter history without shame.

NOTES ON CHAPTER 11

1   *Guardian* (London), 7 March 2002.
2   5 March 2002.
3   *Guardian*, 26 February 2002.
4   *Guardian*, 1 March 2002.
5   *Guardian*, 28 February 2002.
6   *Guardian*, 20 February 2002.
7   *Post* (Lusaka), 19 February 2002.
8   *Herald* (Harare), 19 February 2002.
9   For example in John Sweeney's article in the *Guardian*, 2 March 2002.
10   Correspondence to the author, February 2002.
11   *Guardian*, 28 February 2002.
12   Lucia Matibenga, MDC Head of Women's Affairs, 2 February 2002, quoted in correspondence to the author, 28 February 2002.
13   Cited in information to the author from financial workers, 11 March 2002.
14   The following accounts were all given to the author by voters who had waited in these queues.

15   *Guardian*, 11 March 2002.
16   *Guardian*, 11 March 2002.
17   *Guardian*, 12 March 2002.
18   MDC press release, 'Election Message from MDC President Morgan Tsvangirai', Harare, 11 March 2002.
19   All comments gleaned from the *Guardian*, 14 March 2002.
20   *Guardian*, 15 March 2002.
21   Senior ZANU-PF source to the author, Harare, August 2001.
22   Alison Love, 'Democratic discourse? Realising alternatives in Zimbabwean political discourse', *Zambezia: The Journal of Humanities of the University of Zimbabwe*, XXVII:1, 2000.

A Guide to Further Reading

The aim of this essay is not to provide an exhaustive bibliography of modern Zimbabwean political history. Those seeking such are directed towards the South African Institute of International Affairs Bibliographic Series. Nor is this essay necessarily to underpin a book which has relied primarily on more than two decades of fieldwork. Throughout this book, quotes have been sourced and some pertinent background reading indicated. There has also been a light excursion into both the Zimbabwean academic and creative literatures. This essay, therefore, seeks to amplify both that sense of background and to indicate further Zimbabwean works among those written by metropolitan authors. I have indicated some of my own works, since they have contained more detail than has been possible in the sometimes breathless surveys of this book. Any information borrowed from my earlier writings has been completely rewritten for the present effort.

I have also tried to make this bibliographic essay a critical as well as briefly indicative effort, since not all the works published on Zimbabwe – my own included – are of a high standard. I have divided this survey into thematic groupings which match readily with the chapter progression of this book.

WAR AND ITS PRECONDITIONS

There is a very interesting study of white Rhodesian attitudes in

> Peter Godwin and Ian Hancock, *Rhodesians Never Die*, Oxford: Oxford University Press, 1993

and a fine countervailing representation of black life and aspirations, well before the war of liberation began, is

> Terence Ranger, *Are We Not Also Men?*, London: James Currey, 1995.

The actual war of liberation itself is variously represented. The views of guerilla participants can be found in

> Michael Raeburn, *Black Fire*, London: Julian Friedman, 1978; now, after the demise of Julian Friedman as a publishing house, available from Mambo Press, Gweru, Zimbabwe.

And accounts from the white combatants may be found in

> Bruce Moore-King, *White Man Black War*, Harare: Baobab, 1988

which is an account of war guilt, whereas the novel

> Angus Shaw, *Kandaya*, Harare: Baobab, 1993

which attracted respectful reviews, even from black critics, gives a much more nuanced account as to how the white soldiers saw the war. There has been a glut of very bad novels about the war, usually depicting endless ZANLA victories and superhuman ZANLA officers. These are clearly written by the beneficiaries of liberation, who never fought for it and have no idea of the sheer compromise of carnage. The novel that best, by far, captures the terror and trauma of it all has to be

> Alexander Kanengoni, *Echoing Silences*, Harare: Baobab, 1997

but see also

> Shimmer Chinodya, *Harvest of Thorns*, Harare: Baobab, 1989

and very fine fictional accounts of how the war affected ordinary lives are

> Chenjerai Hove, *Bones*, Harare: Baobab, 1988
> Charles Mungoshi, *Walking Still*, Harare: Baobab, 1997.

Scholarly accounts of the war are well represented in

> N. Bhebe and T. Ranger (eds), *Soldiers in Zimbabwe's Liberation War*, vol. 1, Harare: University of Zimbabwe Publications, 1995
> N. Bhebe and T. Ranger (eds), *Society in Zimbabwe's Liberation War*, vol. 2, Harare: University of Zimbabwe Publications, 1995.

And by far the most cited accounts of the various constitutive elements that made up resistance and rebellion – most cited since this debate and its methodologies, probably more than the war itself, has excited scholars – including the importance of spiritual ceremony and endorsement of the guerillas, are

> Terence Ranger, *Peasant Consciousness and Guerilla War in Zimbabwe*, London: James Currey, 1985
> David Lan, *Guns and Rain*, London: James Currey, 1985
> Norma J. Kriger, *Zimbabwe's Guerilla War: Peasant Voices*, Cambridge: Cambridge University Press, 1992.

NEGOTIATIONS

With the (sometimes large) caveat that, in these BBC interviews, conducted as negotiations proceeded, Rhodesian, Zimbabwean and British political figures were often speaking to reinforce their negotiating positions, and not necessarily the truth, the following book is invaluable

> Michael Charlton, *The Last Colony in Africa*, Oxford: Blackwell, 1990.

The actual final Commonwealth and Lancaster House negotiations have attracted very different accounts indeed. For an account of the centrality of Lord Carrington, see, of course

> Lord Carrington, *Reflect on Things Past*, London: Collins, 1988.

Another pro-Carrington and pro-US-influence account is by a scholar who later became a senior US State Department figure in negotiations to end the war in Mozambique:

> Jeffrey Davidow, *A Peace in Southern Africa: The Lancaster House Conference on Rhodesia*, 1979, Boulder, Colorado: Westview, 1984

with whose account I have pointedly disagreed, in

> Stephen Chan, *The Commonwealth in World Politics: A Study of International Action 1965–1985*, London: Lester Crook, 1988.

There are also somewhat different accounts of the transition period, after formal negotiations had been completed (but informal diplomatic foraging continued), particularly over the role of the Commonwealth observer group that monitored the truce and election campaign, and the elections themselves. See

Anthony Verrier, *The Road to Zimbabwe 1890–1980*, London: Jonathan
Cape, 1986

Stephen Chan, *The Commonwealth Observer Group in Zimbabwe: A Personal
Memoir*, Gweru: Mambo Press, 1985

but perhaps the best and most pointedly objective account is the brief
chapter in

Alan James, *Peacekeeping in International Politics*, London: Macmillan, 1990
(Part 2, Section I).

THE EARLY YEARS

The little book that seemed to enshrine all of the hopes of racial reconciliation was

Victor de Waal, *The Politics of Reconciliation*, London: Hurst, 1990

whereas the first organised retrospective by Zimbabwean scholars,
including of the land issue, was not always hopeful. Certainly it was
mindful of large problems ahead:

Ibbo Mandaza (ed.), *Zimbabwe: The Political Economy of Transition 1980–1986*,
Dakar: CODESRIA, 1986.

A short early warning note about economic difficulties was

Stephen Chan, 'Zimbabwe: Four Years of Independence', *Contemporary
Review*, 245:1422, 1984.

THE FIFTH BRIGADE

An early consideration of dissidence in the Matabelelands, balanced in
the sense that there is a Government perspective, is

Richard Hodder-Williams, *Conflict in Zimbabwe: The Matabeleland Problem*,
London: Institute for the Study of Conflict, Conflict Studies 151, 1983.

At that time, the extent of Government violence was not appreciated. By
far the most moving subsequent accounts of the human effects of this
violence are

Jocelyn Alexander, 'Dissident Perspectives on Zimbabwe's Post-Independence
War', *Africa*, 68:2, 1998

Richard Werbner, *Tears of the Dead*, Edinburgh: Edinburgh University Press, 1991

Richard Werbner, 'In Memory: A Heritage of War in Southwestern Zimbabwe', in Bhebe and Ranger, vol. 2, 1985, op. cit.

For a historical and (again) spiritual contextualisation of war and suffering in the Matabelelands, see

Terence Ranger, *Voices from the Rocks: Nature, Culture and History in the Matopos Hills of Zimbabwe*, Oxford: James Currey, 1999

Jocelyn Alexander, JoAnn McGregor and Terence Ranger, *Violence and Memory: One Hundred Years in the 'Dark Forests' of Matabeleland*, Oxford: James Currey, 2000.

THE 1990 ELECTIONS AND A DECADE'S DISILLUSIONMENT

Almost certainly the best and most considered account of economic and public administration in Zimbabwe, covering the greater part of the first ten years – and dealing, among other things, with the land issue, was

Jeffrey Herbst, *State Politics in Zimbabwe*, Berkeley: University of California Press, 1990

although it was received unfavourably in Zimbabwe itself, for lacking a desirable neo-Marxist methodology. Better received was

Ronald Weitzer, *Transforming Settler States*, Berkeley: University of California Press, 1990

and, while I reviewed and defended the Herbst book, I reviewed and criticised the thesis of the Weitzer book – that Mugabe had borrowed, from the Smith regime, an apparatus of control and repression. My view was that, notwithstanding borrowings, the Mugabe apparatus contained its very own characteristics. In Zimbabwe, however, it was a suitable analysis in the neo-Marxist school to view bourgeois stages of history as part of one essential epoch – and this book fitted in with this analysis, even though it was not so designed. The neo-Marxist view of state development, democracy and progress across epochs was somewhat unevenly stated in

Ibbo Mandaza and Lloyd Sachikonye (eds), *The One Party State and Democracy: The Zimbabwe Debate*, Harare: SAPES, 1991.

This also covered the 1990 elections, and John Makumbe wrote a typically elegant and penetrating critique of them. Having said that, the most comprehensive analysis of those elections was undertaken by a scholar who later became (in)famous as a Mugabe minister. In earlier days, the gap between him and his academic colleagues was not so great, and both Makumbe and the senior MDC official Welshman Ncube were participants in the early stages of the project that resulted in

Jonathan N. Moyo, *Voting for Democracy: Electoral Politics in Zimbabwe*, Harare: University of Zimbabwe Publications, 1992.

As I have waxed on in my text, I feel that the most insightful analysis of Zimbabwe – and academic expression of disillusion – over its first ten years was

Brian Raftopoulos, *Beyond The House of Hunger: The Struggle for Democratic Development in Zimbabwe*, Harare: Zimbabwe Institute of Development Studies Working Paper 17, 1991.

THE BRIEF YEARS OF TRIUMPH AND
SEIZING TRIUMPH FROM TRAGEDY

I wrote a brief account of the 1991 Commonwealth summit in

Stephen Chan, *Twelve Years of Commonwealth Diplomatic History: Commonwealth Summit Meetings 1979–1991*, Lewiston: Edwin Mellen, 1992

and a slightly longer account both of the 1992 drought and Mugabe's excursion to meet Afonso Dhlakama, the Mozambican rebel leader, in

Stephen Chan, 'The Diplomatic Styles of Zambia and Zimbabwe', in Paul B. Rich (ed.), *The Dynamics of Change in Southern Africa*, London: Macmillan, 1994

but came to different conclusions over the respective roles of Mugabe and Nkomo, in the first ministerial contacts with South Africa, from those of

Ulf Engel, *The Foreign Policy of Zimbabwe*, Hamburg: Institut für Afrika-Kunde, 1994.

The preconditions for Zimbabwean mediation in Mozambique were laid out in

Hasu Patel, 'Zimbabwe's Mediation in Mozambique and Angola, 1989–91' and Moises Venancio, 'Mediation by the Roman Catholic Church in

Mozambique', both in Stephen Chan and Vivienne Jabri (eds), *Mediation in Southern Africa*, London: Macmillan, 1993.

The question as to who mediated in Mozambique to what effect has given rise to three major schools. For an emphasis on Zimbabwe's – Mugabe's – role, see

Stephen Chan and Moises Venancio, *War and Peace in Mozambique*, London: Macmillan, 1998

whereas there is a strong school that emphasises the role of the US:

Cameron Hume, *Ending Mozambique's War*, Washington DC: US Institute of Peace, 1994

and a view that emphasises the role of Lonrho and Tiny Rowland:

Alex Vines, 'The Business of Peace', in *Accord* (Special Issue: The Mozambican Peace Process in Perspective), 3, 1998.

THE GREAT SOCIAL ISSUES OF THE 1990s: LAND AND OTHER WOES

Apart from chapters in works cited above, extended work on the land question is recent. The exception is

Sam Moyo, *The Land Question in Zimbabwe*, Harare: SAPES, 1995

One recent approach which explores   using a conceptual framework based on Foucault – the relationship between white commercial farmers and their black workers, is

Blair Rutherford, *Working on the Margins: Black Workers, White Farmers in Postcolonial Zimbabwe*, Harare: Weaver (elsewhere, London: Zed), 2001.

There have been several deep studies, however, of urban labour relations in Zimbabwe – perhaps reflecting the urbanised Zimbabwean intelligentsia – and one author has, in particular, contributed to these studies:

Brian Raftopoulos and Ian Phimister (eds), *Keep On Knocking: A History of the Labour Movement in Zimbabwe 1900–97*, Harare: Baobab, 1997
Brian Raftopoulos and Tsuneo Yoshikuni (eds), *Sites of Struggle: Essays in Zimbabwe's Urban History*, Harare: Weaver, 1999
Brian Raftopoulos and Lloyd Sachikonye (eds), *Striking Back: The Labour Movement and the Post-Colonial State in Zimbabwe 1980–2000*, Harare: Weaver, 2001.

This last book gives some background to the emergence of opposition led by former trade union leader, Morgan Tsvangirai. The condition, not of urban labour but the unemployed and destitute urban poor, is not so frequently studied. An exception is

M. F. C. Bourdillon, *Poor, Harassed But Very Much Alive*, Gweru: Mambo
Press, 1991

which uses as its rubric a quote from Dambudzo Marechera, already recognised as the poet of dispossession. There was, until recently, not a great deal of extended work on women in Zimbabwe. Since the end of the 1980s, this has begun to change:

Alinor Batezat and Margaret Mwalo, *Women in Zimbabwe*, Harare: SAPES,
1989.

This, however, was a very brief effort; and the first extended treatment was prefigured in

Christine Sylvester, *Zimbabwe: The Political Economy of Contradictory
Development*, Boulder: Westview, 1991.

Extended treatments of the role of Zimbabwean women during the liberation war, i.e. women as combatants not as victims and widows, are very recent indeed:

Josephine Nhongo-Simbanegavi, *For Better or Worse? Women and ZANLA in
Zimbabwe's Liberation Struggle*, Harare: Weaver, 2000
Women of Resilience: The Voices of Women Ex-combatants, Harare: Zimbabwe
Women Writers, 2000.

There have been, as far as I am aware, no full-length treatments of AIDS in Zimbabwe. One well-written account which touches Zimbabwe in its regional survey is

Nana Poku, *Regionalization and Security in Southern Africa*, London:
Macmillan, 2001

and there is nothing extended on homosexuality in Zimbabwe. For a flavour of street protests as they began in the late 1990s, see

Stephen Chan, 'Troubled Pluralisms: Pondering an Indonesian Moment for
Zimbabwe and Zambia', *The Round Table*, 349, 1999.

A SELECTION OF NOVELS AND OTHER FICTION

Neither this book nor this essay can be an exercise in literary appreciation. However, I do feel scholars – in amassing evidence – do violence to the expression of those they study by not considering creative writing as an often particularly telling mode of evidence. Having said that, I am not a great expert on Zimbabwean creative writing. I give here some favourites, in addition to those cited in the first section of this bibliography, but do suggest that the time is ripe for more international attention to be given what seems to me an extraordinary national expression.

An early, exceptionally well-written account of the seizure of land from King Lobengula by the emissaries of Rhodes, and of Lobengula's diplomatic embassy to Queen Victoria:

Stanlake Samkange, *On Trial for My Country*, Oxford: Heinemann, 1966.

Banned in Rhodesia, this collection of short stories expresses the weariness and hesitations of the black population:

Charles Mungoshi, *Coming of the Dry Season*, Harare: Zimbabwe Publishing House, 1981 (first published in 1972 by Oxford University Press).

The now accepted epitome of contemporary Zimbabwean frustration, even though published before liberation:

Dambudzo Marechera, *The House of Hunger* (a novella and short stories), Oxford: Heinemann, 1978.

As I have noted in my text, there is now an academic 'industry' around Marechera. Some of this, but also the original intent to introduce a tragic but brilliant writer to the world, may be found in

Flora Veit-Wild and Anthony Chennells, *Emerging Perspectives on Dambudzo Marechera*, Trenton: Africa World Press, 1999

and I have made my own fuller notes to set him, not only in a wider social context but within a context of psychological examination:

Stephen Chan, *Composing Africa*, Tampere: Tampere Peace Research Institute, 2002.

I have already celebrated his novel, but the short stories also contain foreboding studies of the interface between liberation and sanity:

Alexander Kanengoni, *Effortless Tears*, Harare: Baobab, 1993.

The leading woman novelist has produced darkly lyrical novels of township life and womanhood, among them:

Yvonne Vera, *Butterfly Burning*, Harare: Baobab, 1998.

She has recently completed a novel to do with the atrocities in the Matabelelands, even now a delicate topic in Zimbabwean political discourse. For an analysis of her work, see

> Ranka Primorac, 'Crossing the Space-Time of Memory: Borderline Identities in Novels by Yvonne Vera', *Journal of Commonwealth Literature*, 36:2, 2001.

There are few full-length published books on Zimbabwean literature. There is an unpublished thesis by Anthony Chennells, to which many researchers from outside Zimbabwe have turned. However, the most recently published book contains certain flaws: whether for academic or personal reasons, Shimmer Chinodya is not mentioned at all, and he is undoubtedly one of the great Zimbabwean novelists:

> Rino Zhuwarara, *Introduction to Zimbabwean Literature in English*, Harare: College Press, 2001.

The title of this last book of course indicates that there is also a wealth of fiction in Shona and Ndebele.

MATTERS OF THE SPIRIT

The recent, very influential book on the place of the 'irrational' and spiritual in African political and public life has also been controversial:

> Patrick Chabal and Jean-Pascal Daloz, *Africa Works: Disorder as Political Instrument*, London: James Currey, 1999.

In a sense, it follows on from the pioneering works on Zimbabwean spiritual belief in times of war by Ranger, Werbner and Alexander, cited in the first section of this bibliographic essay. Alexander has written of the importance of cleansing as a spiritual ritual and prerequisite for sanity. Ranger has written, in his earlier academic incarnations, of popular ritual and belief in Tanzania and Zambia. Even now, there are still echoes of the 'African historiography' he helped to found, even in neo-Marxist circles:

> Louis Masuko, 'The Zimbabwean Burial Societies', in Mahmood Mamdani and Ernest Wamba-dia-Wamba (eds), *African Studies in Social Movements and Democracy*, Dakar: CODESRIA, 1995.

Having said that, I feel that there are certain oversights possible in this emphasis. The first is to misplace its importance amidst other considerations. After all, African life is composed of a great number of givens and variables. This was Kriger's complaint against Ranger in the work cited in the first section; and I have tried to suggest, very generally, the list of items that must be included in a map of African attempts to navigate a public world in Chan (2002), cited in the previous section.

Second, it is one thing to suggest the importance of the spiritual without expressing how the spiritual works, and another thing entirely to investigate the methodology of entering the spiritual world, or the spiritual world entering ours. This is where

Pamela Reynolds, *Traditional Healers and Childhood in Zimbabwe*, Athens, OH: Ohio University Press, 1996

is of some importance. She describes the practice and rituals of inter-action with the spirit world as a complete and self-contained system of psychological health.

Third, there is a certain question of a political sociology of things spiritual, that is that things spiritual affect not only the political sphere but things political – and otherwise public and social – affect the spiritual sphere. The spirit world can be used as a threat to those not in touch with it – shamans and witches, spirit mediums can misuse their powers, or be themselves persecuted for fear that they might:

Gordon L. Chavunduka, *Traditional Medicine in Modern Zimbabwe*, Harare: University of Zimbabwe Publications, 1994.

Access to spiritual knowledge can be used quite pragmatically – or even corruptly – as a means of dealing with, or profiting from, the political world:

Billy Mukamuri, *Making Sense of Social Forestry: A Political and Contextual Study of Forestry Practices in South Central Zimbabwe*, Tampere: Acta Universitatis Tamperensis, ser. A vol. 438, 1995.

And finally, in the face of modernity people can make choices about how much of either world they wish to subscribe to:

M. F. C. Bourdillon, *Where are the Ancestors? Changing Culture in Zimbabwe*, Harare: University of Zimbabwe Publications, 1993.

Even so, it is a rare conversation in Zimbabwe that does not include reference to the spirit realm and its intersection with our own. When people speak of Mugabe haunted by Tongogara, they allow it possible credence. Here, it is not as if Mugabe could choose whether to be affected by the ghost of Tongogara or not; or at least he chose some time ago; and the balance between one realm and another is that those who are wicked must one day be called upon to pay a price. In the Shona cosmology – I have not read any studies about that of the Ndebele – there is, finally, justice, even if it has not always been readily apparent in the first 22 years of independent Zimbabwe, and the rule of Robert Mugabe.

Index